Thank God My Regiment an African One

Colonel Nathan W. Daniels of the 2nd Regiment Louisiana Native Guard Volunteers. This photograph was taken on January 12, 1864, while Daniels was in Washington, D.C.
Roger D. Hunt Collection, U.S. Army Military History Institute

THANK GOD MY REGIMENT AN AFRICAN ONE

The Civil War Diary of Colonel Nathan W. Daniels

EDITED BY C. P. WEAVER

LOUISIANA STATE UNIVERSITY PRESS
Baton Rouge

Published by Louisiana State University Press

Copyright © 1998 by Louisiana State University Press
All rights reserved

Manufactured in the United States of America
Louisiana Paperback Edition, 2000

Designer: Michele Myatt Quinn
Typeface: New Caledonia
Typesetter: Wilsted & Taylor Publishing Services

Library of Congress Cataloging-in-Publication Data:

Daniels, Nathan W., d. 1867.
    Thank God my regiment an African one : the Civil War diary of Colonel Nathan W. Daniels / edited by C.P. Weaver.
       p. cm.
    Includes bibliographical references and index.
    ISBN 978-0-8071-2566-3 (pbk. : alk. paper)
    1. Daniels, Nathan W., d. 1867—Diaries. 2. United States. Army. Native Guard Infantry Regiment, 2nd (1862–1863) 3. Ship Island (Miss.) 4. New Orleans (La.)—History—Civil War, 1861–1865—Personal narratives. 5. United States—History—Civil War, 1861–1865—Personal narratives. 6. Louisiana—History—Civil War, 1861–1865—Regimental histories. 7. United States—History—Civil War, 1861–1865—Regimental histories. 8. Soldiers—United States—Diaries. 9. United States—History—Civil War, 1861–1865—Participation, Afro-American. 10. Afro-American soldiers—History—19th century. I. Weaver, C.P., 1939– . II. Title.
E510.5 2nd.D36 1998
973.7'463—dc21   98-10522
                                                                             CIP

The paper in this book meets the guidelines for permanence and durability of the Committee on Production Guidelines for Book Longevity of the Council on Library Resources. ∞

Contents

Foreword
by Edwin C. Bearss / ix

Preface / xv

Acknowledgments / xxv

Abbreviations / xxvii

INTRODUCTION / 1

PART I

SHIP ISLAND, MISSISSIPPI

January 12–April 28, 1863 / 25

PART II

NEW ORLEANS

April 29–September 26, 1863 / 107

CONCLUSION / 157

Appendix 1:
Officer Roster / 179

Appendix 2:
Enlisted Roster with Company Officers / 183

Appendix 3:
Ships and Captains / 199

Bibliography / 201

Index / 207

Illustrations

◦‿

Map *(facing page 1)*

Area of Activity, 2nd Louisiana Native Guards

PHOTOGRAPHS AND PRINTS

Colonel Nathan W. Daniels / frontispiece

Sample page of Daniels Diary / xxii

"Ship Island and the Approaches to New Orleans" / 26

Daniels and Major Francis E. Dumas on horseback / 35

Daniels and Dumas / 41

Headquarter buildings, Ship Island / 49

Battery No. 5 / 50

Scene of Ship Island / 53

Company D, 2nd Louisiana Native Guards / 57

Colonel Daniels and ship captains / 74

Colonel Daniels and ship captains in ambulance / 78

Battery No. 6 / 86

Foreword
Edwin C. Bearss

❧

I entered on duty as a historian at Vicksburg National Military Park on September 28, 1955. Although a Civil War buff since the mid-1930s, I possessed scant knowledge or appreciation of the significance of African American soldiers and sailors in our nation's defining conflict. I had grown up in Montana, where I knew two black families—the Proctors and the Englishes—the only ones in the area. I had served in a segregated Marine Corps and attended undergraduate school at Georgetown University, where there were few, if any, African American students in the late 1940s. The first time I met, worked with, and got to know black professionals was during the three and a half years I spent at the U.S. Naval Hydrographic Office at Suitland, Maryland. In 1953–1954, I attended Indiana University and, while there, wrote my graduate thesis, "Patrick Cleburne: Stonewall Jackson of the West." A proposal by General Cleburne to enlist blacks in the Confederate army was suppressed by the government and undoubtedly short-circuited his brilliant military career.

Autumn 1955 was an eye-opening time for a "Yankee" historian to arrive in Mississippi. Seventeen months earlier, the U.S. Supreme Court, in *Brown v. Board of Education of Topeka*, had determined that separate educational facilities were "intrinsically unequal," intrinsically outlawing racial segregation in the nation's public schools, and in August, six weeks before I traveled south, Emmett Till had been murdered in Sumner, Mississippi, his body thrown into the Tallahatchie River.

In familiarizing myself with the Vicksburg campaign, I learned that black troops had seen bloody, no-quarter-asked-or-given fighting at Milliken's Bend, Louisiana, on June 7, 1863. The 11th Louisiana Infantry (African American descent) suffered terrible casualties—30 killed, 119 wounded, and 293 missing. Also while at Vicksburg, I became aware of the significant service in Mississippi during the second half of the war by the 3rd U.S. Colored Cavalry, led by Colonel Embury D. Osband. During the Vicksburg campaign, Osband commanded Major General Ulysses S. Grant's escort. Soon after the end of the war, he was poisoned under still-mysterious circumstances at Greenville, Mississippi; he was buried in the Vicksburg National Cemetery.

In 1963, while undertaking research into military operations in and around Thibodaux, Louisiana, during October 1862, I became aware of the Louisiana Native Guards, whose 1st Regiment was among the participating Union units. The newly organized regiment played only a minor role in this campaign, and Brigadier General Godfrey Weitzel, the officer in charge and a protégé of Major General Benjamin Butler's, treated the unit and its personnel in a patronizing manner. Yet this brief introduction to the Native Guards whetted my interest in the Native Guards, and during the summer of 1965, my last in Mississippi, I had an opportunity to look at a different aspect of that story.

Pierce Reeder, postmaster of Leola, Arkansas, contacted me on behalf of the Grant County Chamber of Commerce. Governor Orval Faubus had recently signed into law legislation establishing Jenkins' Ferry, the site of a bitter Civil War battle, as a state park. Out of this contact came my study *Steele's Retreat from Camden and the Battle of Jenkins' Ferry*, published for the Arkansas Civil War Commission in 1966. Among the battles highlighted in the book were Poison Spring and Jenkins' Ferry. In the former, a disaster for the Union, one of the key participating commands was the 1st Kansas Colored Infantry, which on October 29, 1862, at Island Mound, Missouri, had become the first black unit to see combat in the Civil War (more than six months before the 54th Massachusetts Volunteer Infantry—featured in the movie *Glory*—was mustered into Federal service). At Jenkins' Ferry (April 30, 1864), the 2nd Kansas stood tall, charging and capturing in bitter fighting two cannons manned by Ruffner's Missouri Battery.

A 1967 *Louisiana History* article by Mary F. Berry, "Negro Troops in Blue and Gray: The Louisiana Native Guards," reintroduced me to this unique unit. Until then I had believed that Martin R. Delany, a graduate of Harvard Medical School, had been the first African American officer to hold a field grade, as noted in the popular *American Heritage Pictorial History of the Civil War*, published in 1960. The editors of this work seemingly were unaware of the large number of black line officers and one field-grade officer—Major Francis E. Dumas—in the 1st, 2nd, and 3rd Regiments of Native Guards.

This was to be my last encounter with the Louisiana Native Guards for quite some time. Following my 1966 transfer to the National Park Service's Washington, D.C., headquarters, I did not have an opportunity to revisit them until the late 1970s. At that time I was assigned to prepare a comprehensive cultural history of Ship Island, one of the units in Gulf Islands National Seashore. The most impressive and significant above-grade feature on the island is the third-system masonry fort, commonly called Fort Massachusetts. Commenced in 1859, the fort was largely completed during the war years. Intimately associated with both the barrier island and the fort from January 1863 until their October 1865 muster out of Federal service were the 2nd Louisiana Native Guards, redesignated the 74th Infantry, U.S. Colored Troops, on April 4, 1864.

In doing research for my narrative, which focused on the fort's construction and the cultural history of associated military personnel and civilians, I combed the *Official Records* and manuscript records on file at the National Archives, the Mississippi Department of Archives and History, and other repositories. I revisited Dr. Berry's monograph and other published sources. The available materials enabled me to prepare a satisfactorily documented narrative describing the military and civil history of the island and the associated role of the 2nd Native Guards. Highlighted were the 1863 raid on East Pascagoula (the first Civil War engagement in which African Americans led by black company-grade officers participated), the regiment's duty of guarding Confederate prisoners of war, and the replacement of the black officers by whites.

Missing was the human element. I knew that Colonel Nathan W. Daniels was white, whereas Major Dumas and many other officers were free men of color, members of New Orleans' African American elite. What, then, was life in such a regiment like? How were the officers and men treated, and how did they fare in an environment in which the Lincoln administration, in early 1863, took the bold step of calling on "Africa" for help?

Foreword

The Lincoln War Department during the late winter and spring of 1863 began actively to organize and muster into service black regiments, both infantry and cavalry, and companies of artillery. Known as United States Colored Troops, these units would have white officers—field, staff, and line—with the noncommissioned officers and rank and file being black.

The first months of 1863 were soul-searching times for the five regiments of Louisiana Native Guards, particularly the 1st, 2nd, and 3rd. The Union military establishment, as represented by Major General Nathaniel P. Banks and his examining boards, embarked on a campaign to rid these three units of their original white field-grade officers and replace the black field-grade and line officers with whites. This despite the gallantry displayed by the 1st and 3rd Louisiana Native Guards in their May 27, 1863, assault on an impregnable position at Port Hudson, Louisiana. Conspicuous in the charge was Captain André Cailloux, out in front of his company, urging his men on. His left arm dangled uselessly by his side—a minié ball having shattered his elbow.

This story and others were absent from my *Historic Resource Study of Ship Island*, published in 1984. I was accordingly enthusiastic when in the summer of 1990 John Turner, the director of the U.S. Fish and Wildlife Service at the time and a former member of the secretary of the interior's National Park System Advisory Board, brought my attention to a diary that a friend of his said had belonged to an officer commanding African American troops on Ship Island. Not long thereafter, C. P. Weaver telephoned and asked if I would like to see Colonel Nathan W. Daniels' diary and the accompanying photographs taken of the 2nd Louisiana Native Guards while stationed on Ship Island. This was a dream come true because I had assumed that the Civil War pictorial record of Ship Island was limited to illustrations found in *Harper's Weekly* and *Frank Leslie's*, along with drawings and maps.

Ms. Weaver came to my office in the winter of 1992–1993 with the Daniels diary and the photographs. After scanning the diary, which was difficult because, in the interest of space, the colonel had occasionally employed "cross-writing," I studied the photographs, and my enthusiasm mounted as Ms. Weaver told me that she was considering editing the diary for publication. Next we discussed with Jack Boucher of the Historic American Building Survey how to have the fading photographs copied to enhance their quality and ensure their preservation. Then, recognizing the significance of the Daniels collection, I suggested to Ms. Weaver that when she finished transcribing and editing the journal, she submit it to Louisiana State University Press, as she eventually did.

Coincidentally, in 1995, the Press published *The Louisiana Native Guards: The Black Military Experience During the Civil War*, by James G. Hollandsworth. Written in a graceful and pleasing style, the book provided a welcome and long-needed institutional history of the Native Guards. The following year, the Press accepted *Thank God My Regiment an African One* for publication. I applaud the decision, which with the Hollandsworth work gives the Press a one-two punch in bringing to the attention of the public, as well as academia, the significant history of black soldiers in Louisiana, where there was a long tradition of service by free men of color.

Readers familiar with Joseph T. Glatthaar's *Forged in Battle: The Civil War Alliance of Black Soldiers and White Officers* will find the Daniels diary enlightening, particularly as it focuses on the 2nd Native Guards during a period in which all but one of the line officers, as well as the major, were African American. Colonel Daniels' character and his personal life, along with his rise and fall, are reflected in his relations with southern society and with his colleagues in arms as he challenges racial taboos.

Not only does the diary chronicle the trials and tribulations of a white colonel and the discrimination he encountered from his superiors and peers, but it provides invaluable personal insights into those encountered by African American soldiers, particularly the officers. Many of the blacks in the colonel's regiment, besides being free men of color, were light-complected and had been successful members of a white-oriented society.

Duty on Ship Island, with its isolation and harsh environment, would be a challenge to any military unit, black or white. To compound the situation and relieve the monotonous routine of drills and work details, the officers and men of the 2nd Regiment, during Daniels' months on the barrier island, were allowed to challenge the Confederates only once. As any old soldier knows, much of any war is characterized by the trite saying "hurry up and wait," and nothing will be better calculated to destroy a unit's morale. The Daniels diary, through the colonel's interactions with his superiors and the officers and rank and file of his regiment, gives an excellent overview of the human element in the erosion of a dream and the death of a regiment.

Everyone interested in the African American military experience, which until the late twentieth century was characterized by discrimination, will find *Thank God My Regiment an African One* must reading. It will also appeal to a broad spectrum of the Civil War community. The photographs are poignant as well as informative. Ms. Weaver's editing enlightens without being heavy-handed or patronizing. The book's focus on a black regiment with a scattering of white officers—and they limited to line and staff—and the exceptional photographs combine to give it a special dimension that separates it from the usual unit history or journal.

Preface

Thank God it hath been my fortune to be a participator in the grand idea of proclaiming freedom to this much abused and tortured race. Thank God my Regiment an African one, that I have been permitted to assemble them under the banner of freedom to do and die for their country & liberty—
—Colonel Nathan W. Daniels, March 29, 1863

Civil War Colonel Nathan W. Daniels (1836–1867) is a forgotten man with a forgotten regiment. As the Union white commanding officer of the African American 2nd Louisiana Native Guard Volunteers, he and his men were removed from mainland military activity and confined in obscure duty on Ship Island, ten miles off the coast of Mississippi. Their inglorious existence has earned them little interest from historians of the period, yet they represent a pioneering stage in the history of black troops in the war.

By April 1865, close to 10 percent of the northern armed forces were black males, nearly 179,000 having entered the Union army, and more than 9,500 in the navy.[1] Men of varied backgrounds, free or ex-slave, light skinned or dark, educated or illiterate, joined army regiments organized in different parts of the country, North and South. As one of the first black

---

1. Precise totals of 178,975 for the army and 9,596 for the navy are given by Ira Berlin et al., *Slaves No More: Three Essays on Emancipation and the Civil War* (New York, 1992), 203, 206.

regiments to be mustered, Daniels and his men were at the forefront of this operation.

From 1862 into mid-1863, the sensitive undertaking of bringing blacks into military service moved through an experimental phase in which progress—meaning the simple acceptance of the men as soldiers—occurred slowly in a prejudiced environment. Along with concern over the blacks' fighting abilities there was the critical question of who should lead the newly forming regiments. White officers were chosen to command the black troops from the beginning, but which ones were the most competent for this test? What about subordinate officers?

In the fall of 1862, Benjamin F. Butler, commanding general of the Federally occupied Department of the Gulf, appointed three white officers, each with local ties, to the rank of colonel to command the 1st, 2nd, and 3rd Louisiana Native Guard Volunteers organizing in New Orleans. Often referred to as "free" black units, these regiments in actuality included a majority of former slaves. It was the original enlistment of the 1st Regiment that prompted the term *free,* for it contained a core of historically free people of color, many light skinned, well educated, and prominent citizens in their community. From this nucleus Butler promoted approximately seventy-five men to lieutenant or captain, and one to major, creating a corps of commissioned free black officers. It was a bold move full of promise, for these officers would now command their own men of color; it was also short-lived.[2]

Butler's successor in the Department of the Gulf, Major General Nathaniel P. Banks, came to accept the need for black troops, but he disapproved of their black officers as detrimental to both blacks and whites when serving together. He proceeded to sanction the use of competency

---

2. James G. Hollandsworth, in the most recent study to date, puts the total number of Butler's black officers at seventy-six: Hollandsworth, *The Louisiana Native Guards: The Black Military Experience During the Civil War* (Baton Rouge, 1995), 118. The Native Guards could claim the honor of holding nearly 90 percent of the total number of black officers who would serve in infantry or artillery units in the war. Not until January 1865 did black officers serve again in similar combat groups, and even then only eleven were commissioned, two of whom were recruiting officers. Also receiving commissions as the war came to a close, but as noncombatants, were thirteen chaplains and eight surgeons. Joseph T. Glatthaar, *Forged in Battle: The Civil War Alliance of Black Soldiers and White Officers* (New York, 1990), 9, 179–82, 279–80.

examination boards that methodically removed selected black leaders. This intimidating strategy, plus ineligibility for promotion, inequity of pay, and the ever-present "negrophobic" behavior of white soldiers, created a frustration for the black officers that resulted in their resignations. White officers serving in nearby regiments filled the vacancies.

Not only did Banks encourage removal of black officers from the Native Guards, he also promoted the ejection of the first three white commanding officers. Less than a year after their muster, all three colonels were removed from their commands within weeks of each other. Why? The colonels themselves considered their treatment to be based on frivolous, trumped-up charges within an unreasonable, prejudiced department.

Colonel Nathan W. Daniels and his 2nd Louisiana Native Guards were first assigned, along with the 1st Regiment and a detachment of white soldiers, to a two-month deployment to protect the railroad west of New Orleans. Later, stationed on remote Ship Island, the 2nd was responsible for guard duty at a prisoner encampment and for maintaining the post in a "defensible condition" as a strategic location in Mississippi Sound during the North's blockade of southern ports in the Gulf of Mexico. On April 9, 1863, a portion of the regiment saw its only action, a skirmish on the mainland at East Pascagoula, Mississippi.

On May 4, while on leave of absence in New Orleans, Daniels was arrested under orders from General Banks based on charges preferred by a white engineer officer. The colonel was baffled. Later, additional trivial charges surfaced from other individuals. Daniels remained in the city for five frustrating months awaiting resolution of his situation in a trial that was never to take place. In the meantime, his white lieutenant colonel took over the regiment, his black officers resigned in waves, and the morale of the troops deteriorated. In the end, the worn-down Daniels was able to negotiate an agreement with General Banks that allowed him to resign his commission and leave military service—although today an unchallenged "dishonorable dismissal" remains on his record.

The colonel kept a diary documenting his tour of duty on Ship Island and his time in New Orleans following his arrest. His entries describe a day-to-day life of building fortifications, visiting ships, receiving contrabands and refugees, and enduring false alarms. He reports on the condition of his troops and on the skirmish at Pascagoula, and comments on the progress of the war both inside and outside the Department of the Gulf, with added remarks on various officers of the army and the navy. Intermingled with those notes are thoughts on the struggles and responsibilities of being between the black and white military worlds, of pressing for his men's right to prove themselves, of his defense of his black officers, and of his frustrations in wrestling with his own removal.

In addition to the rare personal narrative, the diary presents equally rare photographs. Although Daniels mentions having sent copies to a few family members and one friend, to date they have not surfaced, including in searches of collections in the National Archives, the Library of Congress, and the Military History Institute at Carlisle, Pennsylvania. Until now, the earliest known date of photographs taken on the island was 1902.

The images show a cross section of subjects: the post's buildings; the dock with men, munitions, and a tied-up ship; one company of the regiment; a few of its officers; and some of the ship captains who frequented the island. Most of the photos are casual, with men on horseback, seated in an ambulance, or grouped together in a relaxed manner. Of particular interest is the only known image of Francis E. Dumas, a light-skinned free black and one of only two men in the total enlistment of United States Colored Troops to reach the rank of major.[3] Dumas is pictured three times with Colonel Daniels; two of the photographs are reproduced here; the third is in unusably poor condition.

It is not known who took these photos. There were several thousand photographers experimenting with their trade by 1861. During the war, itinerant cameramen journeyed to military encampments in search of business, usually in quiet periods between engagements or in colder winter months with little activity. Mathew B. Brady, the famed "photographist," had teams of helpers who eventually spread out to capture scenes from almost every theater of the war, including the Department of

---

3. Dumas was earlier described as having "the complexion of an Italian and features which remind one of the first Napoleon." John William De Forest, *A Volunteer's Adventures: A Union Captain's Record of the Civil War* (New Haven, 1946), 47, quoted in Hollandsworth, *Louisiana Native Guards*, 26 n. 11. The second major, Martin Delany, a dark-skinned black "medical practitioner" and leader of a proposed emigration to Africa in the 1850s, was not commissioned until three months before the end of the war. Benjamin Quarles, *The Negro in the Civil War* (1953; rpr. New York, 1989), 328; Glatthaar, *Forged in Battle*, 9, 179.

the Gulf's Louisiana and Mississippi area. But the early 1863 photos in the diary were more than likely taken by an anonymous photographer from New Orleans, one of many practicing there before Brady's men arrived in the region. Whoever he was, he had to be willing to haul his large, cumbersome wooden camera, numerous 8 x 10 glass plates in dustproof boxes, a myriad of chemicals, and miscellaneous other supplies on board ship for the thirteen-hour trip from the city out to Ship Island. Even though not executed under combat conditions, amid cannon and rifle fire, the process of capturing scenes in a place of constant wind and blowing sand was a feat in itself when one breath of hot air could ruin the sensitive surface of a chemical-coated glass plate or permanently curl a print.

Daniels glued the photographs into his journal. Periodically he referred to the difficulty in getting good pictures of the troops, the batteries, and various other aspects of the military post. He did not seem overly concerned about the images' imperfections, appreciating the prints only as mementoes of his "exile" on Ship Island. The glue and general passage of time have taken a toll on the photos, a few having deteriorated too much for inclusion in this publication. The remaining photographs have been copied then computer-enhanced to reduce flaws and present the historically significant images as clearly as possible, bringing out the details of scenes no one now living has viewed.

There are few published narratives by commanding officers of black troops. The best known is that of Colonel Thomas Wentworth Higginson of the 1st South Carolina Volunteers, a regiment from the Atlantic coastal Sea Islands under Union control. Higginson began his diary in November 1862. He wrote of how his men, of "extreme blackness" and having little or no education, had undergone a sudden metamorphosis from plantation slaves to soldiers. A former clergyman of some literary accomplishment, he expanded his recorded experience into an 1869 work, *Army Life in a Black Regiment*. His diary is an important, sensitive contribution on the black military world of the time.

We know of Colonel Robert Gould Shaw and his heroic black Massachusetts 54th Volunteer Infantry from several publications over the years and from the popular 1989 film *Glory*. Shaw's correspondence and related letters, not a daily journal, provided the basic material. Totally different from Higginson's former slaves, the 54th was the first black regiment from the North, recruited during the winter and early spring of 1863 and made up mostly of educated, free African Americans.

Now the diary of Colonel Nathan W. Daniels, together with its unique photographs, offers new information in the continuing search for the history of black soldiers: a perspective on the early "free" black regiments in the Federally occupied South. Though lacking the eloquence of Higginson or the intensity of Shaw, Daniels in his brief journal deals with an important struggle in a period about which there is little personal documentation from someone of his rank and position. As the white commanding officer of black troops with black officers in a prejudiced military department, the colonel faced difficulties that eventually proved his undoing. With the huge responsibility given to him at the outset of this double experiment, he proceeded in the only way he knew how. Yet from the beginning he was being watched—and judged. For the commanding generals, choosing the right men to lead the people of color, free and freed, was an absolute necessity.

The anonymity of the thirty-one-year-old Daniels and his men of the 2nd Regiment is due partly to their isolation, but partly also to their being overshadowed by their brother regiments, the 1st and 3rd Native Guards, which won recognition for their prominent role in the battle at Port Hudson, Louisiana. But common problems followed all three regiments and their leaders in their respective assignments. If Daniels was the only one of the three colonels to keep a journal of his private thoughts, perhaps he had more time to do so, removed as he was on his "God-forsaken Isle."

Colonel Daniels confiscated the diary from the house of Hamilton McNeil Vance, a Confederate citizen and cotton merchant in New Orleans. Vance and his wife had been writing alternately in the book, describing their fears as the Yankees approached the city after bombarding the forts downstream on the Mississippi River. Abandoning their city home in the last hours before the invaders landed on May 1, 1862, the Vances fled north to Louisiana's Red River Valley. They left their diary behind.

Nearly seven months later, Daniels evidently entered the Vances' vacated house, found the diary, and in all probability due to a scarcity of writing paper, claimed it for his own use. He wrote on the frontispiece, "Captured November 3rd, 1862 from the house of Confederate in New

Orleans." He proceeded to enter several pages of lists concerning "suspicious characters," prisoners, and persons from St. Charles Parish taking the oath of allegiance to the Union. He did not write in the diary again until he and his regiment landed for assigned duty on Ship Island, Mississippi. He then began his entries on January 12, 1863.

Daniels died in New Orleans of yellow fever on October 2, 1867, followed a few weeks later by his year-old daughter. His wife, Cora, moved to Washington, D.C., where two years later she married Samuel Forster Tappan of Manchester, Massachusetts. Daniels' diary came with her to Tappan's New England house. Although Cora and Tappan divorced in 1876, the diary remained in the Manchester attic. Today, I own that house—I am the great-granddaughter of Tappan's sister—and the diary is in my possession.

Note on Editorial Method

The diary is a large hardbound book with nine-by-eleven-inch lined pages preprinted with daily headings in two narrow columns per page, one column per day, except Sunday, which uses a whole page. The columns are transcribed into a full page text with a normal tab indentation for the start of each entry and following paragraphs, instead of the narrow space used by Daniels. Daily headings are made uniform and italicized to differentiate them from the rest of the text.

If Daniels had more to say than space in the narrow daily columns permitted, he continued by writing over his earlier entry at a right angle, creating what I call "cross-writing." This continuation may have been a few sentences, a column, or a complete page—see the diary sample on the next page. Regardless of the amount, I have placed the notation "Cross-written" under the daily heading.

The text as printed in this book remains basically as Daniels wrote it, although some standardization was necessary for clarity and readability. Various marks resembling periods but serving no purpose for understanding the text were omitted. Indistinguishable periods and commas were transcribed according to context. Where there was no punctuation at the end of a sentence, I have added extra space before the beginning of the next. The few words or phrases that Daniels underscored are set in italics.

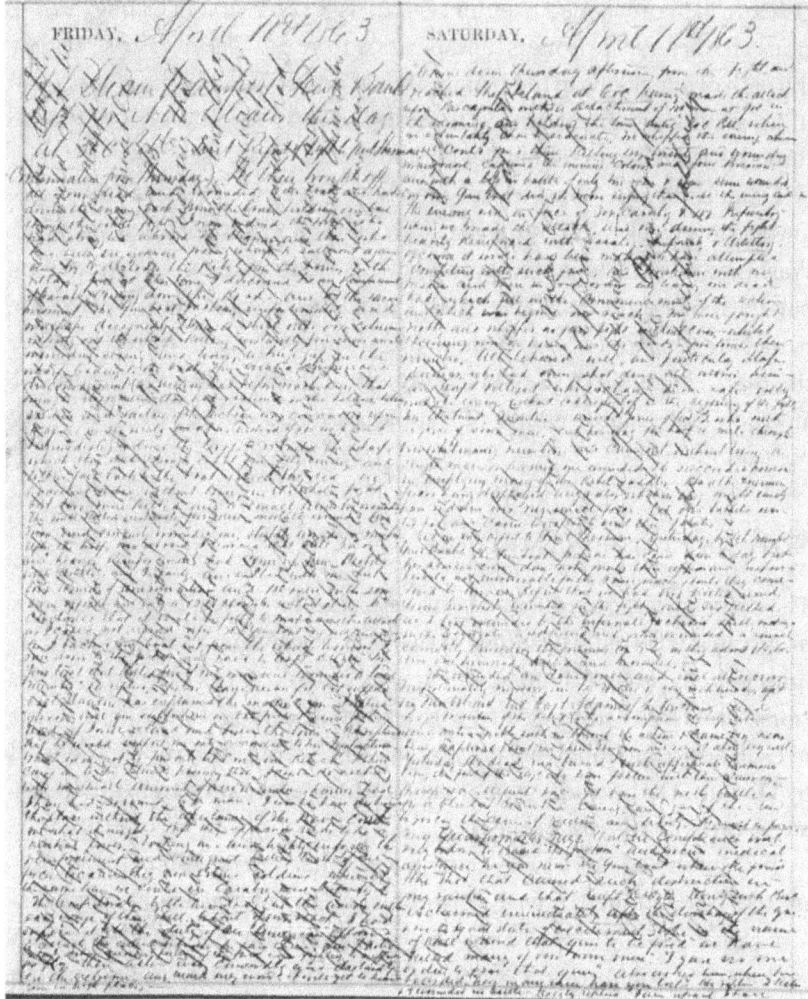

Cross-written page from the Daniels Diary for Friday, April 10, and Saturday, April 11, 1863. The entries describe the 2nd Regiment's battle at Pascagoula, Mississippi.

Daniels' long and short dashes were all made long for consistency. Large lowercase letters that could be read as capitals remain mostly as he wrote them, but where they created ambiguity, I used normal capitalization. Flawed grammar and misspelled words are as Daniels wrote them. Square brackets indicate my conjecture, or inference from the text, as to words or word portions; a question mark indicates doubt in transcription; and dashes indicate the probable number of missing letters. One passage in transcription is noted as being particularly difficult. Two silent emendations occur where Daniels changed a word by writing over it but then proceeded with his thought. I omitted the illegible word as irrelevant to understanding the sentence.

Complete names of nonregimental military personnel are supplied in square brackets if known or noted with a question mark if unknown. Varying spellings for nonmilitary persons are noted at the first variation. Names of ships are as Daniels wrote them, not set off in italics; in a few cases the reader will need to use the context to differentiate, say, the steamer *General Banks* from General Banks, the commander of the Department of the Gulf.

Three appendixes to the book give, respectively, the names of the 2nd Regiment's field, staff, line, and noncommissioned officers; a roster of the enlisted men; and a roll of vessels, naval or otherwise, that called at Ship Island, along with their captains' names, if known.

Daniels pasted several newspaper articles into the diary. Too badly deteriorated for successful photocopying, they have been transcribed into the text. They are set off typographically from the body of the diary entries, as are military reports, refugee accounts, and poetry.

I was unable to locate all pertinent information. Incomplete regimental records often did not include material mentioned in the diary, including correspondence, details on discipline, charges, arrests, orders, and other miscellaneous activity. Some details of nonregimental information also remain unknown, including first names of Daniels' personal friends or acquaintances, first names of various military personnel, the sources of some newspaper articles, and similar data. I take full responsibility for additional knowledge I may have overlooked or in which I am remiss.

Acknowledgments

In addition to a raft of supporting friends and family—especially Dave, Deke, and Mark—I would like to express my thanks to the following, who helped bring the Daniels Diary to life from the earliest stages of my work to the final product:

To Ken Bowling and Charlene Bickford at George Washington University for their historical-editing expertise and encouragement to press ahead. At the University of Maryland, to Leslie Rowland at the Freedmen and Southern Society Project for her sage advice and objectivity. At George Mason University, gratitude to professor emerita of history Josephine Pacheco for her support and council after reading the original manuscript; and to fellow graduate student Kay Kessell for her help with the early transcription. At the National Archives, thanks go to Mike Meier for his inestimable assistance and sense of humor, and to Becky Livingston for digging even deeper. To the National Park Service at the Gulf Islands National Seashore for its interest and concern over the photographs, now enhanced for its museum collection; thanks go there also to Mike Hobbs and particularly to Gail Bishop for her infectious enthusiasm about Ship Island, its men, its fort, and its photographs. To Jim Hollandsworth, deep appreciation for his detailed research into the Louisiana Native Guards and for is unfailing support of Colonel Daniels' journal. Thanks especially to John F. Turner at the Conservation Fund in Washington, D.C., who together with Edwin C. Bearss made this book possible. Additional thanks go to John Easterly and Gerry Anders, editors at LSU Press, whose knowledge and skill made it a reality.

Abbreviations

FSSP   Freedmen and Southern Society Project

LC   Library of Congress

LaNG   Louisiana Native Guards

NA   National Archives

    LR   Letters Received

    LS   Letters Sent

    MSR   Military Service Record

    RG   Record Group

OR   U.S. War Department, *The War of the Rebellion: A Compilation of the Official Records of the Union and Confederate Armies* (128 vols.; Washington, D.C., 1880–1901)

ORN   U.S. Navy Department, *Official Records of the Union and Confederate Navies in the War of the Rebellion* (31 vols.; Washington, D.C., 1895–1927)

USCI   United States Colored Infantry

Thank God
My Regiment
an African One

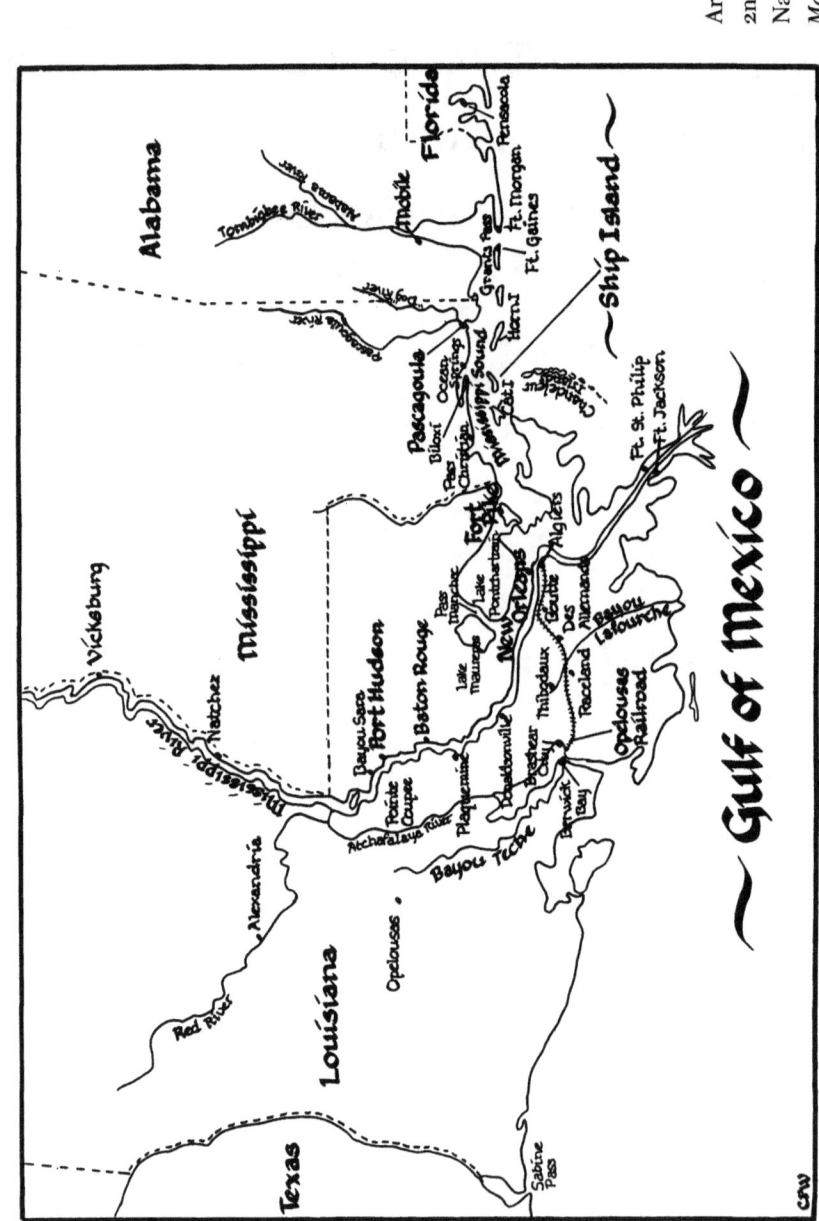

Area of Activity, 2nd Louisiana Native Guards
Map by C.P. Weaver

Introduction

～

In the fall of 1861, Federal forces occupied Ship Island, Mississippi, in the Gulf of Mexico. A small, sandy strip ten miles off the mainland, it was a strategic location for support of the Union's blockade of southern Gulf ports and was the only one of several islands framing Mississippi Sound that could sustain a large encampment of men and provide anchorage for a fleet of ships in its natural harbor. The Yankees restored a fort, a lighthouse, and defenses abandoned earlier by the Confederates, and prepared for an elaborate secret expedition.

In December, thousands of soldiers began arriving in separate detachments, camping in a sea of tents to await instructions from their general, Benjamin Butler, who finally disembarked on the island in mid-March 1862. In late April, Flag Officer David G. Farragut left the island to lead a surprise southern assault on New Orleans via the Mississippi River. Under his command was a blockading squadron as well as a large fleet of schooners, steamers, warships, and gunboats collected from the Atlantic and all over the Gulf. Butler and his infantry regiments, in a coordinated move, departed Ship Island during the navy's week-long attack that began with the bombardment of Forts Jackson and St. Philip, seventy-five miles downstream from the city, and effectively ended when Farragut's ships slipped past those Confederate strongholds by night. The general and his troops followed the navy into a captured New Orleans, arriving May 1, 1862.[1]

Citizens of the city had known of the Federal encampment on Ship Is-

---

1. For background and description of Ship Island, see James Parton, *General Butler in New Orleans: History of the Administration of the Department of the Gulf in the Year*

land from the beginning. The Yankees' presence, however, was not considered a threat because authorities were confident that any attack on New Orleans would come from north of the city, not south: the forts below were very strong, and a "chain raft" obstruction in the river would certainly stop any enemy ship. So sure were the Confederate military leaders of the Federals' northern approach that they sent many of their ships up the river toward Memphis to ward off the anticipated invasion.[2]

New Orleans was defended by a military contingent of only 3,000 men, of whom fewer than 1,200 were armed with muskets, the rest having only such weapons as shotguns or even none at all; ammunition was minimal. Confederate President Jefferson Davis had earlier requested troops and supplies from the seceding states to help in other areas of the South, a situation that left Louisiana, and especially New Orleans, vulnerable. Local white citizens organized into various protection groups, "the Vigilance Committee," "citizen patrols," and "home guards." Within the free black population were the "Native Guards," a militia unique to the city and representative of its historically large component of people of color, the *gens de couleur*.[3]

The United States inherited New Orleans and its interracial, multicultured population with the Louisiana Purchase of 1803. The city already boasted a well-established free black citizenry unlike that of any other urban area, North or South. Foreign domination had influenced the color line from its earliest days. French and, later, Spanish colonists produced biracial children with black slave women. The men openly supported their mistresses and brown-skinned offspring, provided for their upkeep and education, and encouraged the masters to free the women and their children. Divisions between black and lighter-skinned individuals soon established the visible difference between those in bondage and those who were free. Yet dark slaves were also encouraged to buy their freedom, which many did when they could afford to, usually at a relatively mature age. Others were declared free for various reasons—for instance, if they

---

1862 (Boston, 1868), 195–97, 202–203, 208–209; George H. Hepworth, *The Whip, Hoe, and Sword; or, The Gulf-Department in '63* (1864; rpr. Baton Rouge, 1979), 16–17.

2. For the fall of New Orleans, see Gerald M. Capers, *Occupied City: New Orleans Under the Federals, 1862–1865* (Lexington, Ky., 1965), 35–45; John D. Winters, *The Civil War in Louisiana* (Baton Rouge, 1963), 79–99.

3. For New Orleans' defenses, see Winters, *Civil War in Louisiana*, 15–18, 34–35, 75–84.

Introduction

had been abandoned by their masters and had lived independently for several years, or if they had offered to serve the colony under special circumstances.

The new American government tightened the reins on the free blacks' former privileges, slowing their social and economic momentum gained under the French and Spanish. One concern of the Americans was the twofold increase of the black population in New Orleans due to an influx of light-skinned free blacks from Haiti—an educated, French-speaking population that was escaping internal warfare on the island.

As Louisiana's economy began to develop and prosper, however, the free blacks of the city gradually reclaimed the relative prestige and wealth they had realized under foreign rule. The environment helped create an educated, elite class of independent wage earners, from property owners to skilled artisans and tradesmen. Some were planters who owned their own slaves. The *gens de couleur* were a special, separate, free, light-skinned caste whose lifestyle resembled that of their white relatives, although they were also connected to enslaved dark blacks. They were continually pulled in two directions and yet stood apart from both groups.

Over the years, all three countries turned to the free black population when in need of military protection. France fought the Indians and the English; Spain and the United States battled the British. The French not only promised freedom to those who fought for the colony, but also established a free black militia with its own officers. The Spanish continued the French policy and divided the group into sections based on skin color. With U.S. rule, the free black militia expected to be recognized with all its former privileges intact, but instead the whites played a greater organizational and leadership role, thus diluting the blacks' prestige. Before long, the territorial lawmakers deactivated the unit. However, its assistance was again required during the War of 1812: Andrew Jackson utilized the militia to defend New Orleans in 1814. Though he hoped, by promising the men a greater share of American life, to solidify a loyalty still fragmented because of past allegiances to France and Spain, the advertised equality never materialized, and by the 1830s the battalion had again dissolved.[4]

4. For the history of New Orleans' black population and early military organizations, see Ira Berlin, *Slaves Without Masters: The Free Negro in the Antebellum South* (New York, 1974), 109–30, 179–80; Ira Berlin *et al.*, eds., *The Wartime Genesis of Free Labor: The Lower South* (New York, 1990), 348, Ser. 1, Vol. III of Berlin *et al.*, eds., *Freedom: A Docu-*

By 1860, approximately 11,000 of Louisiana's 18,000 free blacks lived in New Orleans, three-fourths of them having mixed racial ancestry. Of the state's approximately 3,000 free black males aged eighteen to forty-five, again the majority lived in the city. At the outbreak of the Civil War, these men felt strongly enough about themselves and their position in the community to want to participate as their ancestors had done in 1814 and before. They felt that they could not only fight, but also lead.[5]

Shortly after the attack on Fort Sumter in April 1861, approximately 1,500 free black men gathered in New Orleans to show support in defense of their homeland. They organized themselves into a regiment called the "Native Guards," which Governor Thomas O. Moore accepted into the Louisiana Militia on May 2. Commissions were issued for black line officers, and the unit joined additional "protection groups," including Spanish, French, British, and other foreign residents who banded together to help guard the city in the event of an attack.

The free blacks joined the Confederate cause more to protect their families, personal property, and existing rights than for any particular allegiance. In fact, they stated later that had they not volunteered, they would have been forced into service by the authorities. Once enlisted, they had to provide their own uniforms, equipment, and muskets, if they had them. Otherwise, they were not issued arms, either because the weapons were not available or were reserved for white troops, or because the whites did not trust the militia with them. Basically, the Native Guards' duties involved monotonous, endless drilling. Gradually their earlier enthusiasm waned in the face of the white population's lack of confidence in their organization, although in November of 1861 a group of 731 black enlisted men with 33 officers marched in parade with white

mentary History of Emancipation, 1861–1867, 4 vols.; Berlin *et al.*, *Slaves No More*, 7–8; Mary F. Berry, "Negro Troops in Blue and Gray: The Louisiana Native Guards, 1861–1863," *Louisiana History* (Spring 1967), 165–67; John W. Blassingame, *Black New Orleans, 1860–1880* (Chicago, 1973), 1–21; Eric Foner, *A Short History of Reconstruction* (New York, 1990), 21–22.

5. For population figures, see Berlin *et al.*, *Slaves No More*, 203; Berlin, *Slaves Without Masters*, 136, 178; Berry, "Negro Troops in Blue and Gray," 167; Blassingame, *Black New Orleans*, 9, 21; James McPherson, *The Negro's Civil War: How American Negroes Felt and Acted During the War for the Union* (New York, 1965), 319; Howard C. Westwood, "Benjamin Butler's Enlistment of Black Troops in New Orleans in 1862," *Louisiana History* (Winter 1985), 6; Winters, *Civil War in Louisiana*, 34.

Introduction

units during a troop review. Then, in January 1862, a state legislative move reorganized the many militias, which then nullified the Native Guards. However, on March 24, after the Federal navy appeared in the Mississippi River below the forts, a concerned Governor Moore quickly reinstated the black unit.[6]

In late April 1862, when the Federal fleet fought its way past Forts Jackson and St. Philip, panic seized New Orleans' citizenry, both civilian and military. Frenzied residents burned or destroyed massive quantities of sugar, molasses, cotton, and supplies that might aid the enemy. Once in the city, the Yankees learned that Mansfield Lovell, the Confederate general who had been governing the citizens under martial law, had refused any part in a negotiated surrender and had left the civilian mayor and city council to discuss terms. Lovell evacuated as much Louisiana state property as possible and ordered the defending state and Confederate military troops to leave New Orleans for Camp Moore, seventy-plus miles north of the city. The Native Guards chose to stay but were ordered to disperse, stash their firearms, remove their uniforms, and return to their families. They were on their own to protect their homes, property, and vested interests accumulated over the years.

Major General Benjamin F. Butler, now commander of the Union's new Department of the Gulf, had been a lawyer and an active politician in his home state of Massachusetts before the war. His instructions from President Abraham Lincoln on arrival in New Orleans were to "run the machine as he found it." Butler found total chaos. He set to work immediately to meet civilian needs, including food, sanitation, citizen discipline, currency, local government, and measures against yellow fever. He ruled the city, however, with an iron hand under martial law, starting with the

---

6. For the Confederate Native Guard organization, see Berry, "Negro Troops in Blue and Gray," 167–70; Ira Berlin, Joseph P. Reidy, and Leslie S. Rowland, eds., *The Black Military Experience* (New York, 1982), 305, 13, Ser. 2 of Berlin *et al.*, eds., *Freedom: A Documentary History of Emancipation, 1861–1867*, 4 vols.; Blassingame, *Black New Orleans*, 34; Manoj K. Joshi and Joseph P. Reidy, "'To Come Forward and Aid in Putting Down This Unholy Rebellion': The Officers of Louisiana's Free Black Native Guard During the Civil War Era," *Southern Studies* (Fall 1982), 328–29; Westwood, "Benjamin Butler's Enlistment of Black Troops in New Orleans," 13; Winters, *Civil War in Louisiana*, 34; Hollandsworth, *Louisiana Native Guards*, 1–11. Hollandsworth found the Confederate black organization to number 870 men and 36 officers in total, of whom 142 were absent during the parade review.

requirement that citizens take the "oath of allegiance" to the United States. People showing disloyalty—which could mean the slightest remark or action aimed against the Union—often found themselves in jail locally or shipped off to distant prison forts.

Butler rescued the disaster that was New Orleans, but he was detested in the community. Women of the city, angry and defiant at the presence of the Yankee invaders, showed their distaste by being rude, insulting, and hostile to the soldiers. Butler's tolerance of their abuse ran out barely two weeks after the northerners' arrival when two of his men were spat upon in the street by a passing woman. The immediate result was the general's infamous "Woman's Order," General Order No. 28, issued May 15, 1862: any Confederate female found insulting Union officers, in word or deed, would be treated as a woman "of the town plying her avocation." This decree absolutely incensed much of the population, male and female. Then, on June 7, Butler made an example of William Mumford, who had shown the audacity to haul down the United States flag that Federal forces raised over the U.S. Mint during the initial takeover of the city. Mumford was hanged in front of a large gathering of spectators for a crime the Confederates hardly felt deserved a death sentence. Heavy-handed actions like these helped seal the general's reputation as "Beast" Butler.[7]

The military forces under Butler's command were now inundated with slaves who had left plantations to seek asylum and freedom within Union lines. "Contrabands" came by the hundreds, then thousands, risking their lives in the swamps, arriving "naked, starving, sick, hunted, scared and scarred." By midsummer of 1862, approximately 10,000 refugee slaves were in the New Orleans area, dependent on U.S. troops for food and protection. Ironically, it was Butler who a year earlier had initiated the contraband situation at Fortress Monroe, Virginia, when he refused to return runaway slaves who came into his lines unless the owners took the oath of allegiance to the Union. When they did not comply, he declared the slaves as property that could be confiscated like any other contraband of war, and put the blacks to work for pay at the fort.[8]

7. For Butler's rule of New Orleans in general, see Berlin *et al.*, eds., *Wartime Genesis of Free Labor: Lower South*, 359; Capers, *Occupied City*, 61–66; Parton, *General Butler in New Orleans*, 324–27; Winters, *Civil War in Louisiana*, 125–48.

8. Berlin *et al.*, *Slaves No More*, 191–92; Glatthaar, *Forged in Battle*, 4–6.

Introduction

The First Confiscation Act in August 1861 supported Butler's move by freeing all fugitive slaves who were taken by occupying Federal forces. The Second Confiscation Act of July 1862 expanded the first to include those slaves who came into Union lines stating their owners were disloyal. They could not be returned to slavery. Under this act, Lincoln was given the authority to use the black population in any way necessary in order to end the war. The Militia Act, which passed at the same time, opened the door for employing competent blacks in any part of military service, guaranteeing their freedom and that of their families, if the latter had also been owned by disloyal masters.[9]

The contraband situation in New Orleans was out of control. At first the slaves worked as cooks, teamsters, laborers, servants for officers, and in the Quartermaster's Department, but there were endless masses of people to handle. The question turned to whether black troops would be effective on the battlefield. Could they be armed? Would they fight? Although General Butler, like President Lincoln, was not ready to experiment with the employment of slaves as soldiers in mid-1862, other Union generals were, including one in Butler's own backyard. For in the spring and summer of 1862, simultaneously and independently, Major General David Hunter in South Carolina, Brigadier General James Lane in Kansas, and Brigadier General John W. Phelps in Louisiana organized bodies of black troops.[10]

In March and April, Hunter, the sixty-year-old commander of the Department of the South, aggressively recruited slaves, often at gunpoint, in sweeping, frightening roundups, attempting to build a black army from the isolated, Union-controlled South Carolina Sea Islands. Once word of his tactics reached Washington, the reaction from President Lincoln and

---

9. Berlin *et al.*, *Slaves No More*, 21, 40–41; Glatthaar, *Forged in Battle*, 4, 7; McPherson, *Negro's Civil War*, 165.

10. For background on the early black troops, see Berlin *et al.*, eds., *Black Military Experience*, 42–45; Berlin *et al.*, *Slaves No More*, 38–39, 195–96; Glatthaar, *Forged in Battle*, 6–7; McPherson, *Negro's Civil War*, 113, 164; Thomas Wentworth Higginson, *Army Life in a Black Regiment* (1869; rpr. New York, 1984), 27, 260–66; Dudley Taylor Cornish, *The Sable Arm: Black Troops in the Union Army, 1861–1865* (1956; rpr. Lawrence, Kans., 1987), 29–92; Hollandsworth, *Louisiana Native Guards*, 17 n; Howard C. Westwood, *Black Troops, White Commanders, and Freedmen During the Civil War* (Carbondale, Ill., 1992), 37–49, 55–68.

Secretary of War Edwin M. Stanton was decidedly negative. Hunter's requests to arm the black recruits, considered the "most backward in the entire South," were repeatedly denied from spring into summer: Lincoln thought that the country was not ready to put muskets in the hands of former slaves. By early August, the frustrated general ordered the men disbanded. In the meantime, the president had softened his stance on the issue but replaced Hunter as commander of Department of the South with Brigadier General Rufus Saxton, in whom he had more confidence and to whom he now gave permission to reorganize the recruits. On August 25, 1862, he gave approval for *only* Saxton's black troops as both laborers and armed, trained men. Saxton then appointed Colonel Thomas W. Higginson of Massachusetts to take charge of the unit, a sensitive commander who would prove to be the consummate white leader of black soldiers. Although enlistment had taken place earlier, and Lincoln later sanctioned its reorganization, the South Carolina regiment was not officially mustered into Federal service until November 1862.

General Lane, an abolitionist, recruited both whites and blacks into his Kansas regiment in midsummer 1862, including fugitive slaves from nearby states and free blacks from the North. He promised equal treatment to both races and persisted in his unorthodox military tactics on the frontier without authority or interference from either state or Federal powers. A detachment of the 1st Kansas Colored Infantry fought Confederates at Island Mound, Missouri, in late October 1862, but the regiment was not considered official until January 1863.

In Louisiana, unbeknownst to General Butler, his subordinate General Phelps, a vocal abolitionist from Vermont who had helped lead the troops from Ship Island into New Orleans, had organized five companies of contrabands from Camp Parapet, just above the city. Butler was aware of Phelps's antislavery stance and of the unrest created among local plantation slaves by the abolitionist's encouraging protection of runaways, who swarmed into his lines. In late May, Butler cautioned the Vermonter to control his men, who purposely made life difficult for planters found mistreating their work force. But it was a request for arms and equipment at the end of July 1862 that alerted Butler to the existence of Phelps's already-formed black companies. The commanding general promptly refused the appeal, stating that "only the President has authority to arm Africans"; he ordered Phelps to put the men to work removing trees used as enemy cover near Lake Pontchartrain. Considering this an insult implying a continued form of slavery, Phelps resigned. In good conscience, he could not obey Butler's orders, and yet he was frustrated by the inability to follow his own convictions. Heated correspondence between the men saw each take a different stand on the issue of arming slaves: Phelps felt to arm them would deprive the South of its work force and turn slave against master; Butler was prepared to use the slaves only for labor until the powers in Washington determined otherwise.[11]

During this exchange between the two generals, a battle was imminent at Baton Rouge, occupied by the Yankees. Both sides had an equal number of troops, but on August 5 the Confederates failed to drive the Union soldiers out. Expecting a second attack, the Federals dug in. They requested additional men from General Butler, who had none to spare. Originally, Butler wanted to hold the capital city, but now he became more concerned about New Orleans as the Rebels' next target. He considered burning Baton Rouge but changed his mind and ordered his men to evacuate, leaving things intact. The troops, however, ignored the instructions and followed their own agenda by going on a rampage, burning and pillaging, leaving behind a swath of destruction as they moved out.

After Baton Rouge, Butler felt threatened by the whole western division of the southern army, plus additional troops from Texas and the western side of the Mississippi River. He needed more soldiers, but manpower was precious. He had all but exhausted the Union white male population in the area, and there were no available regiments for him in the North, as they were tied up with the Peninsula and Manassas campaigns in Virginia. On August 14, 1862, less than two weeks after the latest controversy with General Phelps over arming the slaves, Butler wrote to Secretary Stanton, "I need reinforcements very much.... Indeed we are being threatened with an attack on the city of New Orleans.... If it comes at all imminent I shall call upon Africa to interfere and I do not think I shall call in vain." Stanton had earlier advised the general to use his "eminent abil-

---

11. For the Phelps and Butler conflict, see Ira Berlin *et al.*, eds., *The Destruction of Slavery* (New York, 1985), 192–96, Ser. 1, Vol. I of Berlin *et al.*, eds., *Freedom: A Documentary History of Emancipation, 1861–1867*, 4 vols.; Berlin *et al.*, eds., *Black Military Experience*, 42–44; Berlin *et al.*, *Slaves No More*, 36–38, 196; Cornish, *Sable Arm*, 58–63; Berry, "Negro Troops in Blue and Gray," 170–71; General Correspondence, Box 14, and Letter Book 203, both in Benjamin F. Butler Collection, LC.

ity . . . and enterprise" to hold New Orleans by any means possible, as it was more important than many Richmonds.[12]

Butler had read newspaper reports of the free black Native Guard militia with its own line officers serving in the Confederacy. In May 1862, within a few weeks of his arrival in the city, some of these officers had met with the general in response to his order for a surrender of arms and to discuss the disbanding of their unit. It was at this meeting that Butler inquired as to the men's allegiance. At the time, however, there was a general reluctance by the War Department to allow black troops, let alone black officers; nor was there any immediate military need for them. By mid-August circumstances had changed, and the general now needed men.

In a second meeting on August 15, the Native Guard officers returned to Butler with the declaration that they would now support the Union and felt that a number of the enlisted men would follow their example. The general did not approve of arming slave soldiers, but these light-skinned free blacks were different. He was impressed with their intelligence, urbanity, and appearance, some so light as to seem white. With these men, Butler felt he now had the answer he needed for more manpower. For the general, as well as for the Native Guard officers themselves, there was a vast difference between the black slave and the lighter-skinned *free* black; light skin color was perceived by whites to be associated with greater capabilities. Another important personal distinction for the Guards was that they had been born free before the rebellion, something that separated them from the darker slaves now gaining freedom. In good conscience, Butler could arm these men, and he welcomed them into the Union fold. After their enlistment, he wrote to Major General Henry W. Halleck, general-in-chief of the army, "I have kept clear of the vexed question of arming the slaves."[13]

---

12. Major General B. F. Butler to Edwin W. Stanton, August 14, 1862, in General Correspondence, Box 14, Butler Collection, LC; Stanton to Butler, August 7, 1862, *OR*, Ser. I, Vol. XV, 543.

13. On Butler, the Louisiana Native Guards, and black officers, see Berlin *et al.*, eds., *Black Military Experience*, 312–15; Berlin *et al.*, eds., *Wartime Genesis of Free Labor: Lower South*, 353; Berry, "Negro Troops in Blue and Gray," 172–80; Blassingame, *Black New Orleans*, 34, 38–39; Donald E. Everett, "Ben Butler and the Louisiana Native Guards, 1861–1862," *Journal of Southern History* (May 1958), 208–17; Glatthaar, *Forged in Battle*, 8–9; Joshi and Reidy, "'To Come Forward and Aid,'" 328–29; Hollandsworth,

Introduction

Butler issued General Orders No. 63 on August 22, 1862, allowing the former Confederate Native Guard militia to enter Federal service. In writing to Washington, he pressed for prompt presidential approval, as it was vital for the men's credibility to know the regiments were legitimate—and future recruitment depended on it. Butler's announcement came three days before the War Department's sanction of General Saxton's reorganizing and arming his black slave troops in South Carolina. Although Lincoln was more receptive to the experiment of black soldiers when he approved Saxton's move, he was still cautious about additional troops and remained silent on Butler's request. The general did not receive a reply from anyone in Washington concerning his action until well into November, and when he did hear he was told that "the whole matter was left to the discretion of the Commanding General." He stated that this was all the ratification he got—and all he needed.[14]

The 1st Regiment of the Louisiana Native Guard Volunteers filled in ten days with 1,000 men and mustered September 27, 1862. It was made up primarily of light-skinned free men of color, many from the Confederate Militia, with the darkest, according to General Butler, being "about the complexion of the late Mr. Webster." Although light-skinned and yellow-skinned men were represented among the 995 men who mustered into the 2nd Regiment two weeks later, on October 12, the majority were of "black, dark, [and] brown" complexion, indicating an influx of recently freed slaves. Later with more troops still needed, Butler authorized the 3rd Regiment, which mustered November 24, with even greater numbers of black and dark-skinned contrabands. Thus the first three Native Guard regiments varied considerably in their proportions of historically free men and former slaves, although all three continued to be referred to as "free colored" units.[15]

Louisiana Native Guards, 12–22; McPherson, *Negro's Civil War*, 239; Joe Gray Taylor, *Louisiana Reconstructed* (Baton Rouge, 1974), 10–11; General Correspondence, Boxes, 14, 16 and Letter Books 187 and 203, Butler Collection, LC; *OR*, Ser. I, Vol. XV, 442, 555.

14. *OR*, Ser. I, Vol. XV, 556–57; Berry, "Negro Troops in Blue and Gray," 73; Higginson, *Army Life in a Black Regiment*, 265; Westwood, "Benjamin Butler's Enlistment of Black Troops," 17; Testimony of Major General B. F. Butler before the American Freedmen's Inquiry Commission, May 1, 1863, in Berlin *et al.*, eds., *Black Military Experience*, 313.

15. For information on filling the ranks of the Louisiana Native Guards, see regimental records of 73rd, 74th, 75th USCI [1st, 2nd, 3rd LaNG], RG 94, Records of the Adjutant General's Office, NA; Hollandsworth, *Louisiana Native Guards*, 16–28. Hollandsworth

When Butler, still anxious about slaves versus free blacks, discovered that slaves were being recruited into the regiments, he stated that "no man must be enlisted who has failed to obtain his freedom through some recognized legal channel." But now it seemed anyone could join, "the boldest and the finest," all those who were in good health after fleeing the plantations to declare themselves free once they were within Federal lines.[16] The resulting color line would play a big part within these regiments. Though joining military service instilled confidence and hope for advancement in all people of color, expectations varied widely between

---

states that only 11 percent (108 men) of the 1st LaNG had actually been in the Confederate militia; the remainder included other "free" blacks as well as contrabands who had come into Federal lines. He also states the 2nd and 3rd Regiments were mostly former slaves, some freed by French and British nationals whom Butler ordered to declare their respective allegiances. As Britain and France had already outlawed slavery, the general declared bondsmen owned by these nationals to be free and subject to his needs; Berry, "Negro Troops in Blue and Gray," 174–76. Berry names Chauncey Bassett as leader of the 1st Regiment. Colonel Spencer Stafford was actually commander of the 1st but served as overall organizer for the whole Native Guard organization, leaving his lieutenant colonel, Bassett, in charge of the regiment until they were in the field, when Stafford took over. Bassett commanded again after Stafford's removal in mid-1863. Berry also refers to Major Joseph Giddings as commanding officer of the 2nd LaNG. There was mustering officer Major G. R. Giddings, but Colonel Nathan W. Daniels was already organizing the 2nd Regiment by late September 1862; Colonel N. W. Daniels to Major General B. F. Butler, September 29, 1862, in General Correspondence, Box 15, Butler Collection, LC; Berlin *et al.*, eds., *Black Military Experience*, 313–14; Blassingame, *Black New Orleans*, 38–39; Everett, "Ben Butler and the Louisiana Native Guards," 210; Glatthaar, *Forged in Battle*, 8–9, 176; Joshi and Reidy, "'To Come Forward and Aid,'" 329–30; Westwood, "Benjamin Butler's Enlistment of Black Troops," 14; General Correspondence, Box 14, Butler Collection, LC; *OR*, Ser. I, Vol. XV, 59. See Appendixes 1 and 2 for more information on the makeup of Daniels' 2nd Regiment.

16. Lieutenant William H. Wiegel to Colonel S. H. Stafford, September 11, 1862, in General Correspondence, Letter Book 203, Butler Collection, LC; Everett, "Ben Butler and the Louisiana Native Guards," 215–16; Regimental Records, 73rd, 74th, 75th UCSI [1st, 2nd, 3rd LaNG]; Westwood, "Benjamin Butler's Enlistment of Black Troops," 14; Cornish, *Sable Arm*, 66. August and Wimba Congo of the 2nd Regiment's Company A were part of an illegal cargo of slaves brought from Africa three years earlier. They were sold on arrival but later became "free" under the Federal occupation. Though their English was poor, they wanted to fight as "able-bodied" men. Edwin S. Redkey, ed., *A Grand Army of Black Men: Letters from African-American Soldiers in the Union Army, 1861–1865* (New York, 1992), 140.

Introduction

the historically free, light-skinned, educated, biracial individuals and the dark-skinned, newly freed, illiterate slaves. The service together of these different "classes" reflected by skin color would later present special problems, particularly when on assignment with white troops.[17]

All but one of the line officers of both the 1st and 2nd Native Guards were black. The 3rd Regiment had both black and white officers—determined, as Butler stated, "precisely as I found their intelligence." The actual number who transferred from the Confederate militia to Butler's troops was minimal. Only eleven of the men had held earlier commissions. Ten more were promoted from the ranks, for a total of twenty-one officers. Twenty-six former officers declined to serve the Union, leaving Butler to find others in the free black community to fill the remaining positions. Once enlisted, the black officers were encouraged to recruit whole companies that would remain under their respective commands, a move that fostered strong bonds between the proud leaders and their soldiers/friends.[18]

Butler stated he had no trouble finding white staff, or regimental, officers, selecting them from military men in the area. With strict examining boards for testing new white leaders not yet in existence and no known criteria for this leadership experiment, he found his commanding officers simply through their willingness to take on a free black regiment. He then considered their suggestions for filling the other staff officer positions.

Colonel Spencer H. Stafford, detailed as deputy provost marshal in New Orleans from the 11th New York Volunteers, was chosen to com-

17. Glatthaar, *Forged in Battle*, 86–87.
18. For more details on Butler's Native Guard officers, see Hollandsworth, *Louisiana Native Guards*, 25–28. Hollandsworth states that the 2nd Regiment's 2nd Lieutenant William Peabody, originally with the 8th Vermont Infantry, was the first white line officer in the Native Guards. Peabody volunteered to serve in the black regiment replacing Samuel Lawrence, a local free man of color who did not receive his commission until later and was then assigned as a captain to the 3rd LaNG. Another white officer, 1st Lieutenant Elijah K. Prouty, also of the 8th Vermont, appears in Company H of the 2nd LaNG's original roster (see Appendix 2), but he was soon moved to the staff-officer position of adjutant and replaced by a black officer, Octave Rey. Berry, "Negro Troops in Blue and Gray," 175, states that all noncommissioned officers were black. However, at least two were found to be white in the 2nd LaNG (Appendix 2). Each captain of Daniels' regiment was credited with recruiting his entire respective company. Muster Rolls, Oct. 12, 1862, Regimental Papers, 74th UCSI [2nd LaNG], RG 94, NA.

mand the 1st Regiment. John A. Nelson, of the 30th Massachusetts Infantry, was briefly lieutenant colonel of the 1st under Stafford before being promoted to colonel by Butler and moved to command the 3rd Regiment.

Colonel Nathan W. Daniels of the 2nd Regiment, originally from New York and Ohio, had lived in Pointe Coupee Parish, Louisiana, before the war. At the outbreak of the rebellion he joined the Army of the Ohio, returning to the New Orleans area after his tour of duty. He was in the provost marshal's office of St. Charles, St. John the Baptist, and St. James Parishes when General Butler found him.[19]

The 2nd Louisiana Native Guards organized in late September and early October 1862, with Daniels recommending to Butler the names of several white officers for staff positions. He requested Major Alfred G. Hall of the 9th Connecticut Volunteers to be his adjutant, but Hall instead became his lieutenant colonel. Hall had been aide-de-camp and acting assistant adjutant general to Butler's departed antagonist, General Phelps. Lieutenant Elijah K. Prouty, a transfer from the 8th Vermont, temporarily filled the adjutant post, the appointment not becoming official until the regiment was in the field. Daniels asked for Stephen A. Hodgman as chaplain, a white Presbyterian preacher from Texas who had been held captive by the Rebels for seven months before being released by General Butler. According to his Military Service Record, Hodgman was reported to be the only southern white chaplain who accepted a position with a black regiment.[20]

In what was to be a significant promotion, Daniels recommended Francis E. Dumas, a refined, educated, light-skinned black as his major. As such, Dumas became the first black staff officer not only in the three Native Guards, but in the entire U.S. Army. Though Butler later claimed to be responsible for promoting Dumas from captain to major, it may in fact have been done at Daniels' suggestion. Daniels wrote a letter to Butler on September 29 to "respectfully recommend Francis Ernest Dumas, Cap-

---

19. MSRs of Spencer H. Stafford, Nathan W. Daniels, and John A. Nelson, 73rd, 74th, 75th USCI [1st, 2nd, 3rd LaNG], RG 94, NA. Also, Daniels Diary.

20. Requisition form, August 28, 1862, in General Correspondence, Box 14, Butler Collection, LC; Colonel N. W. Daniels to Major General B. F. Butler, September 29, 1862, *ibid.*, Box 15; MSR of Stephen A. Hodgman, 74th USCI [2nd LaNG], RG 94, NA; Berry, "Negro Troops in Blue and Gray," 175. Berry states that the 1st LaNG also had a white chaplain but he was a northerner transferred from the 31st Massachusetts Volunteers.

Introduction

tain Co. B 1st Reg't La Native Guard, free col'd . . . for Major . . . of the 2nd Regiment of Louisiana Native Guard, free col'd." The general had been impressed with Dumas, a biracial, prosperous, slaveowning planter of French background who spoke three languages in addition to French and English. Dumas enlisted his hundred slaves into one company of the Native Guards, instilling in them the will to "break the bonds of [your] fellow men." Butler felt the man's intelligence and capability might surpass his own, yet he still qualified Dumas' status by placing a price on him in the tenor of the day, proposing the major to be a "man who would be worth a quarter of a million, in reasonably good times." As one of the two highest-ranking nonwhite commissioned officers in the war, Major Dumas holds the honor and distinction of being the only one who saw combat.[21]

Daniels had several line officers who were prosperous and respected in the free black community before the war. Some others made reputations through their military service and, afterward, their political involvement, the best-known of these being Captain Pinckney B. S. Pinchback, who later became—albeit very briefly—governor of the state. The son of a white planter and a biracial mistress, Pinchback, who could pass for white, raised his own company for the 2nd Regiment and was proud of his duty. In entering the war on the side of the Union, he stated that it was "the only time in my life I have felt anything like Patriotism." He and his men could now help free the oppressed.[22]

The three Native Guard regiments organized at Touro Barracks in New Orleans and later moved to Camp Strong Station just outside the city for training. Colonel Stafford took charge, helping to prepare, recruit, and coordinate the initial organization, remaining a strong spokesman on behalf of his troops in numerous situations. From the beginning, while the Guards were still in the city, there were problems. The regiments were a

---

21. Joshi and Reidy, "'To Come Forward and Aid,'" 330; Colonel N. W. Daniels to Major General B. F. Butler, September 29, 1862, in General Correspondence, Box 15, Butler Collection, LC; Blassingame, *Black New Orleans*, 36, 39; Berlin *et al.*, eds., *Black Military Experience*, 313–14; Glatthaar, *Forged in Battle*, 9, 179. The second major, Martin Delany, was a recruiting officer and did not see any action.

22. Ted Tunnell, *Crucible of Reconstruction: War, Radicalism, and Race in Louisiana* (Baton Rouge, 1984), 77; P. B. S. Pinchback Papers, Howard University, found in Blassingame, *Black New Orleans*, 36.

source of pride for the black community, but from white civilians the men suffered indignities that ranged from stone-throwing to abuse of their families. Whites suspicious of the free blacks' flip-flopping loyalty complained to the Department of the Gulf of the black soldiers' behavior. Stafford wrote to General Butler in early October 1862 to explain various disruptions, blaming low-class Frenchmen for the disturbances.

It was the custom of slaveowners to invite free men of color to marry their slave women. The men supplied household furnishings and lived with the women at the owner's property. According to Stafford, since the men enlisted in the Native Guards, owners of the wives had insulted and abused the free blacks and would not let them see their wives and children. The soldiers' subsequent attempts at renting houses for their families met with refusals, a blatant denial of their basic rights. Their immediate reaction was viewed by whites as improper or "insolent behavior." Although these particular problems belonged to the 1st Regiment, they were typical of the difficulties endured by the Native Guards as a whole. It was in this unsettling environment that the men took to the field.[23]

The Federal blockade from Virginia to Texas, declared by President Lincoln at the opening of the war, was supposed to hasten the end of the rebellion by "bottling up" southern products within the Confederacy. Not only were cotton, sugar, and other commodities to be prevented from going out, but nothing, including manufactured materials from abroad, was to be allowed in. New Orleans, as the headquarters for southern commercial activity and the control point for the Mississippi River and the central Gulf area, was a prime target for the North. When the city was taken by the Union, the southerners, in order to move their goods, shifted to the bayous, inlets, and smaller rivers off the Mississippi and used shallow-draft boats to smuggle their materials out to the Gulf. (They also continued trading, although on a reduced scale, via the Mississippi Sound and out of still-Confederate Mobile, often adopting Havana, Cuba, as a haven on the way to or from other foreign ports.) The area west of New Orleans became a hotbed of activity for blockade runners and Confederate troops, from the Red River Valley to the Lafourche region to Berwick Bay, and throughout the cotton- and sugar-rich territory of Bayou Teche.

23. Colonel S. H. Stafford to Major General B. F. Butler, October 8, 1862, in General Correspondence, Letter Book 203, Butler Collection, LC.

Introduction

On September 11, 1862, Butler wrote to Halleck in Washington, "I will endeavor, as soon as I receive reinforcements, to organize an expedition which shall relieve the western part of Louisiana from the presence of any force of the enemy." In late October, he sent forces with Brigadier General Godfrey Weitzel west of New Orleans as far as Donaldsonville to flush out Rebel troops while pressing down into the Lafourche region. The Native Guards were to be part of this operation. The 1st Regiment, under Stafford, was sent into the field to join a detachment of the white 8th Vermont Volunteers. They were to open, repair, and guard the Opelousas Railroad, which ran approximately seventy-five miles from Algiers, just across the river from New Orleans, west to Brashear City. The rail line was then to be maintained for the Weitzel expedition's supplies, as well as for shipment to New Orleans of cotton and sugar from planters who had sworn loyalty to the Union. A later request from Butler shifted the two regiments from railroad duty to establishing a telegraph line along the route between Boutte Station, Thibodaux, and Des Allemands. The 2nd Louisiana Native Guards, under Daniels, were then ordered out on October 30 to replace Colonel Stafford's men on the Opelousas Railroad.[24]

Daniels' regiment of nearly one thousand men left New Orleans, crossed the Mississippi River to Algiers, and marched to Boutte Station along the railroad bed while their knapsacks, supplies, and equipment rode on train cars in the rear. For the next two months, the men restored bridges and made repairs on the important Opelousas line, being responsible for "guarding the track, sidings, wood, water tanks &C."[25]

General Weitzel conducted a successful campaign, his troops sweeping the Lafourche region. Some local inhabitants panicked and evacuated whole plantations, moving their slaves out of temptation's way by driving them across the state into Texas. Other planters stayed and took the oath of allegiance; they could then not only finish growing their crops, but also sell them to the Union. As the general and his troops worked their way

---

24. For Lafourche-region operations in the fall of 1862, see Winters, *Civil War in Louisiana*, 156–64; Berry, "Negro Troops in Blue and Gray," 177–79; Regimental Papers, 74th USCI [2nd LaNG]; *OR*, Ser. I, Vol. XV, 133, 159. Lieutenant R. C. Clarke to Colonel Stephen Thomas, 8th Vermont, October 30, 1862, in General Correspondence, Box 16, Butler Collection, LC;

25. Lieutenant R. C. Clarke to Capt. [?] Craig, October 30, 1862, in General Correspondence, Box 16, Butler Collection, LC.

through the region, the magnetism of promised freedom within Federal lines attracted masses of slaves—men, women, and children fleeing plantations in loaded wagons and rickety carts. At one point, Weitzel thought he had more than twice as many contrabands following in his rear than he had soldiers. He was totally unprepared for the multitude, unable to feed the endless mob. The stragglers were forced to fend for themselves. They lived off the land, foraging and stealing what they could.

In addition to the frustration of being unable to deal with the miles of slaves behind him, Weitzel was uncomfortable with the 1st and 2nd Regiments of the Native Guards under his command. To begin with, he had little confidence in the men's ability to fight, but more important, he was concerned that their presence was a disruptive element in his operations. The surrounding territory had an unbalanced population; blacks far outnumbered whites. Weitzel was aware that the sight of free black men in uniform created havoc for the plantation slaves, to the point of influencing a possible insurrection. He would not be responsible for it. Native Guard soldiers were known to encourage slaves to leave, which then caused plantation owners frustration, exasperation, and ultimately extreme anger as their work force disappeared down the road. Weitzel complained to Butler, voiced the significance of the situation, and asked for the removal of the free black troops under his command.

Butler wrote to Halleck in early November stating that he still had not received any communication, whether approval or disapproval, from President Lincoln or the War Department concerning his establishment of the Native Guards. Therefore, in regard to Weitzel's protest, he found himself "without guide in this matter." In the meantime, Butler proceeded to castigate his subordinate and inquired whether Weitzel thought the Native Guards would cause fewer problems under anybody else. Despite continued silence from Washington, he finally assented to Weitzel's request and placed the 1st and 2nd Louisiana Native Guards in an independent command under the 1st Regiment's leader, Colonel Stafford.[26]

26. Everett, "Ben Butler and the Louisiana Native Guards," 213–15; Brigadier General G. Weitzel to Major George C. Strong, November 5, 1862, OR, Ser. I, Vol. XV, 171–72; Major General B. F. Butler to Major General H. Halleck, November 6, 1862, OR, Ser. I, Vol. XV, 162; Major General B. F. Butler to Brigadier General G. Weitzel, November 6, 1862, in General Correspondence, Letter Book 187, Butler Collection, LC.

Introduction

Colonel Daniels and the 2nd Regiment experienced a few incidents of concern to General Weitzel. In November, while under the leadership of black officers—Captain Hannibal Carter and Lieutenants Frank Trask and George Watson—Company C was guarding a plantation against theft and other depredations at Raceland, halfway between New Orleans and Brashear City on the rail route. Soon trouble arose between the officers and the white plantation manager, J. A. Pickens. Pickens accused Captain Carter's men of stirring up the slaves by telling them they did not have to work, that the government would take care of them. He said the soldiers made threats on his life, caroused with the black women, and as a result he eventually had to shut down the mill. Carter, on the other hand, had Pickens arrested for general abuse of the slave women and cruel treatment of the workers. The manager had also ejected a nursing mother simply because she was a soldier's wife. Carter's rebuttal stated that the reason Pickens had closed down the mill was that the workers were ill. In addition, he suggested that it was not the 2nd, but the 1st and 3rd Native Guards who were responsible for any problems with Pickens' slaves because those regiments were camped closer to the trouble area. In correspondence to Butler regarding the arrest and accusations, Pickens stated his belief that Carter and the other two officers could not control their men.[27]

In late December, the men in Company G, under Captain Joseph Villeverd, were accused by a planter of encouraging twelve of his twenty slaves to leave. The planter also charged the men with ruining his garden, stealing the vegetables, and taking wood, horses, and mules. Daniels' men were also charged with running off with fifteen mules from another plantation.[28]

The black troops not only had troubles with the civilian population, but they endured continued harassment from the white soldiers with whom they were stationed. The 8th Vermont was one of the first regiments to share an assignment with the Native Guards. One night on

---

27. J. A. Pickens to Major General N. P. Banks, January 5, 1863, misfiled with 6th USCI, Regimental Books and Papers, RG 94, NA, found in FSSP [G-285]; Captain H. Carter to Colonel N. W. Daniels, February 8, 1863, *ibid*.

28. Correspondence from William Abbott to Department of the Gulf, February 19, 1863, LR, Ser. 1918, Vol. I, in RG 393, Records of the U.S. Army Continental Commands, 1821–1920, Department of the Gulf, Pt. 1, NA; also Colonel N. W. Daniels to Dept. of the Gulf, March 3, 1863, *ibid*.

picket duty, sentries from the 2nd Native Guards were fired on several times. The next morning it was discovered that a company of the 8th Vermont had camped below but had moved out before daylight. They were assumed to be the guilty party. Later, in Algiers, a white soldier started to enter an ammunition shed with a lighted pipe and was stopped by a guard from Daniels' regiment. The soldier, incensed at being ordered by a black man, jumped the guard from behind, but the sentry's comrades came to his rescue. The melee had to be broken up by the regiment's lieutenant colonel, Alfred Hall.[29]

General Weitzel was aware of these problems, and although he was no longer immediately responsible, he was familiar with the actions of the commanding officers, Stafford and Daniels. In early December, he preferred charges against Stafford and some "other officers" but later withdrew them; it is not known what the charges were, or who else was involved.[30]

By the fall of 1862, Butler's reputation in the Department of the Gulf had deteriorated. "Beast" Butler had become "Spoons" Butler for supposedly appropriating for himself silver confiscated from wealthy Confederates. There were accusations of speculation and underhanded business deals involving his brother Andrew, dealings allegedly abetted by bribed Treasury Department officials. Foreign consuls in the city had mounting complaints against the general for his harsh treatment of their concerns, something that sent warning signals to Washington.

In spite of the increasing allegations, Butler continued to attempt to bring order out of chaos. On September 1 he reported the current conditions in the New Orleans area to Halleck. He was spending around $50,000 per month on food and monetary distributions for the whites of the city and giving the blacks almost twice the amount of food rations he was providing his own troops. Contrabands arrived daily within Federal lines by the hundreds, then thousands, the women and children desperately needing to be clothed. Hundreds of whites were also coming into the city weekly across Lake Pontchartrain from the Confederacy, bringing with them descriptions of the starvation there.[31]

29. Joseph T. Wilson, *The Black Phalanx* (1890; rpr. New York, 1994), 199n, 211–12.

30. Brigadier General G. Weitzel to Dept. of the Gulf, December 5, 1862, LR, II, Ser. 1747, Dept. of the Gulf, RG 393, Pt. 1, NA.

31. Major General B. F. Butler to Major General H. Halleck, September 1, 1862, in General Correspondence, Letter Book 203, Butler Collection, LC.

Introduction

Butler ended his report with the good-natured comment that he had learned "by secession newspapers that I am to be relieved of this Command. If that be so, might I ask that my successor be sent as early as possible, as my own health is not the strongest and that it would seem but fair that he should take some part of the yellow fever season." In actuality, the general's reputation was overtaking his accomplishments, and in mid-November he was notified he would be relieved the following month. On December 16, 1862, Major General Nathaniel P. Banks took over as the new commander of the Department of the Gulf.[32]

Banks's arrival in New Orleans and at the department was almost as traumatic for him as it had been for Butler six months earlier, but for different reasons. Shortly after his arrival, Banks wrote the following to his wife:

> I never desparred [sic] of our country until I came here. Our affairs have been terribly managed here. The strongest government in the world could not bear up under such responsibility and wrong. Everybody connected with the government has been employed in stealing other people's property, sugar, silverplate, horses, carriages, everything they could lay their hands on. There has been open trade with the enemy. No attention has been given to military affairs. I have nothing to fight with, but a small force of raw men, poorly armed and much depressed in spirit. No cavalry, no artillery, no transportation, nothing that is required for the work expected of me.... We can never succeed under such direction.[33]

Like his predecessor, Banks was from Massachusetts and a political general with no military background. In the spring and summer of 1862, he had been defeated by Stonewall Jackson in Virginia, first at Middletown and Winchester, then three months later at Cedar Mountain. Now he was transferred to the Department of the Gulf, where his assignment was to open the Mississippi River with Major General Ulysses S. Grant, clear out the Red River Valley in western Louisiana, gain a foothold in Texas, move into Mobile, and later straighten out the state of Louisiana for Lincoln's planned model of reconstruction.[34]

In December 1862, the Department of the Gulf had almost 40,000

---

32. *Ibid.* See also Winters, *Civil War in Louisiana*, 146.

33. Major General N. P. Banks to his wife, January 15, 1863, in Family Correspondence, Box 5, Banks Collection, LC.

34. Winters, *Civil War in Louisiana*, 167.

troops in Louisiana, with another 2,000 in Pensacola, Florida. Designated as the 19th Corps with four divisions, nearly half were nine-months' men, whose regiments' required enlistment expired nine months from the date of the last company's muster. The significance of this fact would become painfully obvious to Banks in his subsequent military engagements.[35]

Included in Banks's troop totals were the three regiments of the Louisiana Native Guards. Although the general was briefed by subordinates in the department regarding all phases of operations, his knowledge of the free black troops was minimal. He was, however, skeptical of the black officers from the start. One week after Banks assumed command, Chief Quartermaster Samuel B. Holabird wrote to him and suggested that several forts, including one on Ship Island, Mississippi, and Fort Pike on Lake Pontchartrain, could be "two thirds or more garrisoned by negroes," relieving the white troops stationed there, who were weakened from disease. The blacks were considered strong and healthy, used to the environment, and capable of fighting if necessary. Ship Island could easily be defended by a black regiment.[36]

Shortly afterward, on January 9, 1863, the 2nd Louisiana Native Guards received orders as independent detachments within the 19th Corps as part of the Defenses of New Orleans. Three days later, three of the regiment's companies landed at Fort Pike with Lieutenant Colonel Alfred Hall, while the remaining seven companies, under the command of Colonel Nathan W. Daniels, docked at Ship Island with its Fort Massachusetts, "assigned to prison guard duty" on the post.[37]

35. *Ibid.*
36. Colonel S. B. Holabird to Major General N. P. Banks, December 22, 1862, LR, Ser. 1956, Dept. of the Gulf, RG 393, Pt. 1, NA, found in Berlin *et al.*, eds., *Black Military Experience*, 638–39.
37. Regimental Papers and Books, 74th USCI [2nd LaNG], RG 94, NA.

Part I

SHIP ISLAND, MISSISSIPPI

January 12–April 28, 1863

Lord what a wretched land is this, which yields us no supplies.[1]

Ship Island lies ninety-five miles northeast of the mouth of the Mississippi River, sixty-five miles east of New Orleans, and fifty miles southwest of Mobile in a string of widely separated Gulf barrier islands ten miles off shore. The island is continually changing, moving to the west as littoral currents build up one end while whittling away at the other. Violent storms with overwash rearrange large portions of sand, and constant winds carve and shift the dunes. In 1969, Hurricane Camille created a totally new configuration by splitting the island in two, east and west; a cemetery on the island was part of the land lost to water.

In the 1860s the low, desolate sandbar was a continuous strand seven miles long and three-quarters of a mile across at its widest point, totaling two square miles. From a distance it was difficult to distinguish the island from an angry sea when waves broke in white foam over the sandy shore. Scrub oak and pine grew on the eastern end; the western end boasted a deepwater natural harbor. "Fresh water," affected by the rise and fall of the tides, was available from six-foot-deep wells dug into the grassy, vegetative surface. Salty-tasting at best, the water was soon to be tainted with gunpowder and creosote. Walking in ankle-deep sand was a continual

---

1. Parton, *General Butler in New Orleans*, 195.

"Ship Island and the Approaches to New Orleans" as depicted in *Harper's Pictorial History of the Great Rebellion, Part I* (1866).
Library of Congress

challenge, flies were a constant nuisance, and the intense, smothering, ovenlike heat and humidity were "insufferable."[2]

No one relished duty at this post, but it was considered the key to New Orleans and vital as a base for tactical maneuvers in Mississippi Sound. On January 12, 1863, the *Northern Star* docked in Ship Island's harbor, delivering Colonel Daniels and seven companies (B, C, D, F, G, I, and K) of the 2nd Louisiana Native Guards. Companies A, E, and H, under Lieutenant Colonel Hall, second in command of the regiment, arrived at Fort Pike, which guarded the eastern water approach to New Orleans.

Colonel Henry Rust, of the 13th Maine Regiment U.S. Volunteers, was in command of the island post, which included Fort Massachusetts and an encampment of prisoners, many sent over by General Butler from the Department of the Gulf.[3] A year earlier, Rust and his men had been among

2. Ibid., 195–96; Edwin B. Lufkin, *History of the Thirteenth Maine Regiment from Its Organization in 1861 to Its Muster-Out in 1865* (Bridgton, Maine, 1898), 25–26; Hepworth, *Whip, Hoe, and Sword*, 16–17.

3. Fort Massachusetts, under construction during most of the war, was too small to hold army personnel, let alone prisoners. Union and Confederate captives, military and civilian—the latter arrested as political dissidents, and including a few women—were con-

Part I, Ship Island

more than 15,000 soldiers stationed on the island preparing for the assault on New Orleans. Now only companies D and F of the regiment remained on assignment. Also on the island was a miscellaneous temporary detachment from Companies E and G of the 8th Vermont Volunteers, the same white regiment stationed earlier with the Native Guards on the Opelousas Railroad.

Daniels reported to Rust, presenting a memorandum that stated he was to relieve the Maine colonel as post commander and that Rust was to move to a new command at Forts Jackson and St. Philip on the Mississippi River. Rust acknowledged Daniels' arrival but, not having received his own orders, remained in charge, much to the newcomer's frustration. The negrophobic colonel from northern New England was nervous at the arrival of the black troops and wrote in his diary, "'Nigger on the brain.' No I have not got that. It has struck to my stomach and gone all over me. The feeling of certainty that I have got to leave my two good Companies here to come into collision with these niggers has made me feel homesick, and I have serious thoughts of resigning." After observing the relieving post commander and soldiers at drill, he grew even more anxious about his men being left behind to the "tender mercies of a colonel of niggers." Rust made his replacement promise that the black Native Guards and the white Maine companies would be kept separate, assigned different duties under their own officers.

Although Daniels did not note it in his diary, a severe storm struck a few days after his arrival, bringing high winds and rough seas that prevented ships from docking at the wharf. Heavy rains followed soon afterward, causing floodwaters to rise over the commissary's flooring and float miscellaneous debris around the post. Finally, with improved weather and official orders in hand, Colonel Rust departed on January 20, still concerned that he was abandoning his 13th Maine men to an unknown fate in what he perceived to be a tinderbox environment.[4]

---

fined to a camp and stockade more than a mile east of the fort, beyond the lighthouse. National Park interpreter, Gulf Islands National Seashore.

4. Colonel Henry Rust to Lieutenant Colonel Richard B. Irwin, Assistant Adjutant General [AAG], January 12, 1863, LR, Ser. 1756, Dept. of the Gulf, RG 393, Pt. 1, NA; Diary of Colonel Henry Rust, 13th Maine Infantry, Ship Island, Mississippi, July 11, 1862–January 21, 1863, found at Headquarters, Gulf Island National Seashore, Ocean Springs, Miss., original in Commandery Collection, Military Order of the Loyal Legion of the United States, United States Army Military History Institute [hereinafter cited by date as

Daniels' diary entries were sporadic during his first two months on the island—understandably so, considering the high level of activity in Mississippi Sound. He settled down to business quickly, following the regiment's orders: to build batteries, guard prisoners confined to the island, and defend the post.[5] However, on January 26, less than a week after Colonel Rust's departure, a major confrontation erupted between the newcomers and the Maine detachment, a "collision" the former post commander feared inevitable. Evidently Daniels paid no heed to Rust's request for separation and ordered a consolidation of the groups that included the usual battalion drill, dress parade, and camp and guard duties. Although it is normal in the military hierarchy to have captains over lieutenants—in this case the black Native Guards captains over the white Maine lieutenants—the subordinate New England officers complained bitterly. Daniels apparently turned a deaf ear. The Maine officers then refused to obey orders: they did not bring their companies to drill or dress parade and refused guard detail under the commanding blacks. In response, the new post commander arrested the rebellious officers. The companies' command next fell to an enlisted orderly sergeant, who asked the men if they would serve under the Native Guards officers. The northern enlisted troops, following in their officers' footsteps, replied they would not, and refused any further orders. They, too, were arrested and, their muskets and miscellaneous equipment confiscated, were confined to quarters like the officers; all were guarded by black sentries.[6]

Rust Diary, MOLLUS]; Edwin C. Bearss, *Historic Resource Study, Ship Island, Harrison County, Mississippi: Gulf Island National Seashore, Florida/Mississippi*, July 1984, National Park Service, Technical Information Center, Denver, Colo.

5. Regimental Papers, 74th USCI [2nd LaNG], RG 94, NA.

6. Springfield (Mass.) *Republican*, March [?] 1863, in Daniels Scrapbook; Daniels Diary, April 19, 21, 1863. Daniels mentions no problems with men from the 8th Vermont at the post, probably because they were not on assigned duty like the 13th Maine, but paroled prisoners sent there in a disciplinary action. About 140 of the Vermonters were captured on September 4, 1862, in an ambush near Boutte Station on the Opelousas Railroad. General Richard "Dick" Taylor, commander of the Confederate forces in the District of Western Louisiana and son of the war hero and former president Zachary Taylor, not only refused an exchange of the prisoners, but later threatened to kill ten of them because of continued Yankee pillaging of property owned by southerners who publicly promoted the rebellion. Taylor's retaliatory stand undoubtedly was influenced by the 8th Vermont's destruction and looting on August 25 of his family plantation (see n. 94 below). Butler later

Daniels cited a violation of the 9th Article of War in his swift control of the 13th Maine's officers and men: any officer or soldier who should "offer any violence against his superior officer on any pretense . . . or who shall disobey any lawful command of his superior officer shall suffer death."[7] This was not the first time the black regiment was involved in controversy, but Daniels' immediate action with the Maine men caused ripples throughout the military community of the Department of the Gulf, with reverberations to northern New England. The move gave pause to people considering the use of black officers with black troops, especially when posted with white soldiers. "They are in a bad state at Ship Island. The niggers have the upper hand and have the poor whites under arrest," wrote Navy Commodore Robert B. Hitchcock in a February 3 letter to Captain Thornton A. Jenkins, both visitors to Ship Island as participants in the Gulf's Mobile blockade.[8]

From the end of January to mid-February 1863, based on refugee reports and naval observations, rumors circulated of enemy activity near Mobile. There was fear of an attack on Ship Island or some other point along the coast of Mississippi Sound, possibly New Orleans. Soon after his arrival, Daniels had set his men to work creating two new batteries, at Colonel Rust's suggestion, on the east end of the island and in front of the

---

berated Taylor on the tactics of the Rebel "Partisan Rangers," who thrived on lawless violence together with the lack of military honor demonstrated by their false use of a truce flag to capture the 8th Vermont men. Butler was also outraged at Taylor's execution of seven New Orleans Germans, formerly in the Louisiana militia, who had joined the Vermont regiment. In return, Butler promised to kill twice as many Confederate prisoners as Taylor threatened of Union men. The Yankee general demanded that no harm come to the Vermonters and pressed for their return: *he* would punish anyone in his command who was guilty of destroying Taylor's plantation and other properties. The 8th Vermont prisoners were finally paroled on November 1. On November 25, true to his word, Butler ordered them to Ship Island for continued punishment as paroled prisoners. They remained until the War Department's General Orders No. 10 allowed an exchange of prisoners, with regimental Special Orders No. 36, February 5, 1863, returning the men to their regiment at Brashear City (see Daniels Diary, February 11, 1863). *OR*, Ser. I, Vol. XV, 133–34, 565, Ser. II, Vol. IV, 523, 565, 594, 708; Microfilm 594, roll 192, Record of Events, 8th Vermont Volunteer Infantry, NA; Regimental Orders, 8th Vermont Volunteer Infantry, RG 94, NA.

7. Colonel N. W. Daniels to Major General N. P. Banks, February 7, 1863, LR, II, Ser. 1747, Dept. of the Gulf, RG 393, Pt. 1, NA; U.S. War Department, *Revised U.S. Army Regulations of 1861* (Washington, 1867).

8. *ORN*, Ser. I, Vol. XIX, 599.

fort. Now, to bolster the defenses, the men rebuilt existing old batteries and started additional new ones. On February 2, Daniels wrote to General Banks about rumors of "six iron clad rams and gun boats in Mobile" and the fact that the enemy was removing its own obstructions in Grants Pass, the channel near Mobile. "Our gun boats guarding the same have fallen back to this point [Ship Island] and anchored in position expectant of an attack." Daniels requested more guns because he had only eight in working condition, mounted in temporary sand batteries, and those ordered for the fort had not yet arrived.[9]

Letters written February 3–5 between Lieutenant Commander Henry A. Adams of the gunboat *John P. Jackson,* Commodore Hitchcock of the *Susquehanna,* Lieutenant Commander John Madigan of the *Vincennes,* General Banks in New Orleans, and the navy's Rear Admiral David G. Farragut in command of the West Gulf Blockading Squadron, confirmed Daniels' concerns. Banks and Farragut, alarmed at the reports, agreed to additional protection: the admiral would send another gunboat to Mississippi Sound and Banks would send another regiment to Ship Island for its defense.[10]

General Banks had questioned the island's defensible condition shortly after taking over the Department of the Gulf from General Butler in December 1862. Lieutenant John C. Palfrey, the only engineer officer at the time, was in charge of all fortifications in the department, including Ship Island. He had previously been acting under instructions directly from Chief Engineer Major General Joseph G. Totten, in Washington, there being no superior officer in Gulf headquarters. His availability was spread thin between posts, often leaving the fortifications under the responsibility of the local commanding officer. However, Banks now urged Palfrey to concentrate his efforts and work with Daniels to complete the batteries and improve the fort. He asked the newly appointed departmental chief engineer, Major D. C. Houston, for an inspection and to report on the progress he found.[11] Daniels did not mention Palfrey in the diary until three months later, but the engineer was on the island from late Jan-

9. Rust Diary, Jan. 17, 1863, MOLLUS; Colonel N. W. Daniels to Major General N. P. Banks, February 2, 1863, LR, Ser. 1756, Dept. of the Gulf, RG 393, Pt. 1, NA.
10. *ORN,* Ser. I, Vol. XIX, 600–602, 609.
11. Major D. C. Houston, Chief Engineer, to Major General N. P. Banks, January 15, 1863, LR, Ser. 1756, Dept. of the Gulf, RG 393, Pt. 1, NA.

uary into mid-February. During that time, he wrote to Houston requesting permission to move temporary buildings brought and erected on the island almost a year earlier for General Butler's troops before the New Orleans campaign. These structures had later served as officers' quarters and storehouses but were in the firing line of the fort's newly ordered guns that would face Mississippi Sound.[12]

On February 6, Captain Robert H. Dunham, aide-de-camp to the department's assistant adjutant general, Richard B. Irwin, arrived on the island and reported to Daniels and Palfrey amid anxiety over the anticipated Confederate attack. He observed that the defensive preparations were as thorough "as circumstances would allow." He found twelve 9-inch Dahlgren guns inoperable and, as Daniels had written to Banks, only eight useable smaller guns, temporarily positioned, six on the north, or Sound, side and two on the east, facing Mobile. The men drilled several hours daily at the guns, and Palfrey pronounced them "quite expert artillerists . . . but in need of a few good marksmen." Dunham described the fort, with a temporary battery protecting its weakest point, as still needing work; Palfrey was awaiting ordered materials for the permanent structure. Dunham judged the number of "effective" men there sufficient for defense in case of an attack. His only suggestions in his report were the addition of two companies of artillerists, one or two more gunboats to monitor Grants Pass, and the speedy delivery of supplies requested by Palfrey and Daniels.[13]

Shortly after Dunham's visit, headquarters ordered Daniels to return the remaining companies from the 13th Maine, then under arrest, and the paroled 8th Vermonters, to their respective regiments at Fort Jackson, Fort St. Philip, and Brashear City.[14] Though Daniels was concerned that he lacked the manpower to meet an attack, he waited more than a month

---

12. Edwin C. Bearss, *Historic Structure Report, Administrative and Historical Data Section, Fort Massachusetts, Ship Island 1857–1935, Gulf Islands National Seashore, Florida/Mississippi*, January 1984, National Park Service, Technical Information Center, Denver, Colo., 96–97; Lieutenant John C. Palfrey to Major D. C. Houston, January 23, 1863, LR, Ser. 1756, Dept. of the Gulf, RG 393, Pt. 1, NA.

13. Captain Robert H. Dunham to Lieutenant Colonel Richard B. Irwin, AAG, February 9, 1863, LR, Ser. 1756, Dept. of the Gulf, RG 393, Pt. 1, NA.

14. Colonel N. W. Daniels to Major General N. P. Banks, February 13, 1863, LR, II, Ser. 1747, Dept. of the Gulf, RG 393, Pt. 1, NA.

before requesting that his three companies at Fort Pike be reunited with his regiment on Ship Island in order to make the post more secure.[15]

Feeling more confident of the military post's preparation, Daniels sent Banks a report on the latest condition of his fortifications. Banks wrote to General-in-Chief Halleck in Washington that he had done all he could for the defense of Ship Island but that only two sailing vessels were there for protection (the *Vincennes* and *Relief*), along with "one colored regiment." He also mentioned Dunham's suggestion of added artillery. Halleck responded two weeks later offering thoughts on efficiency for the fort but commenting that more artillery would only increase the enemy's temptation to attack.[16]

The threat of the Confederate offensive gradually subsided. Banks never had to send additional troops; however, one of Farragut's gunboats, the *Clifton*, captained by Lieutenant Commander Richard A. Law, arrived temporarily in the Sound to help if needed.[17]

Routine island and regimental business continually demanded Daniels' attention. He passed on to headquarters reports of enemy activity taken from refugees, runaways, and prisoners picked up by gunboats and brought to the post. Contrabands seeking asylum in Union territory created special problems for him after landing on the island. He frequently wrote to newspapers, especially northern publications whose readership supported the use of black troops in the war. He asked for a clerk to help the adjutant, Lieutenant Elijah K. Prouty, and requested an additional surgeon to help Major (Doctor) Samuel Willis. First Lieutenant Ernest Hubeau resigned effective January 22, shortly after he arrived on the island, making him the first black officer to leave the Native Guards. Daniels requested a commission for his present sergeant major, James Noyes, an 8th Vermont transfer, as Hubeau's replacement.[18] Here was the first in-

---

15. Colonel N. W. Daniels to Major General N. P. Banks, March 22, 1863, LR, II, Ser. 1747, Dept. of the Gulf, RG 393, Pt. 1, NA. The request must have been denied, for the detachment remained at Fort Pike.

16. Major General N. P. Banks to Major General Henry Halleck, February 12, 1863; Halleck to Banks, Feb. 27, 1863, *OR*, Ser. I, Vol. XV, 240–42, 690.

17. Rear Admiral David Farragut to Lieutenant Commander Richard A. Law, February 5, 1863, *ORN*, Ser. I, Vol. XX, 602.

18. Colonel N. W. Daniels to Major N. P. Banks, January 20, 26, February 12, 13, LR, II, Ser. 1747, Dept. of the Gulf, RG 393, Pt. 1, NA.

Part I, Ship Island

stance of a white supplanting a black. It is not known whether this request was Daniels' independent decision or was suggested strongly through General Banks at headquarters, but it was to become a widespread movement in the following months.

Approximately two weeks after arriving at Fort Pike in January, Lieutenant Colonel Hall applied to General Banks for an examination board to test the knowledge and capabilities of the officers of his detachment, Companies A, E, and H. If Daniels knew of this request he neglected to note it in the diary. Hall may have been receiving pressure from headquarters to gradually eliminate black officers, and because military protocol had not been established in dealing with the sensitive issue, he took it upon himself to make changes within his own detachment. The fact that he and Daniels were separated geographically in a divided regiment may have offered another reason, as communication was profoundly difficult. The two had a strained relationship as well, based on the colonel's disapproval of Hall's drinking habits, something evident later in the diary.

On February 3, Banks approved a three-member board of Hall, as president, and two captains from the 31st Regiment Massachusetts Volunteers stationed at Fort Pike. The board met on February 9, and "in accordance with the report . . . the commissions provisionally issued" to Captain Monrose Murillion, 1st Lieutenant William F. Keeling, and 2nd Lieutenant Lucien Scott "were rescinded." Although Captain Arnold Bertonneau, 1st Lieutenants Ernest Morphy and Octave Rey, and 2nd Lieutenant Robert H. Isabelle survived the interrogation, they became frustrated with the continuing prejudice and resigned three weeks later. Isabelle cited his hopes, when joining the regiment, that "all past prejudices would be suspended for the good of our Country and that all native born americans would unite together"; he was disappointed and discouraged to find prejudice still existed. Hall later recommended filling the blacks' vacancies with white officers promoted from the 31st Massachusetts.[19]

19. Lieutenant Colonel Alfred G. Hall to Major General N. P. Banks, January 29, March 2, 16, 1863, LR, II, Ser. 1747, Dept. of the Gulf, RG 393, Pt. 1, NA; Office of Adjutant's Regimental Papers, 74th USCI [2nd LaNG], RG 94, NA. The examination tested seven out of nine of Hall's officers. The remaining two were from Company A, Captain P. B. S. Pinchback and the regiment's only white line officer, William Peabody. Pinchback was being held at Ship Island under arrest "for leaving his command and post without

Daniels made no mention in the diary of Hall's change of officers until six weeks later, in a general comment dated March 24—"in regard to change of officers of The Reg't. I regret the Col has taken the steps that he has in the matter"—even though as early as March 2 he had received *and* acknowledged a notification from department headquarters of Hall's action.[20] He did not mention the situation again until April, when he expressed a more intense but less general reaction, condemning *only* the removal of Captain Murillion. He made just one comment on the officers who quit in frustration, a short sentence at having received Robert Isabelle's resignation; otherwise, he simply noted receipt of the special orders that included their move. His support for his officers seems to have been selective, based on no apparent reason, at least none that can be determined from his diary.

While Daniels was preoccupied with the defense of the island, his black officers were concerned about their place in the military. Word of the examination board at Fort Pike traveled to the rest of the regiment at Ship Island. Also, not two weeks after Hall's action, Colonel John Nelson of the 3rd Louisiana Native Guards at Baton Rouge had requested a board for *his* black officers.[21] Knowledge of this intimidating procedure added to the unrest that had been building for months among Daniels' line officers. The educated, light-skinned, free black leaders in the Native Guard regiments were extremely sensitive to "unfair treatment." Their self-esteem caused them to react strongly to inequitable policies that belittled them as gentlemen and officers.[22]

On March 2, coincidentally the same day that Daniels acknowledged Hall's moves at Fort Pike and a few of the officers there resigned, the 2nd Regiment's Ship Island line officers held a meeting to air their grievances. All of them, as well as the lone staff officer, Major Francis Dumas, signed

---

leave" on December 29, 1862, while stationed on the Opelousas Railroad. Peabody was not tested. Regimental Papers, 74th USCI (2nd LaNG), RG 94, NA; MSR of P. B. S. Pinchback, 74th USCI [2nd LaNG], RG 94, NA. The vacancies were not filled until later that summer and into the fall.

20. Colonel N. W. Daniels to Major General N. P. Banks, March 2, 1863, LR, II, Ser. 1747, Dept. of the Gulf, RG 393, Pt. 1, NA.

21. Colonel John A. Nelson to Major General N. P. Banks, February 15, 1863, LR, Ser. 1756, Dept. of the Gulf, RG 393, Pt. 1, NA.

22. Glatthaar, *Forged in Battle*, 111.

Part I, Ship Island

A badly faded photograph of Colonel Daniels (left) and Major Francis E. Dumas at Ship Island. Perhaps as wishful thinking, Daniels drew explosive-looking lines around an imperfection in the print and labeled it "Bomb-shell."

a petition for General Banks. Their listed complaints ranged from enduring "the heaviest guard duty ever known" on the Opelousas Railroad to "continually erecting Batteries, Magazines, and Fortifications, working both day and night" on the island. They had not been paid, and their families at home languished as a result. Promotion once hoped for was not available to them—and now the humiliating examination board. Digging ditches and building gun batteries did not allow them time to "acquire that perfect knowledge of Military" that would prepare them for an interrogating board. As they grasped the strategy behind this whole procedure, it became obvious to them that General Banks wanted them out of military service.[23]

23. The men also learned that Pinchback's white 2nd lieutenant, William Peabody, did not have to undergo Hall's board of examination at Fort Pike, a demoralizing situation in that it was widely known that most of the black officers were far superior to Peabody "in civil or military knowledge." Pinchback, whose name led off the signatures, rejoined his company at Fort Pike shortly after the March petition. Captain P. B. S. Pinchback & 19 sig-

Banks had, in fact, written the U.S. adjutant general, Brigadier General Lorenzo Thomas, in Washington to complain of the black line officers as a "source of constant embarrassment and annoyance." He expressed concern about the "negrophobia" of the white officers and enlisted men in his command. A white lieutenant had stated that if assigned with a negro captain, "I must . . . obey him. . . . I must stand while he sits, unless his captainship should condescendingly ask me to be seated. Negro soldiers are all very well, but let us have white officers, whom we can receive as equals everywhere, and whom we may treat as superiors without humiliation." Banks considered the black officers "detrimental to the service," their presence creating a situation that demoralized both races. He told Thomas he planned to replace them with white officers.[24]

If Daniels was aware of the officers' March 2 meeting and the petition of complaints, he did not mention them in the diary. Although not the most sensitive of leaders, he wanted the best for his men, to help them "prove" themselves, to show them how to do things, knowing they would rise to the occasion; all they needed was "cultivation and refinement." He ordered books for those who wanted to read in their idle time, something unheard of in the later illiterate slave regiments.[25] He was sincerely optimistic of the men's progress and planned to make the regiment "perfect," which of course would also enhance his own reputation.

Perfection means discipline in the military world. In order to instill an awareness of what was acceptable behavior and what was not, Daniels used various forms of punishment. He was harder on some officers than on others and brought charges against offenders, mincing no words in comments on their characters. Within the companies he reduced a few enlisted men in rank and subjected others to the ball and chain plus a reduction in pay—the latter perhaps an idle threat, as the regiment had re-

---

natures to Major General N. P. Banks, March 2, 1863, LR [misfiled 6th USCI], Regimental Books and Papers, RG 94, NA, found in Berlin *et al.*, eds., *Black Military Experience*, 322–23; FSSP [G-287]; MSR of P. B. S. Pinchback, 74th USCI [2nd LaNG], RG 94, NA.

24. Major General N. P. Banks to Brigadier General L. Thomas, February 12, 1863, G-148, 1863, LR, Ser. 496, Volunteer Service Division, RG 94, NA, found in Berlin *et al.*, eds., *Black Military Experience*, 315–16; New York *Herald*, February 4, 1863.

25. Lieutenant Elijah K. Prouty, Post Adjutant, to Major General N. P. Banks, February 13, 1863, LR, II, Ser. 1747, Dept. of the Gulf, RG 393, Pt. 1, NA.

ceived no payment to date. Although he was proud of his command and urged its success in gaining recognition and equality, Daniels appears to have been demanding of his men.

For the black soldiers themselves, officers and enlisted men alike, training, drilling, and artillery practice lost their importance when too much time was devoted to the menial labor of digging canals and building batteries. The officers' March petition was an attempt to bring their concerns to the attention of superiors, in hope that changes would bring their military life more in line with their expectations. It would prove a futile hope.

Daniels' sporadic diary entries settled down to a daily routine after March 9, when life on the island, despite the ongoing alert for enemy moves, must have allowed more personal time. One repeated note of anxiety in Daniels' writing was his acute awareness of the island's isolation and its vulnerability to the ferocity of Gulf storms. Weather determined the ship traffic and emphasized the post's total dependence on outside sources for food, shelter, transportation, and communication. It was a crucial matter if ships laden with rations, supplies, arms, and mail did not arrive when expected. Men were ravenous for any news from the outside world, particularly reports on the progress of the war. Newspapers were their lifeline. Communication with the mainland was infrequent and especially difficult when Daniels needed to send a dispatch of some urgency. Frustrated with the slowness of the large steamers that took nearly thirteen hours to reach New Orleans, he requested the post's own small boat capable of making faster runs.[26]

The colonel's isolation was unique. As the white commanding officer of a black regiment, he already stood apart from other military personnel; being confined to an island compounded the difficulty. Responsibility for all activity on the post lay in his hands, for the local chain of command ended with him. If the enlisted men needed to talk to someone, they could go to their company black officer or to their lone regimental black officer, Major Dumas. The officers' next step was to go to Daniels. If the colonel needed advice, it meant writing to a superior on the mainland; beyond that, he was on his own with a meager support system.

26. Colonel N. W. Daniels to Major General T. W. Sherman, March 13, 1863, LR, Ser. 1756, Dept. of the Gulf, RG 393, Pt. 1, NA.

Personal time and socializing were defined by the isolation. The Native Guards, ship captains, occasional visitors, refugees, prisoners, and contrabands were Daniels' world. Like other Civil War officers in the North and South, he had personal servants, most likely black—his boy Frank on the island, and Levi and William later in New Orleans. Margaret, a beautiful Creole acquaintance from New Orleans, arrived for a poorly timed visit. There was some interaction with those in the prison camp. At one point a "secesh" gentleman gave the colonel a pipe for his kindness in allowing the freedom to walk about the post.[27] Boredom played its role—not unusual for any soldier in the hurry-up-and-wait military, but the island's confines magnified the tedium. Daniels wrote of dining with Captain Joseph Villeverd and the quartermaster, Lieutenant Charles S. Sauvinet, but mentioned only one white staff officer in a social context, his surgeon, Major Samuel Willis, who appeared in several photographs. The colonel's fellowship was mostly with the ship captains, navy and civilian, during their stay in port.

Ship Island was a primary refueling stop for steamers traveling the coastal route linking Key West, Pensacola, New Orleans, and Galveston. Large ships, those of more than 1,500 tons, might remain in the harbor for several days while taking on up to 700 tons of coal. The island also had a machine shop capable of providing vessels with routine maintenance and even major overhauls. Commodore Henry H. Bell's *Brooklyn*, en route from Pensacola to Galveston, stayed at Ship Island for a month undergoing repairs.[28]

The sloop of war *Vincennes* was assigned Ship Island as her home port. The *Vincennes*' captain—first Lieutenant Commander John Madigan, later Lieutenant Commander Henry Adams—was the senior officer in charge of the navy at the post, and all vessels anchoring in the harbor reported to him.[29] The storeship *Relief*, with Acting Volunteer Lieutenant

---

27. Daniels Diary II, January 12, 1864.

28. *ORN*, Ser. I, Vol. XIX, 648; Extract from private diary of Commodore Henry H. Bell, *ORN*, Ser. I, Vol. XX, 753.

29. A change of command ordered Lieutenant Commander Henry A. Adams of the gunboat *J. P. Jackson* to relieve Lieutenant Commander John Madigan as captain of the *Vincennes;* Acting Master N. D'Oyly would relieve Lieutenant Commander Adams on the *Jackson*. U.S. Navy General Orders No. 49, Admiral Farragut to Hon. Gideon Welles, Secretary of the Navy, February 21, 1863, *ORN*, Ser. I, Vol. XIX, 622.

Part I, Ship Island

Benjamin Manton, was also stationed at the island. A Captain Edgerlady, otherwise unidentified, of the government's coal-carrying quartermaster vessel *New England* was a frequent visitor. Captains of all ships stopping at the post called on Colonel Daniels, as was required by military etiquette. Depending on their length of stay in port, Daniels often made reciprocal visits on board their ships. Captains Adams and Manton were mentioned repeatedly in the diary and were to become his supporters and advocates for his black troops. Several photos in the diary show the captains together with Daniels and Major/Doctor Willis.

Even in their isolated duty on Ship Island, the 2nd Louisiana Native Guards continued to be plagued by racial problems. After the departure of the 13th Maine and 8th Vermont companies, the only white group on the post was the prisoners. However, when ships were in port, portions of the crews were often allowed liberty for exercise on the island. The total number of sailors per ship of course varied: 259 on the *Brooklyn*, 162 on the *Vincennes*, 51 on the *Relief*, close to 100 on the gunboat *Jackson*. The navy was integrated in the enlisted ranks, with the number of blacks differing from ship to ship depending on the crew's size requirements. Of the *Jackson*'s crew, 18 were listed as black, 4 as mulatto. Conditions on shore—whether the area was heavily or lightly populated, black or white—often determined the crew's liberty—who went, and how many. The racial makeup of a group landing on Ship Island from the *Jackson* in mid-March 1863 is unknown, but because of subsequent events it can be presumed that the visiting sailors were white—coming ashore where the black Native Guards were in command.[30]

On March 18, Colonel Daniels wrote of a "difficulty between a sailor and a guard": a white sailor evidently committed a serious offense and the black sentinel attempted an arrest. Rescuing sailors overpowered the black guard and dragged their mate to their boats, but not before the guard stuck the white offender with his bayonet. There is no reference to this incident in regimental records, but it may be the altercation Joseph T. Wilson referred to in his 1890 history of African American soldiers. Wilson identified the white sailors as being from the *Jackson* and claimed that *several* were *killed* in a scuffle with black soldiers. Daniels referred to only

---

30. See ship roster for statistics. Muster Rolls for USS *J. P. Jackson*, RG 24, Bureau of Naval Personnel, NA.

one injury—that of the bayonetted sailor—although other sailors were involved in the rescue. He made no comment on any death at the time or later in the diary, when this affair was to play a larger, retaliatory role during a combat situation.[31]

The Native Guards, like the later black regiments, needed the ultimate test of battle to prove their worth and equality as soldiers. Most whites doubted the abilities of black soldiers, feeling that they would run rather than fight. Daniels' regiment, with its mix of historically free men and former slaves, was in the war to fight for rights, for homes, property, businesses, families, for justice for black compatriots, and ultimately for the black race. It was a freedom-or-death question. The colonel's men and officers were "naturally ambitious," filled with eagerness and commitment. Daniels shared their impatience and hoped for a battle to relieve the monotonous assignment on Ship Island. His only concern was controlling his troops in the heat of the moment, for he knew that "defeat in our case is worse than death."

The time finally came. On April 9, 1863, the regiment was called to make a reconnaissance expedition to Pascagoula, Mississippi, where a small force of Confederates was said to be in control. Daniels expected that the mission would secondarily divert enemy troops from Mobile toward Pascagoula, preventing their moving to an anticipated battle at Charleston, South Carolina.[32] He took only two companies, B and G, totaling 180 men, plus their officers, along with Major Dumas and the quar-

---

31. Wilson, *Black Phalanx*, 132n, 208. Wilson spent some time in the 2nd LaNG and was familiar with incidents of the regiment, though he may not have been personally involved. His statements do not always correspond to Daniels' diary entries. A man "without academic training" and writing more than twenty years after the war, he was not always accurate—as evidenced, for example, by his slips in placing the 2nd LaNG at the May assault on Port Hudson and stating that the regiment lost its Colonel Paine (219). The 2nd LaNG was not at Port Hudson, and Colonel Charles J. Paine of the *white* 2nd La. Infantry, though present at Port Hudson, was not killed (*OR*, Ser. I, Vol. XV, 254). Wilson himself was on leave, hospitalized for disease from mid-April into July of 1863 at St. James Hospital, New Orleans: MSR of Joseph Wilson, 74th USCI [2nd LaNG] RG 94, NA.

32. Wilson, *Black Phalanx*, 208, mentions Daniels' mainland objective as being the destruction of a railroad to Mobile that transported Confederate troops toward Charleston. Daniels does not mention a railroad.

Colonel Daniels and Major Dumas.

termaster, Sauvinet. He asked Captains Adams and Manton of the navy along to observe. The *Jackson* was to accompany the expedition to help if the soldiers "were repulsed."

Shortly after landing at East Pascagoula, the men encountered the enemy and fought as Daniels knew they would—bravely, intelligently, with several officers worthy of commendation and all deserving of praise, which he showered on them afterward. Dumas, especially, won acclaim from the colonel for his courageous role in the fighting. Later, Daniels summed up the men's intensity: "one of the privates . . . had both legs blown off by a shell . . . so that his bowels hung from the gaping hole . . . and the remnants of his poor mutilated body was being borne by me upon a stretcher when, he raised up on his elbow, gave the military salute and exclaimed—'don't give up, Colonel, we can whip the d——d rebels yet. God bless you colonel—Fight them to the death.' . . . He died soon after." The men had no white soldiers alongside them with whom to be compared. Only Daniels, the two navy captains, the distant *Jackson*'s crew, and the enemy were white witnesses to the skirmish. Captain Manton, previously skeptical of black troops, came away favorably impressed. Unfortunately, the *Jackson's* sailors, according to Daniels, took this opportunity to retaliate for the incident on Ship Island a month earlier. As the black soldiers withdrew to their boats after being repulsed by greater numbers, the *Jackson*, instead of firing at the oncoming Confederates, fired directly into the retreating blacks coming out onto the wharf, killing several and wounding others. Although livid at this inexcusable act, Daniels in his official report referred to it only as an unfortunate situation and made no mention of any earlier racial problems between the two groups. The account he sent to the New Orleans papers did include the incident, but their edited versions left out the *Jackson's* implication.[33]

The skirmish whetted the appetite of the regimental companies involved. Unfortunately for the eager black soldiers, it would be the only combat the 2nd Louisiana Native Guards experienced. Yet despite its insignificance in the larger theater of war—especially when followed by the 1st and 3rd Regiments' prominent role in the assault on Port Hudson—the Pascagoula battle enlightened and encouraged a skeptical public toward supporting the use of black troops. The men involved were heroes for the moment, creating great excitement for the New Orleans populace, black and white, under Federal control. The brief combat also helped bolster the soldiers' morale, which had been sagging with their bitter disappointment at military life in the blatantly prejudiced Department of the Gulf.

From the beginning, one of the most controversial issues involving black regiments centered on pay. Not only was payment stalled for the first organized troops, but when it did come, it was not as promised. The Native Guards led the fight against this glaring inequity, paving the way

---

33. Daniels Diary II, January 10, 1864; Daniels Scrapbook, Rochester (N.Y.) *Express*, November 24[?], 1864. The retaliation of the *Jackson's* crew may be viewed as an isolated occurrence based on a personal grudge between these particular groups, but nonetheless it had racial overtones. Colonel N. W. Daniels to Brigadier General T. W. Sherman, April 10, 1863, *OR*, Ser. I, Vol. LII, 61. Wilson, *Black Phalanx*, 208, again gives a slightly different version of the action, commenting on Daniels' omittance in the official report of Confederate women's and children's participation in the fight. Daniels did, however, mention them in his diary notes.

for future black troops. At recruitment in the fall of 1862, the men had been told they would make the same pay as white regiments: ten dollars a month plus three dollars for clothing. Later, the amount was changed to seven dollars a month with three dollars for clothes. The soldiers were angry at having to accept less than whites: "Do we not fill the same ranks?" Not only that, but they had not in fact been paid *at all* since their muster in October. Trouble brewed as a result.

Colonel Spencer H. Stafford of the 1st Louisiana Native Guards complained in the fall that families of his men had been arrested for not paying their rent. Three months later, after repeated requests for payment of his troops, Stafford was told that pay would be denied until the paymaster received further instructions. Daniels requested payment for his regiment on a regular basis and at one point wrote to President Lincoln. Finally, at the end of April, the men of the 2nd Regiment did receive pay, but only half what they were due. Two months later, Paymaster William W. Sherman informed his superior that he had "retained one half of the pay of colored soldiers" and asked if he should now allow full pay. The response was that "retention of half their monthly pay is by virtue of orders of the commanding gen'l in absence of law, regulation or orders from the War Department governing the case." With no resolution in sight, the confusion and controversy would continue to create great hardship for the Native Guards and the black regiments that followed, both for the men and for their families.[34]

Besides trying to get pay for his men, Daniels faced continuing disciplinary problems among them. Lieutenant Joseph Jones, who had recently fought at Pascagoula, shot a private in a situation involving negligence on prison guard duty. After reviewing the occurrence, Daniels

34. Glatthaar, *Forged in Battle*, 170–75; Colonel S. H. Stafford to Major George C. Strong, AAG, Dept. of the Gulf, October 23, 1863, LR, Ser. 1756, Dept. of the Gulf, RG 393, Pt. 1, NA; Major R. G. Usher, Paymaster, to Colonel S. H. Stafford, January, 5, 1863, LR, Ser. 1756, Dept. of the Gulf, RG 393, Pt. 1, NA. In an added note Usher stated he was "personally in favor of arming, equipping, subsisting, mustering into The U.S. Service and paying Colored Regiments, or any other set of men that will help crush out this wicked Rebellion." Colonel N. W. Daniels to Major General N. P. Banks, March 3, 1863, LR, II, Ser. 1747, Dept. of the Gulf, RG 393, Pt. 1, NA; Regimental Papers, 74th USCI [2nd LaNG], RG 94, NA. W. W. Sherman to [?], June 9, 1863, LR, II, Ser. 1747, Dept. of the Gulf, RG 393, Pt. 1, NA.

found the officer at fault and promptly issued special orders requiring all ranks not to interfere with sentinels at their posts. Captain William Barrett, who had also been in the Pascagoula skirmish, received charges preferred by the adjutant, Elijah Prouty, and another officer. Daniels later arrested two captains and a lieutenant for disrespect and conduct unbecoming an officer. One had been the reserve captain and fought well at Pascagoula; the other two men had remained on Ship Island. These same three officers a few days later turned around and preferred charges against Daniels. The colonel did not seem to be particularly concerned, as he felt that the three had already established poor reputations at headquarters. If there was any kind of bonding between the white commanding officer and his black officers after having experienced battle together, it does not appear to have enhanced their relationships on the island.

Lieutenant Colonel Hall at Fort Pike had troubles of his own. He was left with only two line officers, his free black captain Pinchback and white 2nd lieutenant Peabody. The expected white replacements had not yet arrived for the seven blacks—two captains and five lieutenants—who had either been removed by the February examination board or resigned shortly afterward. Hall's change of officers created a severe morale problem among the men of his three companies. Daniels noted in the diary that Hall had been drunk for several days in a row. It was around this time that the lieutenant colonel, in an unsteady hand, wrote his resignation to headquarters, citing the "great feeling ... obtained among the officers of the regiment against me, so much so that the interests of the service are injured thereby." Apparently no action was taken in the department, whether because Hall changed his mind in more sober moments or the declaration was not accepted, for Hall remained with his companies at Fort Pike.[35]

A good percentage of Daniels' diary entries show an avid interest in the war's progress as taken from newspapers, military reports, and the inevitable rumors. Some of this information was timely, but most arrived long

---

35. Lieutenant Colonel Alfred G. Hall to Captain Wickham Hoffman, April 16, 1863, MSR of Alfred G. Hall, 74th USCI [2nd LaNG], RG 94, NA.

Part I, Ship Island

after the fact, especially from the northern and eastern fronts and from the sectors of French activity in Mexico. Daniels' first concerns were events in the Department of the Gulf where his troops might be involved but, frustratingly, were not. Led to believe their position was as crucial as any other in the department, in actuality they were in military exile. Movements of the army and navy during the long-drawn-out Vicksburg campaign seemed to involve everyone but the 2nd Louisiana Native Guards.

A key to Grant's overall Vicksburg strategy was the taking of heavily fortified Port Hudson, Louisiana, 240 river miles south of Vicksburg on the Mississippi. While Rear Admiral David D. Porter struggled to open the river north of the city with help from Grant's Army of the Tennessee, General Banks moved portions of his 19th Corps toward Port Hudson. In mid-March 1863, he left New Orleans for Baton Rouge with 12,000 undisciplined, mostly nine-months' men. He was joined there by the 1st, 3rd, and newly formed 4th Native Guards to march north with another division for diversionary action in front of Port Hudson, a coordinated move with Admiral Farragut that would allow the navy to run the river batteries. Daniels eagerly awaited news reports on the action, only to learn that the plan faltered due to miscommunication between the two leaders. The colonel noted the resulting losses in his diary.

Banks found Port Hudson nearly impregnable and his forces woefully inadequate. He abandoned an all-out assault plan, shifting his concentration to western Louisiana in an attempt to cut the fortification's supply lines and halt enemy activity throughout the Teche district, the bayou networks, and the Red River Valley.[36] Daniels followed the general's movements and those of others, including Brigadier General Godfrey Weitzel, under whose command he and his men had been in the fall of 1862.

As the war continued unabated, the value and necessity of black troops gained recognition in the North and with President Lincoln. In March 1863, Secretary Stanton ordered Adjutant General Thomas to begin recruiting blacks in the Mississippi Valley and find "willing" white commanders from existing units. He also ordered Brigadier General Daniel

---

36. Winters, *Civil War in Louisiana*, 166–67, 212–34.

Ullmann to Louisiana to help Banks raise black troops, who would then remain under the latter's command.[37] Banks had already raised the 4th Louisiana Native Guards with white line officers and had plans for more regiments. He hoped these new units would be free of the problems that continued to plague the first three groups with their black line officers raised under General Butler.

In March, before the Port Hudson expedition, Colonel Stafford of the 1st Louisiana Native Guards wrote to General Banks to complain about the difficulty of dealing with the Department of the Gulf. Earlier, in New Orleans, his men had been insulted in the streets by white soldiers. Mothers and wives had been locked in jail because they did not have the passes or papers promised at recruitment. Police continually arrested black soldiers, calling them slaves. Now the men lacked sufficient equipment, and what was issued was of poor quality and left over from other regiments; requisitions were stalled or went unanswered; requested lumber and ammunition did not arrive; most damaging of all, the men had not been paid.[38] Stafford's complaints attest to the hardships of the first three Native Guard regiments, whose commanding officers were trying to prove that blacks could make good soldiers. But the department showed a decided lack of support. Banks tolerated the Native Guard colonels' grumbling but did little for the three regiments, placing more emphasis on the new units to come, free of the troublesome black line officers.

In the spring of 1863, Banks spent a good deal of time in the field, returning to New Orleans only for brief visits. He was back in the city on April 25 and left again five days later for Opelousas and his western expedition. Colonel Daniels left Ship Island for a leave of absence in the city, arriving late on April 29, just missing the general, who departed early the next morning. A letter written April 21 by Lieutenant Palfrey, the department engineer who worked with Daniels on Ship Island, was not noted as received at headquarters until May 3. Brigadier General Thomas W. Sherman, in temporary command in Banks's absence, would address the

---

37. Edwin M. Stanton to Brigadier General Lorenzo Thomas, March 25, 1863, *OR*, Ser. III, Vol. III, 99–103; Stanton to Banks, March 25, 1863, *OR*, Ser. III, Vol. III, 101–102.

38. Colonel S. H. Stafford to Captain Wickham Hoffman, February 23, 1863, LR, Ser. 1756, Dept. of the Gulf, RG 393, Pt. 1, NA, found in FSSP [C-544].

letter's contents, which involved the black regiment's commanding officer. Daniels' long-awaited break from the island's isolation was about to become more than he anticipated.

Ship Island, Miss, a Military Post of U.S.

Monday, January 12th 1863

Came to Ship Island, Miss.—Took command of Post, relieving Col Rust of the 13th Maine Vol, a dreary desolate sandbar. Brought seven companies of my Regiment, 2d La N.G. Volunteers, found two companies of 13th Maine stationed here. They will remain under my Command. Have been guarding The Opelousas R.R. for the last three months, and now come to a drearier duty on this God-forsaken Isle. Col Rust goes to take command of Forts St Phillip & Jackson. Find good Headquarters here, but no barracks for my soldiers.—Sloop of war Vincennes and Store Ship Relief in Harbor with Gunboat Nassau for an intercepting boat.

Sunday, January 13th 1863

Schooner in from New Orleans with Supplies for this Post, ordered Quartermaster to take possession of same, and receipt to officer of 13th Maine.

Monday, January 14th 1863

Col Rust still here and through Etiquette I permit him to retain Command, however shall soon take possession if he does not succeed in getting transportation   Lt Col Hall of my Reg't. at Fort Pike with three companies.—

Monday, January 21st 1863

Col Rust 13th Maine Vol turned over command of Ship Island to me last evening & embarked on steamer Nassau for Fort Jackson.—Have now under my command Seven companies of my own Regiment Two of the 13th Maine—two 8th Vermont—paroled Prisoners, and some Fifty Prisoners of war—making in the aggregate some Twelve hundred men. Am busy at work this morning constructing sand batteries as The Alabama is reported off our southern shore.[39]

Saturday, January 26th 1863

Placed under arrest all of The Commissioned Officers and most of The Privates of the Companies of The 13th Maine Vol at this Post for Disobedience of Orders. Disarmed the soldiers and stationed a guard around their Quarters. Great excitement on The Island in consequence.[40]

Building Batteries above the Light House. Refugees here from Mobile say that the Confederates have the gun boats at that place, two iron plated, heavily armed, & equipped. About 15000 Infantry are there under command of Buckner, 2000 in The Forts Morgan & Gaines.[41]

Wednesday, February 11th 1863

Steamer here from New Orleans with ammunition &C for this Post. Orders from Headquarters to order the detachment of 13th Maine here under arrest to Forts Jackson & St Philip. They left this day on Steamer New Brunswick. Detachment of 8th Vermont also sent to rejoin their Regiment at Brashear City. Recd letters from home.—

39. The infamous *Alabama*, contracted for by the Confederacy and built in Liverpool, England, roamed the Atlantic and Gulf of Mexico threatening U.S. ships. Also known by northerners as the Rebel pirate ship "290," she had just sunk (January 11, 1863) the Union side-wheel steamer *Hatteras* in the Gulf off Galveston Island, Texas, and was rumored to be in the area. *OR*, Ser. I, Vol. XV, 647. She captured, burned, or sank more than sixty ships in her career before she was caught and sunk by the USS *Kearsarge* off Cherbourg, France, in June 1864.

40. Colonel Henry Rust wrote in his Ship Island diary of impending doom should his two companies and Daniels' men be thrown together. His fears were now borne out. Rust Diary, January 12–21, 1863, MOLLUS. A later Rust diary, September 4, 1863–December 26, 1864, begun at Forts Jackson and St. Philip, makes no reference to Colonel Daniels, the black 2nd LaNG, or Daniels' arrest of the Maine men. "Diary and Related Papers of Colonel Henry Rust, 1861–1914," MSS 261, Manuscripts Division, Historic New Orleans Collection, New Orleans. For that arrest, see nn. 6–8 above and related text.

41. Confederate major general Simon B. Buckner (1823–1914) was ordered in December 1862 to fortify Mobile, Alabama, where he remained until April 1863. Ezra J. Warner, *Generals in Gray* (Baton Rouge, 1959), 38; Forts Morgan and Gaines were at the entrance to Mobile Bay, the latter on the eastern end of Dauphin Island, with Fort Morgan on the opposite peninsula, known as Mobile Point (see map facing page 1).

Part I, Ship Island

"View of my Headquarters Buildings, the Fort in the background—Medical Quarters on The Left, Adj't and Quartermasters Departments on the extreme Right. Major Willis and myself mounted in front of my domicile—the buildings having been brought by Gen'l Butler's corp de armee from Vermont—of no interest particularly except as a memory in the future of our locale whilst in exile at Ship Island.—Shall move my buildings to a better location on the Island next week therefore must take the view as what we found upon our arrival at the Post." (Sunday, March 22, 1863)

Sunday, February 13th 1863

Finished to day our three upper batteries so that now we are in a defendible condition. Wrote mother, Katie, Hattie, Mr Childs, and Col [?] Hyde.

Monday, February 16th 1863

Have at this date Four Batteries, mounting six guns on the north side, two batteries mounting two guns on the west side, and two guns on platforms in the Fort on the south side of The Island. Have also constructed rifle pits, barricades, and two large magazines. A considerable change since our arrival as we found the heavy guns lying in the sand, no batteries

"View taken from Battery No Five.—My surgeon, Adj't, portion of Company, and myself in foreground, a decidedly Artistic scene, could it be properly Photographed." (Thursday, March 26, 1863)

in construction nothing done to place the post in a defencible condition, not one gun in position that could be used. Now we can hold the post against 1000 men & all the gunboats that the Confederate gov't can send against us.—

Sunday, February 22^d 1863
[Cross-written]
    Washington's Birthday ordered a salute of twenty one guns to be fired which was done the grand old echoes reverberating for miles on the Gulf causing the secesh across the waters to wonder at our noise—The U.S. Naval Boats The Vincennes, Capt Madigan, The Relief Capt Manton, The Jackson, Capt Adams and The Clifton, Capt Law all fired salutes and for a little while it looked like a real battle. My Batteries led off first & the navy followed. Just as we commenced firing a steamer bore in sight in the offing apparently intending to run outside without reporting at this naval [post]. Immediately the Clifton steamed up and started firing her salute as she went out to sea. It was a beautiful sight and awakened great enthusiasm

both in the Army & Navy. She gained upon the Blockade Runner fast and when off Point ChandeLeur Light House overtook and captured the vessel which she has brought back and which proved to be a light draft steamboat out of Pascagoula—laden with cotton and Confections and bound to Havana. The chase was a beautiful one as the Gulf was as calm as water could be [for] the vessels all the while in sight. Had grand Review and Dress Parade in the afternoon—Then found a barrel of whisky and gave us noble fellows a Washington treat—

Monday, March 9th 1863
[Cross-written]
   Privates as Post Carpenters were busily engaged digging Canal through Island at The Pass so as make the middle Island defensible.—An alarm last night by Gunboats coming down the sound, went to Quarters for two hours, but the same resulted in a friendly sail.—
   Sent to St James Hosp'l New Orleans La Descriptive Lists & Passage for the following sick soldiers of this Regt Joseph Alcide Co D—Rob't Smith Co D—Andrew Bond Co D—Chas Nackir Co C—Abraham Wilkinson Co C—Van Meter Taylor Co C—Robert Jackson Co C—2d Rgt La NG Vol.—Ship with Rhode Island Cavalry aboard left Port for New Orleans.—

Tuesday, March 10th 1863
[Cross-written]
   Steamers Jackson and Clifton went up the sound to Grants Pass last evening. Commenced laying out ground for new street, started new battery. Wrote mother, Sent article relative to the 13th Maine difficulty on the Island to The Boston Transcript. Steamer belonging to Navy and bound to Lake Pontchartrain came in from New Orleans, brought no mail. Bark Houghton, naval store ship, left Port this P.M. for New York.—

Wednesday, March 11th 1863
   Commenced moving Buildings out of range of guns in Fort, and at Light House.—Sent Copy of Article sent Boston Transcript to New York Tribune for Publication. Made out Warrants for Non-Commissioned Officers of the Regiment. Weather cold and windy.—

Thursday, March 12th 1863

US transport Mississippi arrived. Brought the following Despatches
Gen'l Orders from Headqtrs
Special   "   "   "   NO's 64[42]
Letters from Brig Gen'l Sherman.[43]
    "   "   Headqtrs relative to Commission of Lt Smith.
Letter from Pro[vost] Mar.[shal] Dept. relative to soldier in arrest.
Letter from Ordnance Dept N.O.

Found Canal at head of Island, no go.

Commenced moving Headquarter buildings.

Old woman came over from Cat Island, for cook.—

Weather cool, but pleasant.

Had sea-gull cooked for supper and eat the same under the supposition that it was Duck, found it good, but a little tough.

Friday, March 13th 1863

Wrote Brig Gen'l Sherman Reporting force at this Post under my command.

Also Forwarding Information of enemies movements near Grant's Pass, and in the Sound. Asking that a steamer might be sent us to carry Dispatches &C.

Wrote Ordnance Dept enclosing Recpt for 190 Barrels Packing Powder.

Dispatched Yacht to New Orleans with Lt. Noyes with Despatches for Headquarters.

Wrote mother

Gave Lt Noyes letter from Pro Mar Gen'l relative to soldier in arrest

42. Special Orders No. 64, March 5, 1863, included the discharges of Captain Arnold Bertonneau and Lieutenants Octave Rey, Ernest Morphy, and Robert H. Isabelle, as a result of their resignations at Fort Pike. Special Orders, Ser. 1767, Vol. I, Dept. of the Gulf, RG 94, NA.

43. Brigadier General Thomas W. Sherman (1813–1879), the Union's "other General Sherman," assumed command of the Defenses of New Orleans for the Dept. of the Gulf on January 10 and served until May 21, 1863. *OR*, Ser. I, Vol. XV, 5 and Vol. XXVI, Pt. 1, p. 501.

"Scene of Ship Island, but a miserable affair. God knows the place is bad enough, but not equal to this dismal looking sketch." (Sunday, March 29, 1863)

with Instructions to have him Released and Restored to his Co at Fort Pike La—

Gen'l Banks gone up to Baton Rouge with all of his Troops, expect that Port Hudson has been attacked 'ere this. We are ordered to hold ourselves in readiness to move at an hours notice, should he be repulsed, we would doubtless reinforce him. Gen Sherman is in Command at New Orleans, and is somewhat anxious about the city's safety. There are but few troops left, and should the Rebels determine upon an attack, it could easily be taken—

Saturday, March 14th 1863

Took boy Frank into my employ. It would seem as though a combined attack was to be made by our forces at Charleston, Port Hudson, Vicksburgh and below Murfeesborough, so that the next advices must bring us important news. There has been inactivity enough   It is time our troops were now at work. They cannot commence too soon.—

Expecting daily an attack upon this Post from The Mobile forces. Am building two additional Batteries to command the approaches down the sound, and holding my command in expectancy, night and day. I hope the enemy will favor us with a call. We are anxious to test their metal.—The only trouble I fear in a fight is my inability to hold my men well in hand. Their ardor and Impetuosity excels all the Zouaves and [---ces] that were ever organized.—They will fight like bloodhounds, and never surrender. Defeat in our case is worse than Death. Victory the only alternative—my men are well aware of this and will vent themselves accordingly.—

Sunday, March 15th 1863
[Cross-written]

Weather delightful. Dined aboard Storeship Relief with Commodore Adams & Capt Manton. Tried to get Photographs of Batteries and Troops, but could not get good ones.—U.S. Steam Transport Eastern Queen came in last evening from New Orleans with Commissary Stores for us, but no mail. Great stupidity on someones part. Left this morning for Pensacola for troops to take to Baton Rouge. Brings news that Gen'l Banks is at Baton Rouge but has made no advance upon Port Hudson.—He must move soon, or he will have no troops, as they are mostly nine months men, and their time has nearly expired. Sent monthly Regimental Returns, to Washington for February. Review and Dress Parade in afternoon went off exceedingly well   Finished out buildings on Hill for Headquarters.

Canal at Neck of Island a failure. Had it cut through, but the current would not keep the sand out. Large embankment thrown up however, which make a splendid Fortification, so that if the Rebels come down from Mobile as we expect they will some of these nights we shall be tough for them. Can take and enfilade them for a mile and that in a narrow neck of land surrounded nearly by the Gulf of Mexico.

Monday, March 16th 1863
[Cross-written]

Pickets from head of Island threw up white and Red Signals last night at 8 1/2 o'c informing us of danger above. Beat the long roll, had the Artillery at Quarters, and waited in hopes of having a chance at the enemy. Our heavy guns were trained to bear upon anything that might come down the sound, and the men ready with [Lock strings?] in hand to welcome whoever might come. Matters remained in this Position until 10 o'c when a large fire appeared from the same position indicating continued danger. I

Part I, Ship Island

immediately ordered the Light in The Light House, and all other Lights on The Island, to be extinguished, dispatched a courier to the head of the Point, and awaited events. The Navy was also at Quarters, momentarily expecting an attack. At 3 o'c courier returned, Reporting that a Confederate Ram had come out from Biloxi, or rather Ponchatoula River,[44] had steamed over to the lower end of Horn Island, & run aground, but upon seeing the signals, and our lights being extinguished backed off, and made up the sound towards Mobile. A heavy thunder shower came up about 9 o'c and lasted nearly all night. The darkness thereby occasioned and the extinguishment of our Lights undoubtedly prevented our being attacked, as our gun boats were up the sound, and they wished to reap the advantage of their absence—Messenger down from East end confirming last night Report, was plainly a Confederate Ram.—Inspected the Light House and directed the keeper to blind the Light towards the Sound in all directions. He complied by boarding up fire glass on the North, North East, and North west points of the same.—[45]

Tuesday, March 17th 1863

The Ram seen night before last had no smoke stack, was very low in the water, and of very slow speed—but the following item from the NO. Picayune of this date, so it seems the outside world knows something of our position.

New Orleans Daily Picayune

The Confederate Fleet in Mobile—the N.O. correspondent of the Boston Journal in a letter of the 11th ult. says:

Although the enemy has made no demonstration against Ship Island I am by no means convinced that they have abandoned the idea of attacking it, in the manner described in my last. I am informed by a "reliable gentleman" who left Mobile three weeks ago, that there was then one ram, rather a formidable craft and two gun boats afloat, the Oregon and Florida. The

---

44. Daniels misnames the Pascagoula River, twenty-five miles east of Biloxi and directly opposite Horn Island.

45. The loss of the island's beacon proved to be significant. Though Daniels statement implies that the south sides, toward the Gulf, were not blinded, the news reaching New Orleans and later New York was, "The Light at Ship Island has been extinguished." New York *Daily Tribune,* April 13, 1863.

rebels are building two rams at Selma on the Alabama river. They are nearly finished and also are two others on the Tombigbee river and will doubtless make their appearance in due season when, let it be hoped, our navy will be prepared to give them such a welcome as shall effectually wipe out the disgrace of Galveston, Sabine Pass, the escape of the Oreto and the destruction of the Hatteras.[46]

Gunboat Pinola came in last evening from Mobile for repair. She is a beautiful little thing, and as she carries a 11 inch Dahlgren, is a very valuable accession to our defences. Will remain one week.—Wrote Letter to Col Hall Enclosing official Copy of Special Order No 61 from Headquarters,[47] and requesting him to send me names of non-commsd offcrs of the Companies under his Command. Issued order to Light House keeper to blind the Light on North, North East & North west side of the same. Moved my Headquarters up the Island on the high knoll, so that I now have a very pleasant location, airy, cool, and healthy. Schooner Belle of Mobile came in from New Orleans with stores for sutler, a very welcome visitor as we are entirely out of luxuries. Capt Stillwell of The Gunboat Pinola and Capt Adams of The Vincennes ashore and paid me a visit. Went off in the evening with Capt Manton of The Relief to visit Capt Adams.

46. The Galveston, Sabine Pass, *Oreto,* and *Hatteras* events occurred in January 1863. On January 1, a small detachment of Federal troops (three companies of the 42nd Massachusetts Regiment and the 2nd Vermont Battery) in command at Galveston, Texas, surrendered to the Confederates after a surprise 3 A.M. attack. One ship was captured, one destroyed, and two barks lost. The Rebels killed or captured 130 men. *OR,* Ser. I, Vol. XV, 202–203. On January 21 at Sabine Pass, Texas, two Confederate gunboats encountered, pursued, and captured two Federal blockading ships with a loss of thirteen guns, 109 prisoners and a $100,000 in property. *Ibid.,* 237–38. The *Oreto,* or the *Florida,* a Confederate ship built in England, had been bottled up in Mobile Bay, having slipped through the blockade in September 1862. The following January 16, between 2 and 3 A.M. after a passing storm, she slipped out again, passed two Union ships, and evaded the pursuing fleet. Philip Van Doren Stern, *The Confederate Navy* (Garden City, 1962), 128. For the *Hatteras,* see n. 39 above.

47. Special Orders No. 61, March 2, 1863, contained procedures for the Provost Marshal office and division commanders on how to deal with commissioned officers, enlisted men, and nonmilitary personnel arrested in New Orleans. Also, restrictions were to be issued on passes to officers and enlisted men because of past abuse. Five hundred men were confined in early March for no passes. Special Orders, Ser. 1767, Dept. of the Gulf, RG 393, NA.

"Picture presented me by The Capt of Company D, Capt Chase of my Regiment, not very good still well for Ship Island." (Thursday, April 16, 1863)

Had a pleasant game of whist, and comfortable supper. Our fleet now in Port an very pleasantly commanded—

Wednesday, March 18th 1863

Finished mounting Gun in Bat No 3 upon Pivot and Traverse.—So that we now have Three guns upon Traverses & very effective. Schooner went to New Orleans   Sent Despatches by her to Col Hall. Experimented with Battery No 3. Threw shell across the Island and two miles out at sea, so that we are satisfied of our ability to reach any vessel that may come up the Gulf, or down the sound, works beautifully on The Traverse, and is a perfect success.—

Battallion Drill and Dress Parade in the afternoon. The Regiment improve very fast, and maneuver finely. I will make them as perfect as possible 'ere we leave this post.

Sailed up the Island in Yacht to the Canal, find it improving, and an admirable fortification—

Sailor ashore, caught in the act of committing a serious offense. Guard attempted an arrest, but were outnumbered by the Tars, and they succeeded in getting into their boats, an the sentinel could [not] get any assistance. The Sentinel however, put his bayonet into Jack.[48]

Difficulty occurred between sailors and guard, sailor taken forcibly away from corporal by his comrades.—

Thursday, March 19th 1863

Went off and took Breakfast aboard The Gunboat Pinola with Capts Stillwell and Adams. Learned that Capt Adams formerly lived in Pt. Cou-Pee La, my old locale, and knew many of my old acquaintances, had a very pleasant resource of old memories.

Five Refugees from Mississippi came over and delivered themselves up this P.M. some of them had formerly been in the army with Gen'l Bragg,[49] said that they had been captured & Paroled and that the Confederates were now after them again. Represented their country as being in great destitution. Knew nothing of Mobile. Sent them to guard house after administering the oath of allegiance to The United States. Went off to see Mr. Edge aboard Ship New England in Harbor. Had Battallion Drill this P.M. very good, the Regiment improves rapidly.—

Friday, March 20th 1863

The Gunboats Jackson & Clifton came down the sound late last night, and brought a Mobile paper of yesterday's date, which contained an ac-

---

48. A March 9 log entry from the USS *Jackson* states that Joseph Penfield was arrested for "drunkenness and creating a disturbance on shore," and held for trial, which occurred later on April 3 as a "deck trial" on board the *Jackson*. Also on March 9, Joseph Mitchell was added on sick report, where he remained sixteen days; there were no details from the medical or surgeon's reports as to his condition, whether stab wound or other. The ship's log entry appears nine days before Daniels' diary notations. This may or may not be the incident referred to later by Daniels in relation to retaliatory action by the *Jackson* crew at the Pascagoula skirmish, but it is the only incident found reported by both the *Jackson* and Daniels in the same general time frame. USS *Jackson* Ship's Log, Vol. 205, RG 24, NA. See related text of n. 31 above; see also diary entry for April 10. "Jack Tar" was a general nickname for sailors.

49. Confederate general Braxton Bragg (1817–1876) commanded the Army of Tennessee. Most recently before this diary date, he had led the invasion of Kentucky and fought at Perryville, October 8, 1862, and at Stones River (Murfreesboro), December 31, 1862, to January 2, 1863. Warner, *Generals in Gray*, 30–31; James M. McPherson, *Battle Cry of Freedom* (New York, 1988), 515, 519–20, 579–82.

Part I, Ship Island

count of an action at Port Hudson in which the fleet engaged the enemy for four hours, losing The Mississippi and driving back all but The Flag Ship Hartford and Monongahela. The Richmond badly cut up, all in all equal to a defeat. The army under Banks not heard from, but supposed to be repulsed, as they moved simultaneously with The Navy.[50]

Another steamer ran The Blockade at Charleston. Burnside in command at Charleston. Engagements at Yazoo Pass, result not known, an interesting batch of news, but not favorable to us.—This comes through Rebel sources, and is to be taken with due reference to its source, but if it is true Gen'l Banks will return to Washington & shorn of all his laurels.— Admiral Farragut has gone on above in the Hartford, and is now between Port Hudson and Vicksburgh, a critical position should he be disabled, or should their rams be equal to an attack against him, but he is brave and rash, and will probably reach Porter at Vicksburgh.—[51]

Nothing from New Orleans to day. Judge from advices rec'd by Prisoners captured by The Jackson that an immediate raid is contemplated by

50. Banks and Farragut miscommunicated in coordinating their moves. Farragut's ships started their run past Port Hudson before midnight on March 14; Banks apparently thought the attack was to begin the following dawn. The navy suffered heavy losses. The *Richmond,* after receiving severe shelling, retreated and in the confusion mistakenly shot at the *Mississippi,* just beginning her run. The latter ran aground but freed herself, floated downstream on fire, and blew up. The *Monongahela* tried to pass the batteries, but her engines failed and she floated back down under heavy fire with many casualties. The *Hartford,* with help from the gunboat *Albatross,* managed to pass the batteries and continued unimpeded up the Mississippi to communicate with Grant south of Vicksburg. *OR,* Ser. I, Vol. XV, 253; Winters, *Civil War in Louisiana,* 216–17.

51. Major General Ambrose Burnside (1824–1881) at this time was in command of the Department of the Ohio, headquartered in Cincinnati, not with Union forces at Charleston. Major General David Hunter (1802–1886) was in South Carolina as commander of the Department of the South and of the 10th Corps, having resumed the command January 1863 after being removed in August 1862. Ezra J. Warner, *Generals in Blue* (Baton Rouge, 1964), 58, 176; *OR,* Ser. I, Vol. XIV, 376, 391. Yazoo Pass, Mississippi, a flooded inlet off the Mississippi River opposite Helena, Arkansas, was the site of a Federal combined army-navy expedition trying to reach Vicksburg downstream beginning in early February 1863. On March 11 and again on March 13, two Union ironclads were repulsed by the Confederates at Fort Pemberton, near Greenwood, Mississippi. Grant had not heard from his forces at Yazoo Pass and sent Admiral David D. Porter (1813–1891), together with Major General William T. Sherman's ground troops at Steele's Bayou, as a relief expedition. Porter started March 15 but became bogged down in shallow, tree-choked creeks and upon encountering Confederates had to retreat. Winters, *Civil War in Louisiana,* 183–84.

The Mobile forces upon us, as they represent that the two additional rams that were being Iron plated up the River have come down and that they are quite equal to the original Merrimac.⁵² —If so, and they visit us, it will take our heaviest shot, and many of them to have any effect.—10 o'c P.M. a Schooner in the offing towards New Orleans, have sent my boat out and hope she may bring us news.—

Saturday, March 21ˢᵗ 1863

Small boat arrived from New Orleans with man sent by Col Holabird Quartermaster of Gulf Dep't, to take off old brig in the Harbor belonging to The United States Gov't.⁵³

It is about time I think that this matter had been attended to and had not the Quartermaster have turned his attention think I should have had her off with my own force.—

Reduced 5th Sergeant of Company C to the ranks on account of disobedience of orders, and promoted 3rd Corporal of same company to the position. Promoted Private Wm H. Grant to fill the place made vacant by the promotion of such 3rd Corporal.⁵⁴

Newspaper rec'd from New Orleans corroborating the Rebel a/c of the burning of The Mississippi, but it seems she was destroyed by our own forces to prevent her capture. It seems to be understood though nothing

---

52. Daniels sent on a report of the *Jackson*'s captured prisoners to Brigadier General Thomas W. Sherman, Commander Def. of N. O., stating that the ironclads being built at Selma had come downriver to Mobile, had "taken aboard their engines, and have been completely outfitted and are now ready for active service," and that "an attack is now contemplated either upon this post or upon our fleet off Mobile Bay." The original *Merrimack*, a Federal forty-gun screw-steamer, burned and abandoned at the Norfolk Navy Yard April 20–21, 1861, was later resurrected by the Confederates, refurbished, and renamed the CSS *Virginia*. Colonel N. W. Daniels to Brigadier General T. W. Sherman, March 20, 1863, LR, Ser. 1756, Dept. of the Gulf, RG 393, Pt. 1, NA; McPherson, *Battle Cry of Freedom*, 279–80, 314, 373.

53. Union colonel Samuel B. Holabird (1826–1907) became chief quartermaster for the Department of the Gulf December 17, 1862, and remained in that position for the duration of the war. *OR*, Ser. I, Vol. XV, 611, and Vol. LIII, 609–10.

54. Fifth Sergeant Henry Joseph was removed to the ranks and replaced by 3rd Corporal John Woods. William Grant was promoted from the ranks to fill Woods's position. Muster Rolls, Regimental Papers, 74th USCI [2nd LaNG], RG 94, NA.

Part I, Ship Island

is said in the paper, that Genl Banks has been repulsed. Cap's Barrett & Carter over on the schooner Rocky Hill last night.⁵⁵

Sunday, March 22ᵈ 1863
[Cross-written]
The following despatches were rec'd by the Schooner Rocky Hill late Friday night.—

Letter from Lt Col Hall containing names of non-commissioned officers of Detachment under his command and letter containing statement of condition of detachment &C &C. Letter from Col Stafford 1st La N.G. relative to discharged soldiers. Letter from Pro Mar Gen'l stating that one of my Privates was confined under the late order of Genl Banks relative to Desertion in Parish Prison. Letter from Lt R. H. Isabelle Co H Containing Resignation.⁵⁶

Commodore Adams of Vincennes and Capt Stillwell of Gunboat Pinola dined and wined with me to day, rather an interesting communion.

Learn that the order was issued from Headquarters to my Rgt to move up to Baton Rouge, and then countermanded, just as the Steamer was coming for us, on account of the danger threatening this Post and the 1st and 4th Rgts of Native Guards ordered to move⁵⁷—They have gone, and

---

55. Captains W. B. Barrett and Hannibal Carter had been in New Orleans as witnesses in a court-martial. MSR's of William B. Barrett and Hannibal Carter, 74th USCI [2nd LaNG], RG 94, NA.

56. Parish prison was located in New Orleans at the corner of Orleans and Tremé Streets. "Norman's Plan of New Orleans & Environs, 1854," Fillmore Map Collection, No. 29, LC. Lieutenant Robert H. Isabelle, serving in Lieutenant Colonel Alfred Hall's detachment at Fort Pike, survived the February examination board together with Captain Arnold Bertonneau and Lieutenants Ernest Morphy and Octave Rey, but wrote his resignation later on March 3. Second Lieutenant R. H. Isabelle to Captain Wickham Hoffman, AAG, March 3, 1863, MSR of Robert H. Isabelle, 74th USCI [2nd LaNG], RG 94, NA. See n. 42 above.

57. The 1st Regiment and newly organized 4th Regiment, both under the command of Colonel Spencer H. Stafford, received a twelve–hour notice to leave Fort St. Leon for Baton Rouge on the transport steamer *General Banks*. They were to join additional troops with General Banks in front of Port Hudson. Special Orders No. 138, March 17, 1863, by Brigadier General T. W. Sherman, Def. of N. O., LR, Ser. 1756, Dept. of the Gulf, RG 393, Pt. 1, NA; Winters, *Civil War in Louisiana*, 214.

will probably be in at the fight at Port Hudson—I regret the countermanding of the order, as I want to get into a fight with my command—

Steamer Gen'l Banks from New Orleans came in this P.M. also Naval Stores Ship

Recd Letters from Gen'l Sherman and General Orders from Headqtrs. My Quartermaster and Lt Noyes came in Steamer. Bring Intelligence that our Fight at Port Hudson was after all a success as the Admiral passed with three boats and was all right above the batteries. Banks only made a Reconnaissance, a feint to attract the enemies attention whilst Farragut passed up the River. Only The Mississippi was lost.—Rec'd Letter from Chapin and Noble.—Steamer leave early in morning for New Orleans. Gen'l Sherman writes me that my Report is highly satisfactory & to hold my position at all events. That probably my men will not be moved from this position as its importance is equal to any in the Dept.

Monday, March 23^d 1863

Despatched U.S. Steamer Gen'l Banks to New Orleans with Passengers & mail and Despatches to Headquarters. Wrote Despatch to Gen'l Sherman relative to Mobile and Grants Pass. Sent Capt Ringgold to New Orleans with Instructions to go to Pro Marshals Dept and have soldier there in disservice released, also to take discharge papers to soldier in Parish Prison, also to attend to Capt [?] Bdlg's man under arrest. Chaplain, Dr. Gihon[58] and Sergeant Dauchy have leaves of absence to go to city, also sent off all Contrabands on The Island, as we cannot take care of them here.—

Rec'd letter from Pro Mar Dept relative to Wm Gallaher, Private of my Rgt. Wrote mother enclosing Photographs of scenes on Island, also my brother, my niece, Katie Bay, my cousin Mattie Warren and Mr. [?] Young.—

Made Requisition for Ordnance stores and Grape for IX inch guns and ammunition for muskets—Gave Capt Manton of U.S. Relief and Capt Edgerlady of New England Passes to New Orleans on Steamer Genl Banks. Wrote Letter to Gen'l Sherman asking that the Detachment of my troops at Fort Pike might be immediately ordered to this Post.—

---

58. John H. Gihon was the additional (assistant) surgeon Daniels requested on January 20, 1863. Regimental Papers, 74th USCI [2nd LaNG], RG 94, NA.

Equinoctial storm, very rainy, and disagreeable, sent off all contrabands on Island to New Orleans—

Tuesday, March 24th 1863
Terrible storm all day yesterday, new house leaked like a sieve—covered it with tent when it ceased leaking.—My Small boat came in from New Orleans, had stopped at Fort Pike five days on account of adverse winds, so that her news was old—

Rec'd letter from Col Hall relative to death of soldier. Also letters from Capt's Pinchback and Bertoneau relative to Col Hall's movements in regard to change of officers of The Reg't.[59] I regret that the Col has taken the steps that he has in the matter, as they will be likely to seriously revert upon himself. The question as to whether colored officers are not quite as competent when properly instructed, I am not as yet inclined to deny, at least my experience has thus far proved that they are, and their standard of Intelligence is quite as high as that of any line officer of any Rgt that I have yet seen—

Major sends me word that he will be over in next boat with Victor.—[60]

Wednesday, March 25th 1863
Officers drill last evening, went off very well. They improve rapidly.— Sick all day. Hang the military Service and this being confined at one station so long without an earthly chance of being Relieved so that one can go home and see friends, or even to New Orleans &C, if anything should occur whilst I was absent from my Post, I would of course reap the full benefits of such absence.—

59. Captain Pinchback had returned from Ship Island, where he was held under arrest for two months and signed the March 2 petition of the officers' grievances. Now back at Fort Pike, he was concerned, along with Captain Bertonneau, who survived the February interrogation, over Lieutenant Colonel Hall's removal of his black officers. Hall's request for a board of examiners to test his officers' capabilities was approved under Special Orders No. 34. The board's finding created Special Orders No. 55, in which the "provisional commissions" of Captain Monro(s)e Murillion, 1st Lieutenant William F. Keeling, and 2nd Lieutenant Lucien Scott were canceled. Adjutant's Regimental Papers, 74th USCI [2nd LaNG], RG 94, NA.

60. Major Francis E. Dumas of 2nd LaNG, and civilian Francis Victor, who sold provisions to the soldiers as sutler to the post. Muster Rolls, Regimental Papers, 74th USCI [2nd LaNG], RG 94, NA.

No News from Genl Banks troops up the River though we heard continued firing night before last in the direction of Port Hudson—Suppose that another attack has been made—I hope The Genl will be more successful this time, as there is no doubt but that he was driven back before—or at least found it comfortable to resume his original base.—I wish that Major Gen'l Phelps was here, he has great Military Genious and would effect more than any other that has as yet been sent to this Department. Wrote Col Hall enclosing letter of Defense. Wrote Capt Bertoneau.

Thursday, March 26th 1863

Some of my soldiers are working at my Headqrs as carpenters and their music is good, one in particular now singing an opera air reveals a richness of tone in his voice that would make him noted in the world of cultivation and refinement. There are many rough diamonds among this race, and what they need is only cultivation and opportunity. The Bonds of a half dozen centuries could not smother their inherent capacity no more than the political endeavor of present Copperheads can return the once freed to a state of bondage. The taste of Liberty is too sweet and death is far preferable to them than renewed slavery.—To hear these men reiterate "that they will die sooner than be taken," note the flashing eyes, the quivering nostrils and their immovable determination, one can but *know* that they are the men to battle and conquer, one can but feel that in their action is success.

Small boat in from New Orleans—brings bad news—

Friday, March 27th 1863

Small boat came in last night from New Orleans. Brings no mail, but an account that Admiral Farragut has been taken Prisoner above Port Hudson, and sent to Richmond, and his ship The Hartford destroyed. That Gen'l Weitzel has met with a reverse at Berwick Bay. That Gen'l Banks also met with a severe reverse at Port Hudson and is sending his troops back to New Orleans. That bad news has been rec'd from the north by last steamer which the Authorities in the city would not permit to be published. That Banks was seizing all boats to hold himself in readiness to evacuate New Orleans if necessary. That he was fortifying Pass Manchac, and that our forces had evacuated Pensacola—all in all a black news list. I only hope it was from a Confederate lie, but The Clifton, U.S. Gun boat, came over to day from Fort Pike, and has gone around to Berwick Bay, so it seems that there may be some truth in the a/c of Weitzels repulse.[61]—I hope that Admiral Farragut is safe if inland [at?] the Richmond. It will be a very somber affair—

Saturday, March 28th 1863
[Cross-written]

Rec'd Seranade last night from some of Company G of my Reg't, a number of beautiful voices among the seranaders,—and some excellent music was heard—Six Refugees came over yesterday from Pass Christian all telling the old story that they were fleeing from The Conscription Act. Their names were Eugene Jacques—James [Cline?]—Andrew [Gracien?]—Vincent St. John—Francis Schara—and Wm Strausburg. Two of them were deserters from the 5th Regt La Vol at Richmond, rather suspicious looking characters. I have administered the oath of allegiance, but doubt their loyalty notwithstanding. They say there is some 5000 troops at Mobile and two new iron plated Gun boats, don't appear to know much about Confederate affairs, seem inclined to keep all of their knowledge to themselves.—I shall try them again however tomorrow, and may extract some information. Had Target practice this afternoon, fired some 72 rounds and made some excellent shots. Heard heavy firing in the direction of Mobile—sent despatches to Col Hall by boat bound to New Orleans—Jackson went up the Sound again this morning. Rec'd Call from Capts Adams & Stillwell, and present of Beef and Lobster from Stillwell—very acceptable.[62]

61. Rumors flourished, but General Weitzel did meet a reversal. He ordered the gunboat *Diana* to make reconnaissance by Grand Lake north of Berwick Bay. Instead, she chose to go on the Atchafalaya River, right into "the teeth of the enemy." The damaged gunboat was taken by the Confederates. The total of killed, wounded, and captured was 150. Brigadier General G. Weitzel to Major General N. P. Banks, March 28, 1863, *OR*, Ser. I, Vol. XV, 290.

62. Pass Christian, Mississippi, is approximately twenty miles northwest of Ship Island across Mississippi Sound and twenty miles west of Biloxi, Mississippi. The Confederate Conscription Act in effect at this time was adopted April 16, 1862, and required three years' service of all white males eighteen to thirty-five years old. *OR*, Ser. IV, Vol. I, 1095–96. The Confederate 5th Regiment Louisiana Volunteers were at Richmond, Louisiana. Eugene Jacques and James [Cline?], privates in the regiment, were picked up on March 17 from a skiff by the *Jackson*. Andrew [Gracien?] deserted a "camp of instruction." USS *Jackson*

Had a splendid sail this evening in my crack little Yacht Witch—Beat everything among the Fleet.—The waters around the Island, on the sound side especially are usually quiet. The wind in the South blows over the land, and is Just right for swift sailing—This is one of my recreative perquisites [---] which together with my equestrian exercises I enjoy hugely. The only draw back is the want of a few feminine friends and companions to christianize our sports No wonder a man becomes boorish and stupid—Don't catch sight of a petticoat once in three months, and then it is so stupid in Secessionism that the figures will later catch no other patterns but stars and bars.—

Sunday, March 29th 1863
[Cross-written]

Terrible storm last night. About 12 o'clock a gale of wind struck my house and I thought for a few moments that the building would Certainly go over, but it stood well this storm. Cap't Villevert Quarters Just above me blew into a perfect wreck, but injuring no one, also Major Willis' Office went over Lightning as rapid in flashing as the rain that accompanied it, altogether a terrible storm, and one that I do not care to experience often. Wind perfectly loose this morning. Wrote Despatches to Lt Col Hall enclosing Warrants for non-commsd officers of Companies A E & H of my Reg't with Instructions for him to distribute same. Being all the morning finishing up Muster & Pay Rolls of Detachment of my Rgt at this Post. Wrote letters and sent Muster & Pay Rolls of same to Major [William] Sherman, Chief Paymaster of Gulf Dept, also wrote Lt Col Hall to furnish the same of Detachment under his command. Gave Recpt to Capt Stillwell yesterday for his impressions of war. Lent anchor to men Col Holabird sent here to get off wrecked Brig in Harbor. They have pumped her out and got her afloat, but have no anchor to hold her and I accordingly lent them one that we have ashore.—

As I sit in my Headquarters, I can lookout upon the Gulf of Mexico and see the surf breaking,—the huge waves coming nearly up to my feet—tis grand magnificent, the huge men of war are tossed about like playthings

---

Ship's Log, Vol. 205, RG 24, NA. The *Jackson* landed at Dauphin Island the day before after seeing stray Rebel cattle from Fort Gaines. Crew members killed twelve and later gave some of the fresh meat to the *Vincennes* (Captain Adams) and *Pinola* (Captain Stillwell). Ibid.

upon the water. The storm increases with great rapidity, and bids fair to wreck everything off and on The Island tonight. It appears as though, after the sun had set, that its monitor had succumbed to its fury and that its hell hounds were now let loose. The winds are wild children, and when once given the free rein sport with no trifling hand. Their weird voices chant a dismal song and keep hideous wassail to the white sea songs and the long low regimen of the falling rain.—Who would be upon the high sea this night woe betide the unlucky keel that shall meet the gales out of a safe harbor. Tis one of these terrible storms this Gulf is noted for. Destruction to every white winged messenger that crosses its deadly path. But what matters it when in [---] Are we not the same upon the water as we are upon the land, in the hands of an all powerful destiny.—Now comes to me the beautiful excitement embodied in the song of The Tempest which says—

> We were crowded in the Cabin,
> Not a soul would dare to sleep.
> It was midnight on the water
> And the storm was in the deep.
> 'Tis a fearful thing in winter
> To be shattered by the blast,
> And to hear the Trumpet thunder
> "Cut away The Mast."
>
> We shuddered there in silence
> For the stoutest held his breath
> Whilst the hungry sea was reeling
> And the breakers talked with death.
> Sad thus we sat—in silence
> All busy with our prayers.
> "We're lost"—the Captain shouted
> As he staggered down the stairs.
>
> But his little daughter whispered
> As she took his icy hand
> Is not God upon the water
> Just the same as on the land?
> Then we kissed the little maiden

And we spoke of better cheer,
As we anchored safe in harbor
When the sun was shining clear.

Capt Stillwell came and bid me good bye saying that he should start this morning with The Pinola for his station off Mobile but it is so rough that at this hour 12 o'ck he has not weighed anchor. It must be very rough outside. Recd fine present of a quarter of fresh beef from him—very acceptable considering the scarcity of fresh meat at this place. Weather growing colder more like Maine than La. Hunter C came down from head of Island & Reported that a woman with six children had escaped this morning from Rebeldom and came over to this shore. Poor creature, she deserves kind treatment if she has breasted the storm that has prevailed all day and sailed on the rough sound with six small children. Picket also Reports that a schooner came in this A.M. and went down the Sound close into the other shore.—What can our Gun boats be about. Lt Souvinet and Capt Villevert dined with me. Who could imagine that these gentlemen had African blood running in their veins, their skin is as white, their hair as straight as mine, nothing about them indicates Ethiopian origin. Yet what if they have had black skins for Ancestry. I have yet to learn that a noble heart may not beat beneath a sable covering as of one of among tint.—That a manly soul may not exist within the being of its darkest of Ethiop race as of those of snowy skin and Caucasion extraction. Thank God it hath been my fortune to be a participator in the grand idea of proclaiming freedom to this much abused & tortured race. Thank God my Regiment an African one, that I have been permitted to assemble them under the banner of freedom to do and die for their country & liberty—The 2^d Louisiana Regiment of Native Guards will yet have a name in history. The Record of their deeds will emblazen one of the brightest pages of the future's escutcheon.—The originators of this organization will be ranked with Wilberforce, with Wendell Phillips, with Victor Hugo,[63] with all noblemen whose deeds have been for Liberty and the

---

63. William Wilberforce (1759–1833), a member of Great Britain's Parliament instrumental in abolishing that country's slave trade in 1807, led a crusade for the slaves' emancipation in 1823. Wendell Phillips (1811–1884) was an American radical abolitionist, reformer, and orator. Victor Hugo (1802–1885), the French poet, novelist, and playwright, was known for his social consciousness.

Progress of the Human Race.—The hereafter will have more Joy for them with its acknowledgement of a great work accomplished than the present has of misery through [the rest of this sentence is in nearly indecipherable diminutive cross-writing: the (service?) and opposition and (redesign of the?) work of those, who in the darkness of clouded existences, oppose and attempt to overthrow] The cloud is [swiftly?] passing away and very soon the world and particularly this work of ours in America—will awake to the Realization of the fact that there is no more Slavery to be endured, [en----] of Religion, caste or personal liberty.—That the negro and all others are to be henceforward, Free, their own masters—to have an equal chance in the worlds great struggle for civilization, refinement and knowledge.—

Monday, March 30th 1863

The storm continues this morning with unabated fury, thought during the night that it would certainly blow my house down, but it still remains. Small boats in the harbor all wrecked either torn to pieces at anchor, or driven out to sea.—A woman named Mrs Williams with six small children came over yesterday in the fierce gale in a small sail boat with out any protection whatever from Ocean Springs, reached this end of the Island at 11 o'clock last night nearly dead with fatigue and cold, took her into my Headquarters, and gave her shelter. She is truly brave to breast this storm, and it shows what people will do to get out of Secession barbarism. Her husband, a deserter from the army at Vicksburgh, came over here last week, and I sent him to New Orleans and turned him over to The Pro Marshal's Dep't She supposed he was here, and came to find him.—She says the people are nearly starving, that it is impossible to live there much longer without help, that many soldiers whose families are there are deserting from the enemies ranks and coming home to find food for their wives and children and that the cry is food or peace—That the secesh are at their wits ends to procure food and soldiers, and that peace must very soon come or they will all die of starvation.—Oh! that we might gain a few good victories—me thinks the Rebellion would be ended. Peace would again blush o'er the land, and freedom and happiness once more return to bless this benighted country. The woman gave the two boys that brought her over $80 in Confederate money, all that she possessed. I do not know whether I shall permit them to return or not. They swear everlasting fealty, but I am fearful they may act the spy and inform the enemy of our position and force—

Raised Pole at Headquarters for Post Hquarters Flag.

Fight occurred among men of Co B. Sentenced four Privates to 10 days hard labor on Fort with ball & chain, and $5.00 deduction from pay of each, also Reduced Paul Dunbar to the Ranks for being engaged in the same.[64]—Gale still keeps up, no cessation—Old oyster man lost his boat and all his effects, which necessitates my furnishing him another—

Tuesday, March 31st 1863
[Cross-written]

Weather pleasant and storm subsided. Fitted out boat for old oysterman to go to New Orleans as a Despatch Boat. Sent Duplicate Pay and muster Rolls of Detachment Field and Staff and Hospital to Major Sherman, Paymaster in Chief of Gulf Department. Wrote Col Hall to send the balance of The Regt at Fort Pike with the same. Sent Report to Gen'l Sherman.[65] Also Accepted Resignations of Lt Fleury and Lewis of Companies G and I on account of sickness, and forwarded the same to Headquarters.

No boat as yet from New Orleans. I cannot imagine why we do not get some information from Headquarters. Great and momentous events must be transpiring. If the accounts be true that we receive from Rebeldom then must the last efforts of despair be the allotment of our enemy, their dying there is the most terrible and I imagine that it is at hand, if not now transpiring—

Capt Adams Commanding Fleet in Harbor ashore and dined with me.[66] Took horses and rode to the head of The Island.—

64. Fourth Sergeant Paul Dunbar and 5th Sergeant John Calhoun were reduced in rank; 2nd Corporal John [Dubreuil?] was promoted to Calhoun's 5th Sergeant spot and Private Laurel Johnson moved from the ranks to 2nd corporal. The four privates involved in the fight were not noted. Muster Roll Returns, Regimental Papers, 74th USCI [2nd LaNG], RG 94, NA.

65. Paymaster Major William Sherman. The report was sent to General Thomas W. Sherman, Def. of N.O.

66. A February 21, 1863, change of command promoted Lieutenant Commander Henry A. Adams to the captaincy of the *Vincennes,* and as such he became commander of the fleet at Ship Island as the senior naval officer at the post. See n. 29 above.

Part I, Ship Island

Very true the old adage that March comes in like a lion and goes out like a lamb.—This month was inaugurated in a storm, and has expired in a genial balmy southern breeze.

A year ago today I was at Nashville with Gen'l Buell's "Army of The Ohio" making preparations for our descent upon southern Tennessee—Little did we then think that this terrible war would exist another year, and little did I think that I should be on Ship Island at this time—*sed homine propose et Deus disposi.*—[67]

Wednesday, April 1ˢᵗ 1863
[Cross-written]

A general *All Fool's* Day. Every body fooling everyone. Windy and very unpleasant. This morning a small boat came over from Biloxi, Mississippi with Refugees. A man named John Tunbridge boy & little girl are subjects of Great Britain and have papers from The Commd'g Gen'l out of the Confederate lines. The following is an abstract of his Report.

> Left Richmond about Eight weeks ago, came on to Augusta Georgia, am by Profession a Wig-maker. Most of the Confederate forces that were at Fredricksburgh Virginia have been sent towards Petersburgh. Butter in Richmond $2 per lb, Beef 85 cents, Pork $1 per lb & everything else accordingly. Jeff Davis in Richmond, attended the same church that he did, looked well but [cancrine?].—Troops complaining on a/c of food—no pay—wishing war was over.—Foreigners universally for peace.—Americans desirest for war. Return Prisoners to be well treated. About 3000 troops in Augusta. Plenty of Troops in Petersburgh and Richmond. Left Mobile last Thursday, was in the city Five weeks. About Twenty thousand troops in and around the city, down the bay on the shell road strongly fortified, entrenchments all around Mobile. Very large guns, 200 pounds, 6 of them & Ten Batteries. Ten guns to a battery, over 100 guns around the city in various Batteries. On

---

67. Union major general Don Carlos Buell (1818–1898), commander of the Department of the Ohio since mid-November 1861, moved with his army from the north occupying Bowling Green, Kentucky, and pressed into Nashville, Feb. 14–30, 1862. *OR*, Ser. I, Vol. IV, 358; McPherson, *Battle Cry of Freedom*, 394–95, 397, 402. *Sed homine propose et Deus disposi:* Daniels appears to be attempting to quote Thomas à Kempis, *De Imitatione Christi*, "Homo proponit, sed Deus disponit" (Man proposes, but God disposes), or some other version of this variously attributed saying.

Springhill Road about Fifteen Regiments in splendid winter quarters, well clothed, equipped &C. In the River are Four iron clad Rams completely finished each mounting Four large Pivot Guns one on each end, and one on each side.—Sharp Prows extending from each end Eight feet upon the surface of the water. Paddle stern wheel, all machines under water. Boats very low and covered with three platings of two inch strap iron rail on each other in successive layers the same thickness extending one foot under water.— Four of these Monsters are completed in Mobile Bay, all ready armed and equipped, and three more are nearly finished at Selma up the Alabama River, also a large Steamer Frigate has been built and is now ready for service with armament and crew aboard,—also two iron plated floating Batteries fitted to cast loose and float down in case of engagement, all finished for furnaces on top to [-------] far among the Fleet, completely equipped another one opposite Mobile of same description half completed. One of the Rams was anchored some ten miles down the Bay, all crew went ashore. The Frigate fired Repeated Broadsides with test [painted?] rifle balls at her sides. Splendid Results, the balls only making a slight indentation, scarcely a trace effect upon her iron harness. Their Rams are built of splendid white oak. Beams two feet thick—another cotton clad steamboat armed and equipped ready for service and one small Frigate & schooner fitted, completely armed and manned. One mile from Mobile is a very busy store ship having two guns, stored with ammunition & supplies for The Navy. Also Three wooden Gun boats in Mobile Bay near the Forts.

He also Reports that thousands of people are starving in the city. Half of the soldiers are on half rations and no pay has been rec'd, some of them having rec'd nothing but their food since they entered the service. He leaved on Mobile to Biloxi in a carriage passed through the lines by The Comdg Gen'l at Mobile and looks about as nearly dead with starvation and fatigue as a man well could.—Saw the last Pickets at Goods mill in Dog River,[68] Says there are a few Cavalry on The Coast driving in Conscripts. Has his consulor certificate of naturalization. Has a boy, a very intelligent fellow, and a little girl, a beautiful little creature with him.—I have given her a place at Headquarters, and she wanders around like a fairy sprite among the Soldiers. I shall send them to Gen'l Banks for disposal.—Also Rec'd from Capt. of Gun Boat Jackson two Refugees that he

68. The Dog, or Escatawpa, River empties into Pascagoula Bay in Mississippi Sound.

picked up, up the Sound who have been in Confederate Prison for 22 months ever since the war broke out. They are Italian and miserable enough in appearance.—U.S. Naval Supply Steamer Antona came in late this night. Brings Papers from New Orleans, but they contain no news, say that we are on the eve of important events, but that eve has been of so long duration that I fear it will finally result in perpetual national darkness.—

Thursday, April 2^d 1863

U.S. Naval Steamer Antona came in late last evening from New Orleans. Capt. Manton of Relief came over a passenger. Cant Imagine what has become of my mail have not received any letters from home for a long while, since February 11th, 1863.—Settled a ludicrous Question last night between a man who had married two women & the females. It seems that this contraband when he left Biloxi some six months ago, and escaped from slavery to this Island, left a wife and child behind him. After being on the Island some three months and supposing that he would never see his wife again, he took unto himself another Rib with whom he has been living happily since. Last week "a change came o'er the spirit of his dream" in the shadow of his former spouse who had escaped from Rebeldom and came on her way rejoicing in her freedom & in the prospect of becoming reunited to the partner of her Joys and Sorrows, but lo and behold, she found things different from what she expected & when she learned the facts refused to recognize her truant husband, or to give up the result of their married felicity, the baby. Where upon I summoned the party before me, & after learning the evidence, and sifting the love and hope and desires of all concerned, decided that the second marriage should hold good & the original lady of his heart retain her child and [judgements?]—

Friday, April 3^d 1863

Steamer Antona went out last night. Sloop Belle in from New Orleans, brought papers stating that Admiral Farragut and The Hartford were all right between Vicksburgh & Port Hudson playing the devil with the enemies batteries. One of Two boats sent down by Admiral Porter from the fleet above, succeeded in passing The Vicksburgh Batteries to reinforce Farragut. Banks forces still quiet, remarkably so considering the time he has had to operate in, something should have been accomplished 'ere this!

"Photograph of Officers of The Army & Navy at Ship Island. Maj Willis [front left], myself [back left] of my Reg't, Capt Manton [front center] of U.S. Store ship Relief, Capt Adams [back right] of U.S. Sloop of War Vincennes, and Capt Edge. [Edgerlady; front right] of Ship New England, a Jolly crowd taken together." (Sunday, April 19, 1863)

Rumor that The French have taken the City of Mexico—I don't credit it as Mexico is said to be well fortified and comparatively impregnable.[69]

Went off aboard The Vincennes to a whist party with Capt Adams, Capt. Manton & Dr Willis, had a very pleasant time. Terrible weather came up whilst we were aboard & our boat nearly swamped coming ashore, got wet through & through, shant try that operation soon again in a gale—

69. The *Switzerland* was able to pass the Vicksburg batteries. Napoleon III sent French troops to Mexico in 1862 on the pretense of collecting unpaid debts; his real interest was in creating a French colony. French troops captured Mexico City in June 1863. McPherson, *Battle Cry of Freedom*, 553, 683.

Saturday, April 4th 1863

Weather pleasant and agreeable once more. Sent Refugees over to Cat Island to make Tar.

Three Refugees came in from Pascagoula and Mobile. One of them is a Federal soldier belonging to The 4th Reg't Ohio Cavalry. He was taken Prisoner at Tullahoma previous to the battle of Shiloh, but succeeded in escaping to Mississippi at which place he remain some time, where he was conscripted, and put in Confederate Gun boat Selma, where he served some six months, but succeeded in getting leap of absence to go to Mobile from which place he escaped to this Post in company with a union Alabamian. Gave the name of Col Kennett of his Reg't whom I know very well, and his story appears to be credible, also gives me information of certain events which happened in our Divn in which I at that time was, which makes him reliable—[70]

Sunday, April 5th 1863

Had General Inspection and Review today. Steamer Antona in from Pensacola with Officers of The Army and Navy. Sent Adjutant with Despatches to Headquarters aboard of her to New Orleans.—

Gunboat Jackson came down from Grants Pass with four Prisoners of war, soldiers captured from Fort Morgan, sent guard of four soldiers with them to New Orleans on Steamer Antona.—

Schooner Venturi in from New Orleans with Major Dumas, Mr. Victor as passengers and sutlers stores. Brings no mail to me. Papers contain no news, everybody seems to be in *status quo*, and the country going to the devil through "masterly inactivity"—Major tells me that "Margaret" is coming down on Schooner.[71] God only knows what could have possessed her to come here now. She is much better off in the city and will have to immediately return—Sergeant Dauchy comes in the schooner, brings news that Gen'l Banks is not well disposed towards the Reg't in truth although he acknowledges our excellent Condition and Value. Thank God there are powers above him that are willing to recognize our efficiency

---

70. Tullahoma, Tennessee, is approximately fifty miles southeast of Nashville. The battle at Shiloh, April 6–7, 1862, was the bloodiest to date, with both sides claiming victory. Colonel John Kennett commanded the 4th Regiment Ohio Cavalry.

71. Margaret is Daniels' Creole acquaintance. See diary entry, April 24.

and who will take good care to neutralize all the evil he can effect us. U.S. Schooner Rocky Hill in from Pensacola. Sent Refugees to Pro Marshal and Gen'l Sherman.—John Tunbridge son and daughter to Gen'l Sherman with abstract of their Testimony, as I consider it the most important yet rec'd.

Sent Twelve Refugees on Rocky Hill including John Tunbridge & son, besides woman & four children—

Monday, April 6th 1863
[Cross-written]

Inspection and Review. Men in good condition, arms and equipments equally so. Refugees came over this evening from Biloxi. This is the substance of their story.

> Louis Blas, Constance Blas, and Louisa Blas, Germans. Miss Louisa is a very good looking female, says that They came from Biloxi last night—by profession a Gardener—subjects of Germany. Have Passports from French Consul. Lived in Montgomery Alabama, left there one week ago last Saturday—March 28th 1863 & came down Alabama River to Mobile, stayed in Mobile three days. Saw Forts and one iron plated Ram. Most of the troops have gone to Charleston, not more than 200 in the city, and two companies at the Forts.
>
> Took away our papers at Biloxi and our trunk. Are building iron plated Gun boat at Montgomery, will be completed in three mo's   No soldiers now in Montgomery. Have no defences there. Provisions very scarce. Plenty of gold and silver in Banks, the same brought from Mobile and New Orleans, also plenty of cotton, people very much afraid that our troops are coming up from Pensacola to take their city.
>
> Met an Englishman Mr. Patterson at Mobile who had passport from French Consul to go to England   We got our German Passports at same place—all came together to Pascagoula by carriage where we found one hundred cavalry who told us we couldn't go to the Yankees, stayed one day when they took away Mr. P.'s Passport claiming that he had sold the same papers once before.
>
> I then sent my father to Biloxi with our baggage, we remained at Pascagoula one day longer, then started the next day in small sail boat for Biloxi. Sent Mr. Patterson down the shore with instructions that when we got clear

of the soldiers, he should get into our boat with us, which he did, got nearly to Biloxi when we found a boat in pursuit with soldiers, put Mr. P. out on Deer Island and came on to Biloxi when the soldiers in boat followed us claiming to be in pursuit of Mr. Patterson and saying that we had carried him off in our boat.—This occurred last Friday. The same night I got the man who brought us down to go up to Deer Island and put Mr. P. over on to the main shore. The next day the soldiers went up and searched the Island but found no one. He promised to see that Patterson was sent safely over here. I have not seen him since. Came over here from Biloxi last night. The cavalry were at Biloxi when we left. They wanted to get Patterson when they would have forced him to Join the army.

I gave these people plenty to eat, and a house to live in. They wish to go to New York by the first opportunity. The girl is good looking and *rather pleasant* chatty companion.—

Tuesday, April 7th 1863
[Cross-written]
Steamer Circassian belonging to U.S. Navy, one of the Captured prizes and a beautiful craft, came in this morning from New York bringing supplies to the Navy. She brings N Y [files?] to the 19th but no new intelligence except the expected attack upon Charleston which was to come off last week, and which will be one of the most decisive events of the war. Officers from this steamer came up to Headquarters and we had a very sociable time of it. Admiral Dupont says he will have nine iron clads besides an immense fleet of wooden ships, and cannot but succeed in the Reduction of the city. The Army is still under Gen'l Hunter, but is not expected to cooperate.[72]

72. Union rear admiral Samuel F. DuPont (1803–1865) planned an earlier attack on Charleston, but the battle did not take place until April 7. He expected to demolish the city but "met with a sad repulse" through the sheer strength of the monitor-class ships, ironclads modeled after the original *Monitor,* which sank December 31, 1862, off Cape Hatteras. Assistant Secretary of the Navy Gustavus V. Fox asked DuPont "not to let the Army spoil it." Major General David Hunter and his troops were not to be included except to stand by afterward to "pick up the pieces." Robert U. Johnson and Clarence C. Buel, eds., *Battles and Leaders of the Civil War* (4 vols.; New York, 1887), IV, 32–41; Shelby Foote, *Fredericksburg to Meridian* (1963; rpr. New York, 1986), 225, 227–32, Vol. II of Foote, *The Civil War: A Narrative,* 3 vols.; McPherson, *Battle Cry of Freedom,* 646.

"... had our pictures taken in Ambulance—rather a delapidated looking crowd. Capt Adams, Capt Manton & Capt Edge [Edgerlady] of The U.S. Navy and Major Willis and myself of The Army." (Sunday, April 26, 1863)

Had Battallion Drill this P.M. very hot and hard work. Wrote letter to Gen'l Banks relative to Capt Murillion's matter, stating that I consider his dismissal a great outrage upon the Gentleman, and a disgrace to the American service, and Respectfully requested that he might be restored to his original position immediately.—I don't know how this will be taken, if it gives offence I can't help it, a great injustice has been done to Capt Murillion through a miserable prejudice by this Department—and I'm damned if I don't see it Justified if it takes an appeal to Washington & a full expose of the matter to accomplish the work.—[73]

Wednesday, April 8th 1863
General Banks U.S. Steamer Transp't came in this morning from New Orleans, brought Despatches and mail.

[73]. Monro(s)e Murillion, captain of Company E stationed at Fort Pike, was one of the three black officers removed in the February board of examination requested by Hall. Daniels received notification of Murillion's dismissal, along with those of Lieutenants William Keeling and Lucien Scott, more than a month before this diary entry. See n. 19 above and related text.

Part I, Ship Island

Rec'd letters from Gen'l Banks requesting Report of date of my muster with service, also Commission of three Lieutenants for 2d Regt La. Vol.—not intended for my Reg't, also various orders, but no private mail.—

Planned Expedition to Pascagoula to capture Confederate troops said to be in possession of the place in a small force. Embarked on Steamer Gen'l Banks with 180 men, with my major & Quartermaster of my field and staff, and three captains & the Lieutenants. Steamed up the sound to Horn Island leaving Ship Island at 3 o'c P.M. Had the 12 lb. Howitzer of the Sloop of War Vincennes with nine rounds of shell and nine rounds of grape [canister].—

Came to anchor off Horn Island, intending to go into Pascagoula early tomorrow morning.—

Thursday, April 9th 1863
[Cross-written]

Left Horn Island this A.M. at 4 o'c steamed up to Round Island when we found The U.S. Gunboat Jackson blockading The Pascagoula River. Brought her letters & orders to Join our expedition and open fire in case we were repulsed. Together steamed for Pascagoula and made the town at 9 o'clock in the morning when I landed two Companies, B and G and took possession of The Hotel, hoisted the American colors upon the Cupola and threw out Pickets, one half mile back of the Hotel.[74] Capt. Barrett advanced with a part of his company to the left of the place, and Lieut Jones with the balance of the Detachment occupied the Left.[75] Capt Villevert held the Hotel as a base with his company [in tow?]. I called out The Reserve Capt Carter & sent him to the extreme left to hold the Pascagoula River Road, a squad of Company G maneuvered the Howitzer on the Steamer. The Gunboat Jackson laid out in the sound about one mile from the shore—after taking possession of the Hotel I ordered the colors to be hoisted, & made fast. We had hardly thrown out Pickets when the lookout gave the alarm that The Confederate Cavalry were coming down upon us. I myself saw them from The Cupola of The Hotel coming down the Mobile Road in heavy force with banners waving, cutlass's flailing, evidently

---

74. The town was actually East Pascagoula, Mississippi.
75. Daniels corrects himself later in this entry; Lieutenant Jones was on the right.

intending to make an immediate attack. I immediately ordered the Retreat to be beaten, in order to mass my forces at The Hotel, but the enemy came down so suddenly that it was impossible for all my pickets and their supporting squads to get within our base—however they fought on bravely and succeeded after long fighting in getting to their companies.—Immediately after the Retreat was beaten The Cavalry came upon the extreme left in large force outnumbering us five to one and commenced the attack. Company B gave them a number of volleys when they fell back and came down the Right upon Major Dumas and Capt Villevert & myself with small Detachments of Companies B & G. This firing was rapid & excellent but our men stood fast, and though greatly outnumbered & without cover succeeded in fully repulsing them. They formed again and came around the Hotel in the extreme Right where they found Lieut Jones with a part of Company—six men—He succeeded in emptying many of their saddles and on driving them back. Up to this time we had lost one man killed and five wounded whereas the enemy had lost a large number in killed & wounded.—Capt Carter was now attacked on the extreme left, a large number of Infantry having occupied the houses & being between him and the Hotel, attacked by almost overwhelming numbers both of Infantry and Cavalry,—he slowly retired to the end of a wharf leading out into the sound & off into the extreme Right. Here he maintained a continuous firing for an hour when I sent boats and had him brought to the Steamer. This was at 12 oclock. Skirmishes were constantly kept up as often as the enemy saw fit to come within the range of our guns from The Wharf and Hotel.—The woods here but a few yards in the rear of our position & they kept within such cover & fired constantly upon us.—I had expected up to this hour that The Gunboat Jackson would have opened with shell upon the woods in our front where were stationed large forces of Cavalry and Infantry within sight but beyond the range of our guns. I asked Capt Manton for God's sake to go aboard and ask The Army Officer to commence firing. From the distance that my boat was obliged to be at the wharf, my Howitzer was useless—she could not reach the enemy. They (the Confederates) were armed with Sharps Revolving Rifles,[76] and had a great advantage over us in range. The Gunboat now fired three shell, but with no effect, appearing to care little whether we were overcome or

---

76. Sharps rifles, *not* revolving.

not.—I then ordered my men to hold the place until we could recover our wounded & dead which we did—

Friday, April 10th 1863
[Cross-written]

 U.S. Steam Transport Genl Banks left for New Orleans this day at 3 o'c P.M. Sent Report of Fight to Genl Sherman.

 (Continuation from Thursday). We then brought off all of our dead and wounded to the boat and had driven the enemy back from the lines holding our base through the whole fight I now ordered the troops who had struggled aboard The Steamer and those who had been engaged in freeing wharf to sally out again and try to dislodge the Rebels from the houses in the village. Just at this time I discovered heavy Reinforcements of Cavalry coming down the Road,—and at the same moment The Gun boat Jackson unfortunately and mayhaps designedly, threw a shell into our column moving out the wharf killing instantly five men and wounding seven, and leaving a huge gap in the wharf leading to the boat. This created confusion & discouragement (as rumors had before reached us that owing to difficulties that had occurred on the Island between soldiers and sailors, if The Jackson was ever called upon to assist us she would fire at us instead of for us)[77] and I immediately ordered the troops to rebuild the wharf which they did through a hot fire of the enemy, and to then fall back to the boat which they did in excellent order without losing in the whole fight but two men killed and a small number wounded. The shell killed instantly five men, mortally wounded two men, and seriously wounded one, slightly wounding a number. After the troops were aboard, I learned that still more and heavier Reinforcements had come up from Mobile with artillery and Infantry, and as I had with me but two rounds of ammunition and 180 men with some seven officers and only a 12 lb Howitzer without shell, I concluded that it would be folly to make another attack as I could not depend upon The Gun boat in any emergency. As I backed my boat out from the wharf, however, I ran down to The Jackson and said to Capt D'Oyly "Sir your last shot killed five of my men and wounded a large number." He replied, "Yes sir, I am aware of it, but supposed Capt Manton has explained the matter to you." I replied, "Yes sir, will you support me in the

---

77. See diary entry, March 18; see also nn. 31, 33, 48 above and related text.

fullest sense of the word if I will reland and burn the town." He replied that he would support me only according to his Instructions which were not to fire only but cover our Retreat. I then came on to This Island knowing that I could do nothing with my small amount of ammunition, however had I have had 20 rounds to a man, I would have destroyed the place without the assistance of The Navy cost one what it might—But they appeared more like a neutral power looking on, and highly enforcing the reinforcement and consequent falling luck of my forces because they were colored soldiers, when at the same time we could see Cavalry and Infantry of The Confederates by the hundreds in the woods within easy range of their shell, but out of our reach. I had supposed it to be the duty of an American Officer to attack the enemy whenever he saw them and particularly when another portion of the force was fighting to support the flag. Their action was cowardly and dastardly in extreme—and mark my word, it will yet be heard from in high places—

I had omitted to write that in the last remark that the Capt of The Gunboat Jackson made he also stated "that he would not be guilty of firing into women and children." Upon this his sailors clapped their hands and really appeared to rejoice over this damnable Cowardice and malignant action towards our troops.—They had dared to throw a shell into my troops knowing that it could by lying and chicanery perhaps be excused, but they had not dared to come within rifle shot of the enemy or make an attack even when they saw that the enemy had taken shelter in the houses and had used the women and Children as bulwarks to fire upon us. Even the women themselves fired upon our troops and were seen actively loading the guns and assisting the Confederate soldiers.—

Saturday, April 11th 1863
[Cross-written]

Came down Thursday afternoon from the fight and reached Ship Island at 6 o'c having made the attack upon Pascagoula with a Detachment of 180 men at 9 o'c in the morning, and holding the town until 2 o'c P.M. when we voluntarily chose to evacuate. We whipped the enemy when we could find them, killing over twenty and wounding many more, captured the enemies colors and four Prisoners,—and with a loss in battle of only two men & some seven wounded. Our own Gun boat did us more injury than all the enemy combined. The enemy were in force of 300 Cavalry &

100 Infantry when we made the attack, and were during the fight heavily Reinforced with Cavalry, Infantry & Artillery. Of course it would have been madness to have attempted competing with such force, and I withdrew with my prisoners and men in good order only leaving one dead body which fell in the commencement of the action and which was beyond our reach.—My men fought nobly and whipped as fair fight without cover,—whilst the enemy were in houses and the woods—five times their number. All behaved well, and particularly Major Dumas who had men shot down all around him—and Capt Villevert who exchanged seven rapid volley with the enemy without a single loss in the beginning of the fight, his Lieutenant Martin—and Lt Jones of Co B who with a force of seven men, cut his way for half a mile through overwhelming numbers, and came out without losing a single man, or having one wounded. He succeeded however in emptying many of the Rebel saddles.—Had the enemies forces have displayed any valor whatever, they might easily have ridden over my small force, but our bullets were too hot and came too often to suit their palates.—

Sent in my Report to Gen'l Sherman yesterday by U.S. Transport Gen'l Banks. The Gunboat Jackson has come down today, but her cursed crew dare not make their appearance ashore—I would not [be] answerable for the consequences should they come.—Find by Surgeon's Report that we had two killed and Seven seriously wounded in the fight and six killed and two wounded by the infernal Jackson's shell, making in the aggregate Eight killed and nine wounded—a small casualty considering the enemies loss to be, as they admit it to be, over one hundred killed and wounded.—

The wounded are doing well and will all recover. Unfortunately my surgeon Dr. Willis is very sick and has left for New Orleans, but Capt Adams of The Vincennes and Capt Manton of The Relief (who accompanied the expedition and acted nobly with us through the action & came very near being captured) sent me their surgeon and we got along very well.[78] Yesterday, the dead were buried with appropriate ceremonies being the first of the Reg't who have fallen with their armor on.—Though of a different race, yet have they nobly battled for a blue [tag?] countless cause,

---

78. The surgeons were Dr. [?] Skinner from the *Vincennes* and Dr. Ceise Pierucci from the *Relief*.

and gave up their lives to rescue the cause of freedom and Liberty. *Requiescat in pace.* My Quartermaster says that in compliance with my order to Board The Jackson and procure medical assistance, he was near The Gun boat when she fired the shot that caused such destruction in my ranks and that Capt D'Oyly learned such But exclaimed immediately after the discharge of the gun, & in a great state of excitement "who in the name of Hell ordered that gun to be fired, we have killed many of our own men."— "I gave no one orders to fire that gun." Also asked him, when he boarded, "how many men have you lost"—He replied 2 killed & 5 wounded in battle—D'Oyly replied "I am afraid I have done you more harm than the Rebels have—I did not order that gun to be fired."—

This is all very well, but the other shots that were fired preceding came very near my men on the Boat near the lower wharf and appeared to be designed for them instead of the enemy—Five shots were fired altogether by the Gun boat—one only reaching the woods, the rest either falling short or damaging my men—

Sunday, April 12th 1863
[Cross-written]
Below I give a copy of my General Report sent on the 11th to Brig Gen'l Sherman, Commanding Defences of New Orleans, of Engagement at Pascagoula, Miss April 9th 1863.—[79]

> Headquarters, Ship Island, Miss. April 10th 1863.—
> Brig Gen'l Sherman, Commdg Gulf Defences, New Orleans, La.
> Sir: I have the honor to Report that I embarked with a Detachment of my men, 180 strong, of my Regiment in United States Gov't transport Gen'l Banks, yesterday at 9 o'clock A.M.—Made an attack upon Pascagoula, Miss.—Landed my forces and hoisted the American colors upon The Hotel.—I immediately thereafter was attacked by the Confederate Cavalry, some three hundred strong and one company of Infantry. Repulsed them

---

79. Daniels' published report to General Thomas W. Sherman varied slightly from the diary entry in editorial detail and the report of five, rather than four, "slightly wounded" in the battle. *OR*, Ser. I, Vol. LII, 61. The New Orleans newspaper the *Era* (see diary entry for April 15) reported two killed and five slightly wounded. Regimental records list two killed outright and six wounded, two of whom later died of their wounds. Seven of the eight were from Company B. Killed were James Moore and Alexander Green; wounded, John Fransura, Joseph Turner, Robert Swan, Thomas Scott, William Baron, and Colman Washington (Co. G). Fransura and Turner died shortly after the action.

after a severe fight, killing twenty or more men, and wounding a large number—capturing three prisoners and the Confederate colors.—Held the town until 2 o'c P.M., frequent skirmishes occurring meanwhile when I withdrew my forces to the boat upon learning that large reinforcements had arrived from the camps up The Pascagoula River.—Loss in battle two (2) killed and four (4) slightly wounded. In covering the Retreat of the Troops to the Transport, The U.S. Gunboat Jackson which accompanied the Expedition under orders not to take part in the attack, supposing us to have been Repulsed, unfortunately threw a shell directly into the column moving out the wharf, killing four men and severely wounding five others of my force.—The expedition otherwise was a perfect success as the enemy was in every attack Repulsed, a large number killed and wounded—Prisoners and the Confederate Colors captured—with the slight loss of two men—The expedition has also materially changed the plans of The Mobile forces as they were about sending the weight of their numbers to Charleston S. C.—This attack caused them to send heavy Reinforcements towards Pascagoula—I forwarded the Despatch in great haste by Transport Gen'l Banks and will send Report of details by next opportunity.

Most Respectfully, your Ob't Servt

N. W. Daniels Col 2^d Rg't La NG Vol Comdg Offcr

Wrote Gen'l Banks relative to my muster into service, also sent Lt [?] Hill Chief of Ordnance Recpt for Ordnance Stores for Post. Returned Commissions of Lieutenants of 2d La Reg't as not having been sent to the correct place. Sent Despatches today by Despatch boat of old man. Wounded men doing well. Buried yesterday the last of the dead of "Pascagoula"— Guns of two men brought in which had been shot to pieces, some of the flesh of the poor fellow is upon one where the cursed shell did such execution—Have hung out the Confederate Colors that we captured beneath our glorious flag, as an emblem of our success.—

The poor devil of a Prisoner that we captured rec'd a bad wound in the shoulder in the fight. One of Capt Villeverts men stationed in the woods as a Picket was attacked by nine cavalry at once. He succeeded in whipping the whole party, killing five and dispersing the rest.—

Wrote the following address to my Regiment and delivered same at Dress Parade this P.M.

Headquarters
Ship Island, Miss
April 10th 1863

"An excellent Photograph of Battery No 6 constructed at this Post by my Regiment. On the extreme left is The U.S. Store ship Relief then her Captain B. F. Manton—then myself with Company D of my Rgt in the background—then Capt Villevert, The Artillery Officer of the Post and Director in The Construction of Batteries, and the sentinels in the foreground with musket and colors, and the sea in the distance. Three IX inch Columbiad comprise the battery, and they are terrible weapons at close quarters with shell or shrapnel"— (Thursday, April 30, 1863)

Fellow soldiers.—

For the first time in your military existence have you experienced the glories and the dangers of the battle field.—

You have known what it is to meet the enemy face to face, and to overcome five times your numbers in a hotly contested action.—

You have snuffed the perfume of Powder—heard the key note of the bullets shrill music and are now conscious of the attractions and the horrors of *grim visaged war.*—

You have tested the question of your nations valor, and demonstrated to its fullest extent the capacity—the bravery—the endurance and the nobility of your race, and taught the milignant foe that a centuries oppression has not extinguished your manhood or suppressed your love of Liberty, and that you have still a hand to wield the sword, and a heart to vitalize its blow.

Proudly have you borne the banner of Freedom—the delight of the true warrior's soul—through the thickest of the fray—its folds pierced and pierced with the leaden hail—without paling a star or defacing a stripe—

its tattered condition the true emblem of your work, and your brave endeavors.

Heroes have you proven yourselves in the strife—nobly sustaining your countries honor and gloriously maintaining the valor of your profile.

The brave ones, whose spirits winged their way to brighter spheres during the fierce struggle, are true martyrs in the holy cause of Freedom—They have offered themselves nobly upon the shrine of their countries existence, and their deeds are their glory—their glory their reward.—Their names shall deck the page of history, and their process emblazen the escutcheon of our coming Republic.

Though mouldening now within the silent Tomb, yet ever their souls as noble and as great as e'er rise to heaven from The battle field. Their spirits as brave as ever e'er unwrapped by clayey tenement.—

Monday, April 13th 1863
[April 12 continuing]

Let us then Remember their fate and their Reward.—Let the name of "Pascagoula" be wrought within the folds of our colors—a Page in the history of our career, an emblem of our achievement and an ernest of what the world may expect of those whose first deeds have been so valorous, whose acts have been so brave.—

Your Colonel

Tuesday, April 14th 1863
[Cross-written]

Men all eager for another expedition, but as no boat is at hand, cannot well make another attack. Have learned that the places on the other side of The Sound have all been strongly reinforced, & The Mobile forces sent this way, creating a Diversion from Charleston, which place they had prepared to assist in the great battle that is now being fought there. This was my main object in my attack upon Pascagoula—preventing the sending The Mobile troops to take part in the Great Charleston battle, and I have fully succeeded. There is no telling what an important effect such Diversion may have though small in its design, still may it entirely change the result of the Great Fight.—[80]

80. The battle at Charleston took place two days before the Pascagoula skirmish. It is not known if Daniels' claim of diverting Mobile's Charleston-bound troops had any effect on activity there.

No boat yet in from the city since the action of my troops. Would like to know whether a correct Report has been published or not Whether The Press will over come their unjust prejudice against colored troops sufficiently to enable them to do them Justice.—

Margaret came on Schooner Eliza Anne from New Orleans last Friday, the day after the fight, April 10,th 1863, am glad she came, had a Pass from Col Chandler[81] & have taken her into my domicile, and established a family.—

Of my Field and Staff present at the fight were Major Dumas & Quartermaster Souvinet, both acted bravely and did their duty well.—My Adjutant is and has been in the city for the last week My Surgeon was sick so I was obliged to call upon The Navy for medical aid to my wounded which was immediately furnished and of the best description.—

Wednesday, April 15th 1863

No boat yet from the city.

Dispatched small boat to the city with mail & Despatches to Headquarters. Rumor on The Island that Genl Banks has fought a battle in The Bayou "Teche" and gained a victory.—[82]

Small boat in from the city with papers. My adjutant came down—See that The Newspapers have published my Report of The Pascagoula Expedition only they have left out the Gunboat Jackson's share of the murder.—Officers in from the city Report that our affair created great excitement until the Report was published in "The Era"[83]—Then they were all astonished—Confeds decidely down in the mouth and unbelieving.—

[Newspaper article attached]

---

81. Colonel J. G. Chandler was assistant quartermaster, 19th Corps.

82. Banks's forces pressed up Bayou Teche beginning April 8 or 9 and on April 13 encountered intense enemy artillery at Bisland, northwest of Brashear City and Berwick Bay. The Confederates, under General Richard Taylor, were outnumbered and retreated westward. After another battle, on April 14 at Irish Bend (Nerson's Woods) near Franklin, they escaped by making a forced march to New Iberia. Winters, *Civil War in Louisiana*, 223–31.

83. The *Era*, formerly the *Delta*, was under the control of the Federal military government at the time of this report. "Update," Vol. VII, 1988, Manuscripts Division, Historic New Orleans Collection, New Orleans; Lieutenant Colonel Alfred C. Hills, 4th LaNG, detailed in charge of *Era* office, to Colonel Richard B. Irwin, AAG, February 16, 1863, LR, Ser. 1756, Dept. of the Gulf, RG 393, Pt. 1, NA.

An Expedition against Pascagoula
Creditable exploits of the 2nd Native Guards

A rebel rumor has been in town for some days to the effect that the Second Native Guards, Col. Daniels, had landed at Pascagoula, Mississippi, and had been captured by the rebels. Not having any definite accounts from that quarter, we have refrained from giving currency to any of the flying reports, not deeming them reliable.

We now have, however, an abstract of the official report of Col. Daniels, which places the affair in a very different light. On Thursday, the 9th inst. last, Col. Daniels, with a detachment of about 180 men of his regiment, left Ship Island, on board the U.S. transport steamer Gen. Banks, on an expedition to Pascagoula, Miss. He reached that place and landed his force about 9 o'clock the same morning, took possession, and hoisted the stars and stripes upon the hotel. Immediately after this, he was attacked by a force of 300 rebel cavalry, supported by one company of infantry. After a severe fight, in which twenty or more of the enemy were killed, and a large number wounded, the rebels retreated leaving three prisoners and the Confederate colors to the victors.

Col. Daniels held the place until 2 o'clock in the afternoon, when hearing that large reinforcements had arrived from the camp up the Pascagoula river, he withdrew his forces to the boat and sailed for Ship Island.

The expedition was a perfect success, resulting in the repulse of the enemy in every engagement with considerable loss, while only two of Col. Daniels's men were killed and five slightly wounded.

This movement against Pascagoula has materially changed the destination of the rebel troops stationed in and about Mobile, as we have since learned that the enemy was about to send heavy reinforcements to assist in the defense of Charleston, S.C. This has caused the weight of these reinforcements to be thrown in another direction, and have been ordered to go to the relief of Pascagoula. We hope to hear of substantial benefits resulting from this well conducted affair.

Thursday, April 16th 1863

Boat in from the city with intelligence of Gen'l Banks late fight on Bayou "Teche" in which he burnt The Gunboat Diana & captured some Prisoners.—Admiral Farragut up at Red River blockading that stream, said to be between the batteries and unable to get either way, in a tight place—but the brave old veteran will find some way to get around the Rebels.[84] Great change in public opinion relative to the bravery of the colored troops, Thank God. They are coming to their senses and will be willing to do Justice to these oppressed people after they have gained our [victors friend?]

Friday, April 17th 1863
[Newspaper article attached]

A Cry for Bread or Peace
A Demand for Blood Threatened

Posters, of which the following is a copy, were pasted up in the most public places of Mobile on the 6th inst. It is one of the unmistakable signs now becoming quite common, that the distress of the people in the rebellious states has reached a point that is almost unbearable:

"It has not yet come to be a question of bread or peace with us, but we are fast coming to it. If our government can compel a man with a family of children to fight for it for $11 per month—it can compel, and MUST, those who stay at home and enjoy their ease now, and will enjoy our freedom when achieved—to feed the poor children of poor fathers—the widows, whose only sons are fighting the battles and enduring the terrible hardships of the march and camp, foodless, clothesless and shoeless. Forbearance will soon cease to be a virtue.

"Our wives, sisters, and little ones are crying for bread! Beware!! lest they cry for BLOOD ALSO!!! We have had enough of extortion and speculation; it is time the strong arm of the law was extended.

"The people will rise, sooner or later! There are lamp-posts and rope enough to cure this worse than treason—and the remedy will be supplied by an outraged people."

(Signed) "Brutus II"

---

84. The Union's damaged gunboat *Diana*, lost to the Confederates in March (see n. 61 above), was repaired and operating for them, only to be crippled by Banks's advancing troops in the battle of Bisland on April 13. The next day at the battle of Irish Bend, the disabled *Diana* was abandoned and burned by her crew. Winters, *Civil War in Louisiana*, 224–28. Rear Admiral David Farragut, who ran the batteries at Port Hudson on March 14 and remained between there and the batteries upstream at Vicksburg, asked Porter for assistance in blockading the Red River. *Ibid.*, 217.

Part I, Ship Island

[Cross-written]

Copy of Handbill stuck up in Mobile, one that I sent to Gen'l Sherman and I see it published—it is a strain that shows the current of the secession trend of Rebeldom.—Rec'd letter from Gen'l Sherman acknowledging Recpt of my Report and Mobile papers. He says my Report gives great satisfaction and that the Handbill indicates a great deal to the Confederate disadvantage—If they permit such Incendiary documents to be put up publicly in their streets, then indeed must there a volcano of Rebellion within the Rebellion, be smoldering, ready to break forth at the first opportunity. My God, what a state of anarchy must prevail in such places— God grant the day may soon come when the suffering people will be released from such thraldom.

Saturday, April 18th 1863
[Cross-written]

Steamer Gen'l Banks in from New Orleans, brings mail and some passengers. My orderly "Monroe" came down from the city. Says that thousands of people attended the funeral of the soldier Joe Turner who was killed by the shell at Pascagoula[85]—Says there was great excitement at New Orleans over the fight and that the Regiment had gained great laurels—and that every wounded soldier was a hero and the lion among his circle of friends.—Sent off yesterday the Refugee families that had come over from the enemies lines. Sent Mrs. Robison & family by The Gen'l Banks which left today. Also sent charges against Capt Barrett for conduct unbecoming an officer, and disobedience of orders preferred by Lts [?] Andrews and Prouty to Major [G. N.] Lieber Judge Advocate of Gulf Department. Schooner Wm Hunter came in with coal from Philadelphia commanded by Capt Timothy Baker & an old friend, as I came around once from New York to New Orleans in her & had a very pleasant voyage.—Gave the old Capt a permit & free pass on The Gen'l Banks to New Orleans—Thus this an excellent opportunity to send Margaret to the north to some good school where she can make something of the Refinement and ability that nature hath so bountifully blessed her with.—

---

85. Monroe Coleman, aged twenty-seven, was detailed as orderly to Colonel Daniels from the ranks of Company B on October 15, 1862. Regimental Papers, 74th USCI [2nd LaNG], RG 94, NA. Private Joe Turner of Company B was in charge of the government's

Sunday, April 19th 1863
[Cross-written]

Rec'd letter by yesterday's mail from mother, Cousin Mattie Warren and Carrie, all well & happy. Mother has written me before, but my mail has failed to reach me. She enclosed portraits of herself & baby which I very much regret to have lost. I trust the missing mail will yet turn up somewhere.—She has been making a visit to my brother at Cincinnati, which partially accounts for the non-receipt of any letters lately from her hand.—

Cut out the following account of the trouble that I had with the 13th Reg't Maine Vol—some two months ago—a one-sided version of the affair and not in accordance with the facts, still as it does not take issue with the excellency of my troops, I have nothing to say. If there was a blunder committed as the article would seem to infer, it was not of my making. The Commanding Gen'l placed me in command of the Post, my Rg't's a Regularly organized Rg't of U.S. Troops, & by the eternal—as good as though they were of Caucasian blood, & my orders must be obeyed, if there was a blunder it was in throwing the white and black troops together.—

[Newspaper article attached]

The Ship Island Troubles

The following are the names of the members of Co. F, 13th Maine Regiment now under arrest at Ship Island, as given in a letter published in yesterday's Argus:[86]

Capt. C. R. March, Lieut. R. T. Jordan, Lieut. W. P. Freeman; Privates L. Bridges, W. T. Bridges, J. Burns, J. Bragdon, C. A. Coston, M. D. Chapman, E. J. Caruthers, T. Crocker, J. H. Davis, A. G. Dunham, F. Soloman, E. Grant, J. Harmon, C. H. Hilton, C. A. Jackson, J. W. Jackson, H. D. Jackson, W. F. Libby, L. D. Lowell, S. Robins, J. Staples, E. H. Seavey, H. S. Thrasher, C. G. Thrasher, J. H. Winslow.

The origin of the trouble is as follows, as we condense from the letter referred to. Jan. 20th Col. Daniels landed at Ship Island with seven companies of the 2nd Louisiana Native Guard (colored) with orders to supercede Col. Rust and staff who were to go to another command. Col. Daniels, it seems, issued an order for the companies to appear at guard mounting, in

---

post horses; he died April 10, the day after the Pascagoula battle. Muster Roll Returns, Regimental Papers, 74th USCI [2nd LaNG], RG 94, NA.

86. The *Argus* was a newspaper in Portland, Maine.

which they were to drill side by side with the colored troops, whose officers were to take turns with the white officers. The white companies—a portion of them—refused obedience to the order, were disarmed for disobedience, and put under arrest. Such is the statement.

We are informed on authority which we have no reason to doubt, though we do not avouch for the correctness of the statement, that the commanding officer who gave the offence to the white soldiers, is not a colored man, but a French soldier, a New Orleans volunteer, educated, refined, and gentlemanly, worth his hundred thousand dollars, but, having long resided at the South, is not afflicted with prejudice against color, and can scarcely be expected to appreciate the fastidiousness of the Yankee in this regard.

One thing is clear: the negro troops are not answerable for the Ship Island trouble. THEY were there to obey orders and to do their duty. They are not responsible for the color of their skins. They are to be blamed for the troubles only as true loyal men at the North are to be blamed for the rebellion, or as the Christian Master was to be blamed for the un-godly conduct of the Jews towards him. The whole affair shows the value rather than otherwise, of the colored troops; and if any blunder has been committed from which has resulted the difficulty referred to, it is only a blunder in the details of the camp, and not one that touches the real question, either of the value of negro troops, or of the expedience of using them in crushing out this infernal rebellion.

This is a beautiful day and one that is peculiarly characteristic of The Sunny South.

Busy all day making detailed Report of Pascagoula Expedition—and in making up Dispatches for Headquarters.—Old man came in from New Orleans this morning with passengers & mail in Despatch boat, brought Bodman, my Quartermaster sergeant who reports that Just as he left the city a rumor was flying through the city that Gen'l Butler had Just arrived in the steam ship[87]—God grant it may be him, then we shall see little more active service in this Department, and a little of the old & favored [*require?*]—

Wrote to Major Lieber withdrawing charges that I had Preferred

---

87. Butler was home in Lowell, Massachusetts, during the month of March 1863. On May 1 he testified in Boston before the American Freedmen's Inquiry Commission. Benjamin F. Butler Collection, LC.

against The officers of the 13th Rg't, my reasons for so doing being the requirement of all our forces at present in the department as I did not wish to embarrass the Administration by any further prosecution of the matter as the correction of the offenders would have destroyed the Regimental organization, which ought not in the present be interfered with—

Monday, April 20th 1863
[Cross-written]
Sent following letter to Major G N Lieber Judge Advocate of Gulf Dept—

Sir—I hereby withdraw my charges against The officers and Privates of The 13th Reg't Maine Vol. and decline further prosecution of the matter. My reasons for so doing are that in the present active duties of The Department I do not wish to embarrass the same by a prosecution that partakes more of The Political than military element or to disturb the organization of The Regiment to which the accused belong, as I think it the duty of all *now* to give every aid in their power to the successful prosecution of The war, and to avoid by every possible means any act that may have the least tendency to affect unfavorably the same. Most Respectfully, Your Obd't Serv't,
N W Daniels, Col 2d Rg't La NG Vols
Comd'g Offcr

Recommended the following officers to Gen'l Banks to fill vacancies in my Regiment—Rufus Kinsley, corporal Co. F 8th Ver. to lst Lt. Co. H—O. H. Putnam, musician Co. B. 8th Ver.—2d Lt of Co. H—Augustus P. Hanby 1st sergeant of Co. C 8th Ver.—lst Lt. Co E—Henry Pollard Private 13th Rg't Maine Vol. 2d Lt Co. E—James Welch, Sergeant Co. G 8th Ver't - lst Lt Co. A—W. F. Peters, 8th Ver't Co. D, 2d Lt Co. A of 2d Reg't La. NG Vols. Sent this day by Quartermaster. Also sent "The Southern Pilot," a damnably treasonable sheet confiscated here, to Brig Gen Sherman with suggestion to suppress the same.—Sent letter to President Lincoln Recommending James Forter Bray for Captaincy of Co. E of my Rg't and also asking that he would issue orders for the payment of our troops.—[88]

88. Daniels suggested five white enlisted men of the 8th Vermont and one from the 13th Maine to replace black officers Octave Rey, Robert Isabelle, Ernest Morphy, Lucien Scott, William Keeling, and Arnold Bertonneau, who were removed or resigned at Fort

Wrote mother this P.M. Boat gone to city with my Despatches. Quartermaster and Surgeon Willis gone to New Orleans, all went this P.M. Sent full Report of Pascagoula Expedition to Gen'l Sherman—Sent copy of Pascagoula Expedition Report to "The Union" of New Orleans and to "The New York Tribune"—also copy of "address to soldiers" to "The Union" for publication—Gave them to Quartermaster to translate.[89]

Funeral this P.M. of soldier who died from effect of Pascagoula fight—& of little babe of my cook.—Signed Quartermaster papers today up to January 1st 1863. Sent letter to Dr. Alexander relative to the Engineer Department and my Medical Staff protesting against the connection of the two.[90]—Finished Battery No. 7 last night, an excellent one.—Recommended Lt Noyes wife as a suitable person to come out and take charge of Post school—and asked the Dep't to give her free transportation.

Tuesday, April 21st 1863

Lt. Palfrey came down on last steamer to superintend Engineer Department.—[91]

[Newspaper article attached]

Prejudice Against Colored Soldiers
Ship Island, Jan. 30, 1863

The Government tried, for some eighteen months, to prosecute the war and crush the rebellion, without attempting to destroy slavery, the cause of the war. But finding that either the Union or slavery must perish, the Proc-

---

Pike after Hall's board of examination. Hall had earlier recommended men from the 31st Massachusetts, stationed with him at Fort Pike, to fill the vacancies. James Forter Bray was to replace Captain Murillion, also removed by Hall at Fort Pike. This is the first time Daniels mentions payment for his troops, but he had regularly requested it, the most recent appeal being March 3 to General Banks. See n. 34 above and related text.

89. The *Union* (*L'Union*) was a free-black, French-language newspaper in New Orleans. Quartermaster Charles St. Albin Sauvinet was fluent in four languages. Hollandsworth, *Louisiana Native Guards*, 16 n. 15, spells the name "Sauvenet"; however, it is found to be Sauvinet.

90. Dr. Richard H. Alexander, chief medical officer ("medical director") of the Department of the Gulf.

91. Although this is the first time Daniels mentions Lieutenant John C. Palfrey, the engineer officer had been on the island with the colonel three months earlier rebuilding the post's fortifications. After this April 21 visit, Palfrey wrote a letter critical of Daniels to department headquarters in New Orleans. See n. 5 and related text Pt. 2.

lamation of Emancipation was issued, and now they have invoked the aid of the slave population to put an end to the war and save the Union. This being the case, it strikes me that every patriot ought, so far, at least, to overcome his prejudice against color as not to refuse to stand in the same ranks and to fight under the same glorious flag with them, for the preservation of our national existence and our republican institutions. For my part, I know how to appreciate that species of patriotism which allows an American soldier to resign his commission, or lay down his arms, and refuse longer to serve his country, simply because African soldiers have enlisted in the same cause, and are marching in the same ranks with him, against the common foe.

There are on this island, at present, nine companies of soldiers, viz: Seven companies of colored soldiers of the second Louisiana Native Guards, and two of white soldiers, Companies D. and F., belonging to the thirteenth Maine Regiment, all under the command for the time being, of Col. N. W. Daniels, the officer in command of the island and the fort. Now, it so happens, that in detailing soldiers for guard duty, a white Lieutenant has sometimes to receive the word of command from a colored Captain. I will say of these colored Captains that they were born free and never were slaves; that they are, some of them, men of rather more than ordinary shrewdness and intelligence; that they received their commissions under General Butler, and that they enlisted in the service from patriotic motives. For refusing compliance with this order, the commissioned officers and most of the privates in these two white companies have been suspended, and placed under arrest, till the decision of General Banks shall be known. I was not aware that the distinction of castes existed in this country under our benign republican form of government. It has existed, I know in some of the Southern States, for years. But, I hope it is to be abolished, so that our country shall be emphatically an asylum for the oppressed children of Africa, as well as the oppressed of every other land. It is what, I believe, God designs this country to be. For my part, I would not say to any free man politically, Stand aside, I am better than thou, because his skin happens to be a shade darker than mine. Socially, I am not bound to make the African my companion and equal, any more than I am the Indian or the Mexican.

It is to be regretted that such a strong prejudice against color should be imported South from any of the New England States, which have ever been the home of the most liberal and enlarged spirit of philanthropy as well as patriotism. The General Government is now endeavoring to carry out that

Part I, Ship Island

enlarged spirit of philanthropy, which I may say, has its birth in the New England States, and I trust that no opposition will be made to that effort, by any who claim to be descendents of the Pilgrim Fathers who settled those states.

Finished sailboat—ready for use. Weather beautiful and getting warmer. Went off aboard Ship New England, had a pleasant call upon Mr. Edge.—No boat in from New Orleans. Can't imagine why in the devil the Steamers don't come unless The Department intends to cut us off from all city communication.

Boat brought over intelligence day before yesterday that Gen'l Butler had returned to the city, a new rumor heard Just as the boat left the wharf, but too good, I am assured to be true. Gen'l Butler would seduce the imbecility that characterizes the present administration.

Wednesday, April 22^d 1863
[Cross-written]

This article was written by the chaplain of my Regiment, Stephen A. Hodgman, and is a brief statement of the arrest that I made of certain Maine officers and soldiers some three months ago.—He takes the right view of the matter and one that the people at the south are fast coming to—Every fight, in which these troops show their bravery, only hastens their full recognition as soldiers—They have had but few opportunities as yet but have gloriously made everything of the same.—

[Newspaper article attached]

History records the fact that there were African soldiers in the battle of Bunker Hill; that in the States of Rhode Island and Connecticut, numbers of black soldiers were enlisted, and that no distinction of color was made; that Washington himself, that great and good General, decided to sanction the enlistment of free negroes, and that his decision was approved by Congress; that in Rhode Island, not only were the names of colored men entered on the rolls with white soldiers in some of the regiments, but that a distinct regiment was made up of this class of persons; that the Legislature of New York authorized the enlistment of colored soldiers, and that Maryland during the same year, resolved to raise seven hundred and fifty soldiers, to be incorporated with the other troops. Thus it was that African soldiers helped our Revolutionary Fathers to obtain that glorious boon of liberty which we enjoy; and I trust there will be none found among their descendants so weak as to be unable to rise superior to that absurd prejudice against color which the slaveocracy of the South have labored so assiduously for years to create. It is enough that the poor African had been so long crushed and enslaved by these natural tyrants and haters of liberty. Let us not make ourselves the slaves of the absurd notions which they held and propagated. S.A.H.

Steamer Gen'l Banks came in early this morning from New Orleans. Lt. Jones shot Private on Guard this morning in some difficulty relative to a Prisoner. Placed them all under arrest for investigation. Steamer Circassian of U.S. Navy in from New Orleans, gone to New York. Gen'l Banks brought papers containing news of Gen'l Banks great victory in Western Louisiana,—in which he captured 2000 Prisoners and conquered & dispursed some ten thousand troops Confederate.[92] An attack has been made upon Charleston by The Monitors but unsuccessful. Vicksburgh not yet taken—no movement of armies in the north. Steamer Tennessee in from Pensacola, also Steamer Union—so that we have quite a harbor full.—Steamer Gen'l Banks gone to Pensacola—will be back probably tomorrow. Beat to Quarters when the Naval Steamers three of them, two outside and one inside the Sound. It looked very much like an attack. Three large steamers coming down upon us at once—Had my heavy guns trained upon them from the moment they came in sight until I learned their true colors—could have whipped twice the number.

Thursday, April 23^d 1863
[Cross-written]
U.S. Steam Frigate Brooklyn Commodore Bell Commandg came in last evening from Pensacola, will remain some time for repairs.[93]—U.S.

---

92. Daniels issued Special Orders No. 108 the same day as this incident: no one was to interfere with a sentinel on duty; all ranks were to respect sentinels; sentinels were not to leave their posts or talk to anyone except in the line of duty; sentinels must be strict with prisoners—no conversation unless for duty; and no profane language. Regimental Books, Vol. B, 74th USCI [2nd LaNG], RG 94, NA. Though the figures of prisoners and troops may be exaggerated, they represent Banks's continued pursuit of Taylor up the Teche and his arrival at Opelousas April 19 after a long push. See n. 82 above.

93. Commodore Henry H. Bell and the *Brooklyn* arrived at 8 P.M. April 22, 1863, from Pensacola for repairs and remained until May 18, when they left for Galveston. *ORN*, Ser. I, Vol. XX, 756. See n. 28 above.

Part I, Ship Island

Naval Transport Tennessee also. Col [Isaac] Dyer of 14th Maine Vol and Dr. [?] Morris, Medical Director of Pensacola Dep't both stationed at Pensacola called on me this morning—are on their way to New Orleans—

Wrote Dispatch to Brig Gen'l Sherman now in command of New Orleans asking leave of absence to go up to city—Wrote Chas Sumner, Boston—Enclosing Bill of Sale of negro girl to Gen'l Zachary Taylor, a trophy captured from Brig Gen'l Dick Taylor's Plantation in Confederate service—Rec'd letter from Col Hyde of NY and Miss Lizzie Searles with card de visite of both—an excellent one. Had visit last evening from Dr. [?] Wells of U.S. Steamer Tennessee—Commodore Bell Commanding U.S. Steam Frigate Brooklyn with Capt Adams of Vincennes called upon me this afternoon—A very pleasant visit. The old Commodore is an old veteran. Is a great stickler for ceremony, came up in full dress with sword et cetera, whilst I was in fatigues.—Is like Gen'l Scott Considerable fuss and many feathers, but still a hard old man and competent—Has carried The Brooklyn through many a hard fight and always victorious.—[94]

Placed Capt Wilkinson, Capt Carter and Lt Glover under arrest this morning for disrespect and conduct unbecoming officers and gentlemen. Shall go to New Orleans next week & have the gentlemen dismissed the service—shall then select officers in whom I can place reliance.—[95]

94. Charles Sumner (1811–1874), the Radical Republican senator from Massachusetts, was a tireless crusader for abolition. General Richard Taylor's family plantation was in the Boutte area swept clean by Union troops. On August 25, 1862, the 8th Vermont devastated the homestead, killing or running off stock, plundering stored foods, wines, clothing, jewelry, weapons, and tobacco, and scattering "correspondence and official documents of the old Genl. while President of the United States" (see n. 6 above). Winters, *Civil War in Louisiana*, 156. The 2nd LaNG could not have been there—they had not yet mustered—but they were later assigned with the Vermonters, which is doubtless when the bill of sale passed into Daniels' hands. Winfield Scott (1786–1866), war hero of 1812, became general-in-chief of the United States Army in 1841 and showed his military prowess in the Mexican War. He remained chief of the army until November 1, 1861, when at age seventy-five he was replaced with Major General George B. McClellan by President Lincoln. Warner, *Generals in Blue*, 429–30.

95. Captain Samuel Wilkinson and Lieutenant Calvin Glover of Company K, and Captain Hannibal Carter of Company C, remained in the regiment only to leave at their own discretion: Carter resigned with Glover and five others effective May 30; Wilkinson on July 20.

Friday, April 24th 1863
[Cross-written]

Went off and took breakfast with Capt Manton, aboard U.S. Storeship Relief Weather getting very warm. Old man came over from Biloxi with strawberries and garden sauce, don't like to permit this passing the lines, but we must have something fresh in the eating line or all die of scurvy.

Went up with Margaret and had her Photograph taken, she looks very finely indeed—I shall send her to New Orleans by next boat and when I go to the city make arrangements for her to go to New York to attend school for the next few years. Her history is a strange one and demonstrates the strangeness of everyday Reality as it sometimes makes itself manifest to us. A slave on a Plantation in Western Louisiana, belonging body and soul to an old wealthy French Planter, I found her a charming, beautiful Creole woman, with not enough dark blood in her veins to bust their surface. Long beautiful black hair, rosy cheeks, a complexion like alabaster, contour of features French yet very pretty.—Refined and intelligent—Gladly did she welcome The Yankees Coming although the pet of the southern household & the companion of the master & family. Her father was The Overseer of The Place, her Mother a slave—A family of white sisters by another marriage of her father lived upon the place, and she was a lady and free in every thing but her liberty. She came to me and wished me to take her into a country of Freedom & I did so—and she is now attached to me as her preserver from a life of infamy and shame—as she was intended for by her unfeeling & devilish master.—

U.S. Transport Gen'l Banks came in from Pensacola. Sent Margaret to New Orleans with Monroe on the boat. Left 11 o'clock at night.—

Saturday, April 25th 1863
[Cross-written]

Weather Insufferably hot. Finished Preliminary Examination of Lt Jones Shooting sentinel case—Find the Officer entirely in the fault. Sent Margaret over to New Orleans on Steamer last night with Monroe to fit out for northern trip.—Sent Copy of Official Report of Pascagoula Expedition to "The Boston Liberator"—also wrote Chas Sumner relative to organizations of colored soldiers, as he has taken so much interest in their affairs and is one of The Leaders of the movement. Permitted old Refugee to go back to Pascagoula—Wrote letters to Cousin Mattie Warren, Col

Part I, Ship Island

Hyde and my friend Miss Lizzie Searles of New York—Permitted a part of the crew of U.S. Steam Sloop of War Brooklyn to come ashore for excercise—have to take great precaution to guard against difficulties between the soldiers and sailors as the old Pascagoula affair has not yet been forgotten and will not be whilst I command this Island and the infamous Jackson & her still more infamous officers & crew continue to navigate the waters hereabouts.—

[No name written] of Brooklyn paid me a visit. He married a relative of My old friends The Bentons in Syracuse and knows all of my old chums in Salem[96]—so it was a very pleasant visit recalling old scenes et cetera—

Sunday, April 26th 1863
[Cross-written]

Weather delightfully cool and pleasant. High Pressure Steamboat Came from New Orleans around the point of The Island and was proceding along by The Post without stopping when I ordered a shot fired which was done, when she came about very quickly—and awaited my boats boarding. Learned that she was Just from New Orleans, brought news that our Expedition against Charleston had been abandoned That The Gen'l Banks had arrived safely at New Orleans yesterday and would probably be over here tomorrow.—That Expedition against Vicksburgh was also abandoned—*Mones Parturiens nascitur ridiculus mus.* Thus ends the Great Reduction of The two Rebel strongholds—given up without a show of a fight.[97] Would to god the spirits of our Revolutionary Famed

---

96. This may be today's Salem Corner, approximately ten miles east and slightly south of Syracuse, New York. The name Brooklyn here apparently refers to the ship just mentioned as being in port.

97. The failure of Grant's first Vicksburg campaign, involving many attempts over the winter to reach the city via canals, swamps, and bayous, led people to think he had given up. However, at this date he had already started his second campaign by marching two of his three corps south of the city down the west side of the Mississippi River. With minimal losses, the navy's fleet of eight gunboats and seven steam transports under Admiral Porter challenged and passed the Vicksburg batteries in order to meet Grant's army downriver and ferry them across the Mississippi to approach the city from the south. McPherson, *Battle Cry of Freedom,* 626–27; Winters, *Civil War in Louisiana,* 190–96. *Mones Parturiens nascitur ridiculus mus* should read "Parturient montes, nascetur ridiculus mus": Mountains will go into labor, [and] there will be born [only] a ridiculous mouse. Daniels misquotes and misspells the famous adage from Horace's *Ars Poetica,* line 139.

Waynes Putnams Knoxs and Washingtons could influence and vitalize our paralyzed and worthless Commanders.—I suppose they will delay taking Mobile until it is a second Sebastopol—where as it might now be taken with three iron clads and ten thousand men.—[98]

Had Grand Review and Dress Parade this afternoon witnessed by naval officers who said it was equal to any they had ever before witnessed.—

President Lincoln has set aside next Thursday the last day of The Month as a day of fasting and Prayer throughout the Army and Navy of The United States.[99] I have instructed my chaplain to prepare a discourse for the occasion and shall give the soldiers the benefit of freedom from all drill and duty not strictly necessary in their official capacity.—

I understand that some of my officers, the ones whom I have disgraced and will Court martial have preferred charges against me, & sent the same into Headquarters all of which amounts to nothing as their characters are well known at Headquarters and I have but to say the word, and out they go of The United States service. It has only been the respect I paid to their Companies & the fact of their being poor ignorant devils that has prevented my doing so long ago—but now they must go—[100]

98. Revolutionary War generals Anthony Wayne, Israel Putnam, Henry Knox, and George Washington. "Mad Anthony" Wayne (1745–1796) was known for his courage in leading the recapture of the British-held Hudson River post Stony Point, in New York, as well as his commands and participation at Brandywine and Germantown in Pennsylvania, at Monmouth, New Jersey, and Yorktown, Virginia. Israel Putnam (1718–1790), a fierce opponent of British rule, was an experienced soldier at the outbreak of the war from his earlier participation in the French and Indian War where he was captured by Indians and later dramatically rescued. He fought at the battles of Lexington and Bunker Hill in Massachusetts, rising to the rank of major general. Henry Knox (1750–1806) crossed the Delaware leading Washington's troops on the march to Trenton, New Jersey. He also fought at Brandywine, Germantown, Monmouth, and Yorktown and later became Washington's secretary of war. Sebastopol, an important port on the Black Sea, endured an eleven-month siege, falling to the allies of Great Britain, France, and Turkey in the Crimean War, 1854–1856.

99. President Lincoln issued a proclamation designating April 30 (Thursday) as a day of "National Humiliation, Fasting and Prayer." Captain R. T. Dunham, to Lieutenant Colonel R. B. Irwin, April 27, 1863, LR, Ser. 1756, Dept. of the Gulf, RG 393, Pt. 1, NA.

100. The officers were Captains Samuel Wilkinson and Hannibal Carter, and Lieutenant Calvin Glover. See n. 95 above. Daniels reference may be to the contrabands of Companies C and K.

Part I, Ship Island

Monday, April 27th 1863

Appointed Color Bearer and color guard for the Regiment, one corporal out of each company at the Post as follows. Color Sergeant Henry Joseph of Co C— Color Guard—

[John] Car[r]y	Corporal	of	Co	F
A[E]mile Duval	"		"	G
Joseph La[use?]	"		"	[blank]
Orrill [Laurel] Johnson	"		"	B
Wm Black	"		"	C
Louis Estare	"		"	K
Joseph Labaud	"		"	I
[blank]	"		"	D

a magnificent looking color guard.—

Schooner in from New Orleans with papers of Saturday, no news except the abandonment of Charleston, and the forming a new expedition to Vicksburgh. Gen'l Banks is still moving on towards Alexandria, our gun boats having captured that place. Brig Gen Thomas Adj't Gen'l of War Dept. is in the western Army at Memphis and below, organizing Colored Regiments, so it appears that Gov't has at last awoke to the efficacy of such organization.[101]

Tuesday, April 28th 1863
[Cross-written]

Wrote letters to my Cousin Mattie Warren and to Mrs Young of Toledo.—Sent them both Photographs of The Island scenes.—Made formal call upon The Commodore Cmdg U.S. Steamer Sloop of War The Brooklyn—

Heard rumor of an intended expedition that was to land here and attack Mobile from this point. Hope it may prove to be true.[102]

---

101. Admiral Porter was in the area of Alexandria but did not take the city with his gunboats until May 7. Banks arrived later that day. Winters, *Civil War in Louisiana*, 235. For Brigadier General Thomas, see related text of n. 37 above.

102. The rumor did not prove to be true, but the people of Mobile were concerned for their lack of defense. "We are nearly stripped of soldiers. . . . The enemy has large forces in Louisiana and has command of the sea. It is in their power to land a sufficiently large num-

See The Gen'l Banks U.S. Transport Steamer is in sight trust she may bring me good news.—Intend going on her to New Orleans—

Brought Dispatches from Headquarters. Instructions from Genl Sherman to furnish surgeon to Engineer Department, also a quantity of Gen'l Orders.—Rec'd letter from mother with good Photographs of herself and baby boy. They are as precious to me as precious can be and are some consolation when I cannot see the originals.—Letter also from Mary Drumm.—

Dr Willis and assistant Surgeon with Quartermaster came over from New Orleans on Steamer. Went off this P.M. and made ceremonious visit upon the Commodore on The Brooklyn Rec'd ordnance blanks from Washington and distributed them among the companies.—

---

ber of men on the Mississippi coast and by rapid march threaten us in the rear. . . . The loss of New Orleans has delayed our recognition. . . . By water we are probably safe, but our land works ought to be guarded. . . . Charleston and Savannah have everything they call for: Mobile gets but little." P. Hamilton, Chairman of Committee on Safety, to His Excellency John Gill Shorter, Mobile, Alabama, May 12, 1863, *OR*, Confederate Correspondence, Ser. I, Vol. LII, Pt. 2, p. 471.

Part II

New Orleans

April 29–September 26, 1863

A closed shutter was the sign of a rebel. . . .
Packed up all his goods and gone beyond the lines.[1]

New Orleans had been under Federal rule two days shy of one year when Daniels arrived from Ship Island. He was familiar with the city from his visits during his time in Pointe Coupee Parish before the war. He had returned to the region after leaving the Army of the Ohio the spring of 1862 and was still there when General Benjamin Butler discovered him for the Native Guards that fall. Now, on his first return since his recruitment, he found New Orleans noticeably changed. The hustle and bustle were gone and things seemed "dead in business and appearance" compared with before the takeover even though General Banks, on assuming command of the Department of the Gulf from "Beast" Butler, had relaxed the Federal grip on the city, allowing more leniency for the population. Some stores had reopened, churches closed because their pastors had refused to pray for President Lincoln were again holding services, and more women and children were seen in the streets. However, martial law was still in effect, and Daniels had to acquaint himself with restrictions placed by the Defenses of New Orleans upon the city's people: There were no public gatherings, except for worship, without permission; groups of more than three people found

---

1. Hepworth, *Whip, Hoe, and Sword*, 88.

talking together on the street were dispersed; all clubs were shut down until further notice; and bar rooms, coffee houses, and shops closed at 9 P.M., after which hour only police, Federal military officers, and soldiers with passes were allowed to be out.[2]

In spite of the restrictions, Daniels was glad to be back in civilization with friends he had not seen for a long while, especially his many female acquaintances. Putting first things first, though, he attended to regimental business. En route from Ship Island he had stopped at Fort Pike to check on his detachment under Lieutenant Colonel Hall, lecturing Hall for his excessive drinking and its effect on the men. Once in the city, he reported to Brigadier General Thomas W. Sherman, in command at Defenses of New Orleans, General Banks having just returned to his troops in the field at Opelousas. The colonel and Sherman had a long visit. The next day Daniels requested a board of examination for his black officers at Ship Island, a move he had disapproved of earlier with Lieutenant Colonel Hall and the Fort Pike companies. Was this a change of heart? Or had Sherman, known for his displeasure with black troops and black officers, and perhaps speaking on his own in the absence of Banks, made a strong suggestion?[3]

On Sunday, May 3, 1863, two days after the meeting with Sherman, Daniels received news that shocked him. Lieutenant John C. Palfrey, the engineer officer who had worked with him on Ship Island, had preferred charges against him for his use of a large amount of lumber to build batteries at the post. Daniels was astounded and thought the charges ridiculous—how else was he supposed to defend the island? He planned to fight the man and his accusations all the way to Washington if necessary. Nevertheless, Daniels was placed under arrest by order of the absent General Banks. Frustrated at this turn of events, the colonel wrote to Banks May 5. Stating that he had reported to the provost marshal as required, he anxiously requested an interview in which he could explain circumstances to

---

2. Fred Harvey Harrington, *Fighting Politician: Major General N. P. Banks* (Philadelphia, 1948), 92–93; General Orders No. 18, Brigadier General William H. Emory, Def. of N. O. July 3, 1863, LR, Ser. 1756, Dept. of the Gulf, RG 393, Pt. 1, NA.

3. In the temporary absence of General Banks, General Sherman had the authority to make moves relative to the needs of the department, including the issuing and approval of orders. *OR*, Ser. I, Vol. XV, 1112. Colonel N. W. Daniels to Major General N. P. Banks, May 2, 1863, LR, II, Ser. 1747, Dept. of the Gulf, RG 393, Pt. 1, NA.

Part II, New Orleans

the general and "clear up the fog that now [circles?] around my Regiment and its affairs."[4] What Daniels did not mention in his diary was that Palfrey's charges stemmed from the engineer's return trip to Ship Island April 19 when he observed what he felt to be Daniels' poor conduct and a lack of discipline among the men. Apparently, the lieutenant had little respect for this commanding officer and for the black officers.[5]

Colonel Daniels' leave of absence came to an abrupt halt. His life, after a few days of freedom, must have been complicated, certainly frustrating. On May 7, three days after Daniels' arrest, Lieutenant Colonel Hall left the detachment at Fort Pike and arrived at Ship Island to assume command of the main body of the 2nd Louisiana Native Guards. In reporting this move to headquarters, Hall requested a board to examine the officers at the new post now under his control. More than likely he had no knowledge of Daniels' application, nor did the men. However, his action did not earn him a warm welcome from the island officers.[6]

Colonel Daniels did not write any further entries in his diary for May, and only one each in June and July, before picking up again on a regular basis in mid-August.

A general concern continued over the use of black officers, but there was progress for black enlistment, now viewed as a necessity by Union authorities. On May 1 in Boston, General Butler appeared before the American Freedmen's Inquiry Commission, an advisory council that studied the question of how to deal with slaves freed under President Lincoln's Emancipation Proclamation of January 1, 1863. As former commander of the Department of the Gulf, Butler offered his perspective and experience on raising the Louisiana Native Guards the previous fall. He testified to the need for the troops, adding that his black soldiers were as capable as any man. He described his process of choosing some of the officers simply according to their intelligence. He commented on the late newspaper reports, if correct, as unfortunate, that "a great wrong has

---

4. Colonel N. W. Daniels to Major General N. P. Banks, May 5, 1863, MSR of Nathan W. Daniels, 74th USCI [2nd LaNG], RG 94, NA.

5. Lieutenant J. C. Palfrey to Dept. of the Gulf, April 21, 1863, LR, II, Ser. 1747, Dept. of the Gulf, RG 393, Pt. 1, NA.

6. Lieutenant Colonel A. G. Hall to Major General N. P. Banks, May 7, 1863, LR, II, Ser. 1747, Dept. of the Gulf, RG 393, Pt. 1, NA.

been committed... in the Department of the Gulf, in making all the coloured officers resign."[7]

General Banks had been concerned over the black officers since his assuming command from Butler. He referred to their being the "main defect" in the black regiments, of having "incorrect ideas" and questionable leadership. The men under them were poorly disciplined and caused unnecessary controversial situations with other troops. New regiments needed "good officers," not like the present "generally poor men" who were in command. In a letter to his wife, he stated that "this will be rendered soon."[8]

The same day that Butler testified in Boston, Banks announced his General Orders No. 40 incorporating the Native Guards with newly forming black regiments into the "Corps d'Afrique," where all future commissioned officers would be white. The Corps expected to have eighteen regiments, consisting of infantry, artillery, and cavalry units, each regiment to total five hundred men instead of the usual one thousand. Banks felt there was a greater dependency of black troops on officers for training and discipline, the men being "unaccustomed to battle"; the smaller the companies, the more manageable the regiment as a whole. He already had partially organized groups near Berwick Bay and Brashear City and was prepared to turn them over to General Ullmann, who had recently arrived to recruit in the area, as requested earlier by Secretary of War Edwin M. Stanton. In writing to his wife, Banks called Ullmann a "poor man who will make us all the trouble he can," although Banks was willing to be "patient with him" and wanted to cooperate with instructions from Washington. Ullmann raised his own brigades, and on June 6 the Corps d'Afrique became official: the 1st, 2nd, 3rd, and 4th Regiments of Louisiana Native Guards kept those numbers as infantry regiments of the Corps d'Afrique, while Ullmann's 1st, 2nd, 3rd, 4th, and 5th Regiments were redesignated the 6th, 7th, 8th, 9th, and 10th Regiments of Infantry of the Corps d'Afrique (a regiment forming in Pensacola was to be

---

7. Testimony of Major General B. F. Butler, American Freedmen's Inquiry Commission, May 1, 1863, LR, Ser. 12, RG 94, NA, found in Berlin et al., eds., *Black Military Experience*, 312–15; FSSP [K-86].

8. Banks to his wife, May 30, 1863, in Family Correspondence, Box 5, N. P. Banks Collection, LC.

the 5th Regiment).[9] In May the War Department had taken another step toward the future organizing of black soldiers by creating the Bureau of Colored Troops. The following year, the bureau would redesignate the Corps d'Afrique and all new black regiments as part of the "United States Colored Troops" (USCT).[10]

One of the arguments for the initial recruitment of blacks in the Department of the Gulf was their alleged resistance to diseases: they could be assigned to less healthy areas, sparing the supposedly less tolerant whites. A June 1863 departmental medical report claimed to document blacks' ability to withstand malaria, typhoid fever, diarrhea, and dysentery. The incidence of illness was stated as eleven sick whites to one sick black. This ratio proved to be erroneous later in the war, with blacks far outnumbering whites. By the end of June, close to ten thousand of Banks's men, including the Native Guards, would be wounded or sick, "nearly half the whole command and this without any special epidemic."[11] More than likely these numbers, together with the high percentage of nine-months' men, played a role in the general's movements at Port Hudson.

On March 29, General Grant began his second Vicksburg campaign while Banks remained in western Louisiana, clearing out pockets of Confederate activity wherever he found them. Banks boasted to his wife that his moves through the Teche area were the "cleanest . . . best conceived campaign of the war," and asked if people up North were impressed with his sweep of the territory. His troops alternately attacked and pursued Confederate major general "Dick" Taylor, sending him scurrying farther north, into central Louisiana. Along the way, Banks's army gathered provisions and spoils—cotton, sugar, molasses, horses, mules, and cattle—

---

9. *OR*, Ser. I, Vol. XV, 716–17; *OR*, Ser. I, Vol. XXVI, Pt. 1, p. 539. By September 1863, U.S. adjutant general Lorenzo Thomas thought that the existing regiments could now fill again to the maximum of 1,000 men before recruiting new regiments. Brigadier General Lorenzo Thomas to E. M. Stanton, September 5, 1863, *OR*, Ser. III, Vol. III, 770.

10. *OR*, Ser. III, Vol. III, 215–16; Regimental Papers and Books, 74th USCI [2nd LaNG], RG 94, NA. Infantry units were designated as USCI.

11. Peter Pines, Medical Inspector, to Brigadier General William A. Hammond, Surgeon General, U.S. Army, June 30, 1863, LR, Ser. 1756, Dept. of the Gulf, RG 393, Pt. 1, NA; W. A. Hammond to Edwin M. Stanton, June 30, 1863, *OR*, Ser. III, Vol. III, 454–55.

not to mention freed slaves who became camp followers. The stragglers who followed in the rear ransacked plantations and farms, and though ordered not to pillage and destroy, did so in spite of the directive, taking with them all they could collect and carry. Those accused of the "mischief" made off with "gold pencils, silver spoons and large rolls of Confederate bills . . . and relics enough to fill a good-sized museum."[12]

In mid-May, Grant requested the assistance of Banks's troops. Banks declined the appeal as an unfeasible logistical nightmare because he was bogged down with assorted booty and followers and could not get to Grant using available transportation. Though he refused the request, Banks was still unsure of his next move. His indecision and the delayed, misunderstood communication between the two men left each going his own way: Grant attempted two assaults on Vicksburg, May 19 and 22, and Banks finally committed his army to the taking of Port Hudson. General Halleck in Washington was irritated with Banks for his "eccentric movements" and wrote scolding him for chasing Taylor up the Red River when he should have been working with Grant on the first priority of opening up the Mississippi River by taking the two Confederate strongholds.[13]

In between corresponding with Grant and deciding on his next operation, Banks made a quick trip to New Orleans sometime before May 20, returning to his troops May 21. If there was any communication in the city at that time between the general and a languishing Colonel Daniels under arrest, the latter did not note it in his diary. Banks had more pressing matters on his mind: for one, placing Brigadier General William H. Emory, formerly in the field, in charge of Defenses of New Orleans, relieving Sherman, Daniels' possible nemesis, who had been in command there since January and who now went to the field at Port Hudson.[14]

Once Port Hudson finally became the objective, the 1st and 3rd Louisiana Native Guards and one black engineer unit marched from Baton Rouge under orders and arrived to join Banks's troops on May 25. The first

---

12. Banks to his wife, April 21, 1863, in Family Correspondence, Box 5, N. P. Banks Collection, LC; Harrington, *Fighting Politician*, 120; Winters, *Civil War in Louisiana*, 232, 236–37; Hepworth, *Whip, Hoe, and Sword*, 279–80.

13. Winters, *Civil War in Louisiana*, 239–41; Harrington, *Fighting Politician*, 121; Major General H. W. Halleck to Major General N. P. Banks, May 23, 1863, *OR*, Ser. I, Vol. XXVI, Pt. 1, p. 500.

14. Winters, *Civil War in Louisiana*, 240, 241; *OR*, Ser. I, Vol. XXVI, Pt. 1, p. 501.

assault on the fortifications took place May 27. The 1st Regiment led the attack, the 3rd behind, negotiating an exposed pontoon bridge, downed trees, and a swampy, underbrush-clogged area beneath bluffs that hid enemy guns. They had minimal artillery support from white Union troops and essentially were on their own, fighting desperately. They never were able to break through the Confederates' position and had to retreat after repeated hard-fought attempts. On the whole, the Native Guards impressed all who witnessed their aggressive charges at the enemy. General Banks, who continually thought his army inadequate, was especially pleased and later wrote his wife, "My force is too weak for the work it has to do . . . I had 11,000 men, needed 20,000. . . . I had three regiments of Negroes—two in the fight and one at work as Engineers—They fought splendidly! SPLENDIDLY! Everybody is delighted that they did so well! Their charges upon the rebel works of which they made three, exhibited the greatest bravery." He also commented, "I am glad to see that the Regiments mostly composed of slaves exhibited equal courage and capacity with those who had been free." A New York *Times* article two weeks later helped spread the word to the North that black soldiers could, and would, fight. This was their *first* battle of any significance, preceded only by the unheralded skirmishes of the early South Carolina and Kansas black regiments and the brief, if not already forgotten, Pascagoula fight of the 2nd Louisiana Native Guards. In spite of the black regiments' valorous performance, however, the Port Hudson assault was a failure for the Union due to poor timing, unclear instructions, and uncoordinated moves between commanders.[15]

Grant's unsuccessful assaults at Vicksburg and Banks's at Port Hudson caused both generals to settle in for sieges of their respective fortifications. Banks tried another futile attack on Port Hudson June 14, but was again repulsed, his leaders ineffective, his own credibility weakened. Low morale consumed his green, undisciplined troops. Only a portion of the 1st and 3rd Native Guards saw additional brief action when Banks ordered a few more vague attempts, but the siege continued.

15. Berry, "Negro Troops in Blue and Gray," 186–90; McPherson, *Battle Cry of Freedom*, 637; Glatthaar, *Forged in Battle*, 126–30; Hollandsworth, *Louisiana Native Guards*, 53–58; Winters, *Civil War in Louisiana*, 252–61; Major General N. P. Banks to his wife, May 30, 1863, in Family Correspondence, Box 5, N. P. Banks Collection, LC; New York *Times*, June 11, 1863, found in Glatthaar, *Forged in Battle*, 130.

At Vicksburg, approximately thirty thousand trapped and weakened Confederate troops waited to be rescued, desperate for food. The soldiers' already minimal daily rations had been reduced to "one biscuit and a small bit of bacon," occasional mule meat, and indigestible pea bread. A private, fearing a possible mutiny, wrote to the commanding officer, Lieutenant General Joseph C. Pemberton, that the men did not want to starve and "if you can't feed us, you had better surrender us." On July 4, before a relief force could attack, Vicksburg surrendered to Grant. Word reached Port Hudson three days later, and the Confederates there, knowing that they could not survive once Vicksburg collapsed, surrendered on July 8. "Port Hudson surrendered to us today," wrote General Banks to his wife, noting that it was four months to the day since he began the campaign. He added that it had been six months since he assumed command of the Department of the Gulf.[16]

The 2nd Louisiana Native Guards had been in existence for two months prior to Banks's arrival in December 1862. Their history had been no better, no worse, than that of the other two early black units, but now frustration reigned at an all-time high. They did not have much to show for themselves. Their Pascagoula encounter paled in comparison with Port Hudson, where their brothers in the 1st and 3rd Native Guards had proved to themselves and to a wider audience of skeptics and "sneerers" that blacks were capable of fighting in this war. The 2nd's commander, Colonel Daniels, was under arrest in New Orleans. The arrival on Ship Island of the heavy-drinking, not very popular Lieutenant Colonel Hall as the new commander immediately precipitated resignations among the black officers, as did his newly ordered examination board for them. Meanwhile, the regiment's assigned duty ten miles off the coast in isolation was probably not going to change. It was only natural that the morale of the men deteriorated.

Daniels lost four black officers, three to sickness, while he was in command on Ship Island from January to the end of April. During the six months when Hall was in charge, thirteen officers resigned at the post, five of them in the first week after he arrived in May. Captain William

16. *OR*, Ser. I, Vol. XXIV, Pt. 3, pp. 982–83, 987; Johnson and Buel, eds., *Battles and Leaders*, III, 481; Winters, *Civil War in Louisiana*, 205, 281–83; McPherson, *Battle Cry of Freedom*, 633, 636–38; Major General N. P. Banks to his wife, July 8, 1863, in Family Correspondence, Box 5, N. P. Banks Collection, LC.

Barrett, who fought well at Pascagoula but whom Daniels had later charged with disobedience of orders and conduct unbecoming an officer, wrote to General Ullmann, whom he assumed to be taking over command of the Native Guards in Banks's reorganization plan for the Corps d'Afrique. Barrett was concerned about the continuing removal of black officers and pleaded his case as one of the first who offered his services to General Butler, having recruited his own company in New Orleans of "bona fide freed men, and not contrabands." He received a noncommittal response from someone other than Ullmann and resigned in frustration two months later. Captains Samuel Wilkinson and Samuel W. Ringgold resigned on the same date in July, objecting to the examination board and the fact that the officers chosen for the detail were of inferior rank, "whose promotion would be effected by our dismissal." Major Francis Dumas, whom Daniels praised for his combat performance at Pascagoula, wrote his resignation to Lieutenant Colonel Hall on July 3.[17]

Captain P. B. S. Pinchback, of Company A, was the only black officer left with the detachment of Companies A, E, and H at Fort Pike. The others had been removed during the February purge or had resigned in disgust shortly afterward. Lieutenant William S. Peabody, the single white line officer in the regiment, also remained in Company A. When Lieutenant Colonel Hall was called to Ship Island in May to replace Daniels, Pinchback took over the detachment's command with Peabody assuming adjutant duties. All was going well at first with the three companies. An inspection report found no major problems. Drill and discipline were "good," as were cooking, camp police, personal cleanliness, and clothing. Arms, however, were in "fair to bad" condition, horses and equipment somewhat deficient, and quality of flour rations poor along with the

17. Regimental Papers, 74th USCI [2nd LaNG], RG 94, NA; Captain W. B. Barrett to Brigadier General Daniel Ullmann, May 17, 1863, MSR of William B. Barrett, 74th USCI [2nd LaNG)], RG 94, NA; Captains S. Wilkinson and S. W. Ringgold to Major General N. P. Banks, July 7, 1863, MSR's of Samuel Wilkinson and Samuel W. Ringgold, 74th USCI [2nd LaNG)], RG 94, NA; MSR of Francis E. Dumas, 74th USCI [2ndLaNG], RG 94, NA. Barrett, Ringgold, and Wilkinson, having already resigned, were pallbearers in New Orleans for the late July funeral of 1st LaNG Captain Andre Cailloux, killed at Port Hudson. Daniels, under arrest in the city at the time, made no reference to this elaborate event attended by thousands of blacks lining the streets for more than a mile to pay respects to their hero, who once called himself the "blackest man in New Orleans" and was a popular leader within his regiment and the black community. Wilson, *Black Phalanx*, 214–17n.

amount of medical supplies. In mid-July, Pinchback reported to General Banks that the organization was deteriorating due to a lack of officers. Company H refused to drill under an officer of Company A, black or white; they wanted their own officers—black officers. Pinchback had heard that no new officers would be appointed until *he* resigned. This confounded him, as Banks had advised him the previous December not to resign under charges that were then briefly imposed on him, stating "I will give you every opportunity to prove the efficiency of yourselves and men." Now he realized that Banks had no intention of supporting him, that perhaps "none of us are fit to command."[18]

In early August 1863 there was renewed fear of an attack on Ship Island from Confederate forces at Mobile. During this time Chaplain Stephen Hodgman wrote Banks to express concern over failing discipline among the troops under Lieutenant Colonel Hall as officers at the post continued to resign. At the same time, Hodgman himself reluctantly preferred charges against one of the officers. He had hoped someone else would do it first; he knew the necessity of harmony, especially during periods of threatened enemy activity. "Our regiment is going down for the want of discipline although the common soldier is composed of as good material as can be found in any regiment." In an added note, the chaplain stated that he expected to resign in the near future.[19]

Those who observed the regiment from the outside found Hall to be competent and the men under control. The fact that Daniels was under arrest should have meant that the second man in command would be an improvement. The Department of the Gulf's chief engineer, Major D. C. Houston, familiar with the free black troops, suggested that the 2nd Louisiana Native Guards and the 2nd Louisiana Engineers at New Orleans

---

18. MSR of William S. Peabody, 74th USCI [2ndLaNG], RG 94, NA; Inspection Report, Detachment of 2nd LaNG at Ft. Pike commanded by Captain P. B. S. Pinchback, Adjutant's Regimental Papers, 74th USCI [2nd LaNG], RG 94, NA; Captain P. B. S. Pinchback to Major General N. P. Banks, July 15, 1863, Adjutant's Regimental Papers, 74th USCI [2nd LaNG] RG 94, NA. Pinchback finally resigned on September 10, 1863, because of conditions he felt were hostile to him as the lone black officer at the post. MSR of P. B. S. Pinchback, 74th USCI [2nd LaNG], RG 94, NA.

19. Major N. P. Banks to Commodore H. H. Bell, August 4, 1863, *OR*, Ser. I, Vol. XX, 434; Chaplain Stephen O. Hodgman to Major General N. P. Banks, August 5, 1863, Adjutant's Regimental Papers, 74th USCI [2nd LaNG], RG 94, NA.

combine. It would be an efficient way of raising eighteen hundred good workers who needed no training. Many of the blacks were mechanics, more intelligent, and a "better class of men" than the former slaves then being recruited. In keeping with the tone of the Department of the Gulf, Houston added that the black officers would have to replaced. Colonel Daniels, then under arrest, would not make a "suitable colonel," but Lieutenant Colonel Hall, in command at Ship Island, was a "most efficient officer."[20]

In another outside observation a few weeks after the chaplain's complaint, a summer inspection on the island found the men well drilled and disciplined. Their health had been good until scurvy arrived near the beginning of August. The only negatives were the bad condition of the wharf and the need for another small boat to speed up communication and supplies, a change Daniels had requested months earlier.[21]

Whether it was Hall's lack of attention or the presence of scurvy on the post, the 2nd Louisiana Native Guards failed to respond to an August inquiry regarding the condition of the Corps d'Afrique. Twenty-two regiments sent in reports—every regiment except Hall's.[22]

Daniels' removal from his regiment was painful for him. Although he did not take the charges against him seriously and still considered himself the 2nd's leader, the longer his absence, the more frustrated his diary entries. His situation in New Orleans, with good housing and among friends, was alternately comforting and maddening. He seems to have had personality conflicts with certain people, although his female acquaintances served to meet his needs, emotionally and on occasion physically. Spiritualism and dream interpretation became part of his daily life. He did not return to his diary with any regularity until August 19, by which time other events had added confusion to his ongoing struggle.

Lieutenant Elijah K. Prouty, Daniels' adjutant, who had transferred

20. Major D. C. Houston to Lieutenant Colonel R. B. Irwin, AAG, July 25, 1863, LS, Ser. 1818, Dept. of the Gulf, RG 393, Pt. 1, NA. Evidently no action was taken on Houston's suggestions.

21. Lieutenant Colonel W. D. Smith, Assistant Inspector, to Captain D. S. Walker, AAG, Aug. 25, 1863, LR, Ser. 1756, Dept. of the Gulf, RG 393, Pt. 1, NA.

22. Brigadier General George L. Andrews to Lieutenant Colonel R. B. Irwin, August 21, 1863, LR, Ser. 1756, Dept. of the Gulf, RG 393, Pt. 1, NA.

from the Eighth Vermont the previous fall, was arrested and supposed to be promptly dismissed from military service after an incident on August 7. During an outing near New Orleans, Prouty was accused of "conduct unbecoming an officer and a gentleman in grossly insulting an officer of the Navy by use of indecent language while he was in the company with a lady."[23] Daniels wrote about the affair briefly in the diary more than a week later with harsh remarks on the lieutenant's character. He commented on interceding for Prouty, although apparently the two had a trying relationship. What the colonel did not mention at any time in the diary was his own involvement—he was with the lieutenant at the time and was also charged in the incident.

Daniels may not have been very concerned over the new accusation, as he already had the Ship Island charge to deal with. Although the incident would continue to plague him, and although a few additional piecemeal, petty charges would later surface in a seeming plot, it was Lieutenant Palfrey's accusations from the island that demanded the colonel's time and attention. It was these charges on which a court-martial was to be based and from which he wanted to clear his name. The frustration of dealing with witnesses, depositions, court cancellations, sickness of the judge advocate, and a lack of a jury quorum kept him in New Orleans for five long months. One delay followed another, excuses from officials multiplied. This was not your usual military case. It was an experimental situation involving a white commanding officer of a black regiment.

The colonels of the 1st and 3rd Louisiana Native Guards experienced difficulties not unlike those of Daniels. Colonel Stafford of the 1st Regiment had a lengthy list of minor problems going back to recruitment in the fall of 1862. He was finally charged and later arrested for his behavior in front of troops at a picket line in Baton Rouge on May 14, 1863. Although his arrest is recorded as coming on August 1, he was apparently detained near the May date because it was his lieutenant colonel, Chauncey Bassett, who led his troops during the May 27 assault on Port Hudson. Like Daniels, Stafford considered the complaint frivolous and wrote to General Banks offering an explanation and requesting an interview. Colonel Nelson of the 3rd Regiment had a few troubles along the way be-

---

23. MSR of Elija K. Prouty, 74th USCI [2nd LaNG], RG 94, NA.

Part II, New Orleans

fore his petty charge of appropriating property belonging to a local widow near Port Hudson.[24]

Daniels' frustration at being detained turned in two directions, first in anger at General Banks for allowing the matter to drag on so long, and second, toward thoughts of release from his predicament by resigning his commission. The anger came out in the denunciation of what Daniels perceived to be Banks's habit of letting his political activity overshadow his duties as general.

Banks's background before the war, as a Massachusetts governor and congressman, certainly played a part in his motivation and in his attitude toward many of his duties as commander of the Department of the Gulf. He had a politician's ego, a concern for appearances, and a need for praise. He confided to his wife, "People talk very kindly to me . . . that at some time or other in some way or other the destinies of this country [will] fall into my hands." After eight months of straightening out the turmoil in his department, he passed on another comment to her, this one from an admiring friend: "I may say in the spirit of friendship and not to flatter you that it is the universal opinion in Washington, and so far as I know in Massachusetts, that your administration, civil and military, has been the greatest success of the war."

Banks initiated a peace movement in mid-1863 when he sent secret messengers to both Jefferson Davis and President Lincoln. The attempt never took hold, as Washington radicals opposed anything other than the sheer destruction of the Confederacy. Much to the general's dismay, Lincoln and his cabinet never credited him for this delicate undertaking. Dr. Isaac Zacharie, one of the spies in the endeavor, felt strongly about the general and encouraged him to consider becoming a presidential candidate.[25] Banks certainly made politically adroit moves as viewed by Daniels during the colonel's time in the Department of the Gulf. But even though he may have been entertaining thoughts of higher office, the gen-

---

24. MSR's of Spencer H. Stafford and John A. Nelson, 73rd and 75th USCI [1st and 3rd LaNG], RG 94, NA. See n. 42 below.

25. Major General N. P. Banks to his wife, September 19, 1862, August 27, 1863, in Family Correspondence, Box 5, N. P. Banks Collection, LC; Harrington, *Fighting Politician*, 126–27; Dr. I. Zacharie to Major General N. P. Banks, July 30, August 8, 1863, Military Papers, Box 79, N. P. Banks Collection, LC.

eral was also deeply entangled in Louisiana's problems and in trying to please Lincoln by making the state a model of reconstruction.

One of Banks's political actions turned out to have an indirect effect on Colonel Daniels' thoughts about resigning. On August 6, 1863, the general released nearly all the political prisoners in the Department of the Gulf, most of them having been sentenced by General Butler and confined since the previous fall on various posts, including Ship Island. Banks felt that he could not let them go earlier because there was so much "uproar excited about affairs here." He combined the release with one of President Lincoln's thanksgiving proclamations, a political move that he felt "marks the day as well as signaling our victories and policy at the same time."[26]

Among those released from Ship Island was prisoner number 45, James George Brown, former private secretary of General Butler, arrested by his boss and sent to the isolated post for "betraying official business confided to him."[27] Brown knew Daniels from the island and upon his release visited the colonel in New Orleans. Brown at this point in his career was a fledgling Union spy whose motives were not so much patriotic as monetary. He offered his services as needed to individual generals, and having been rebuked by Butler, he was now hoping to work for Banks. Brown knew a lot about Butler's fraudulent activities in administering the department, information Banks could use in a political arena, should he choose to do so. But at the moment Banks had other plans for the spy.[28]

Colonel Daniels' stagnating situation somehow became a bargaining chip between Banks and Brown, though on the surface it appeared that the former prisoner, out of the goodness of his heart, offered to help the colonel. Lieutenant Palfrey's original Ship Island charge still held. Daniels' diary barely mentions any additional charges against him; notably absent is any reference to his personal involvement in the incident with Lieutenant Prouty, now dismissed from the service. He seems not to have been troubled by a new comment from Brigadier General Godfrey Weit-

---

26. Major General N. P. Banks to his wife, August 9, 1863, in Family Correspondence, Box 5, N. P. Banks Collection, LC.

27. Return of Prisoners in Confinement at Ship Island, Mississippi, December 15, 1862, LR, Ser. 1756, Dept. of the Gulf, RG 393, Pt. 1, NA.

28. Robert Scott Davis, "The Curious Civil War Career of James George Brown, Spy," *Prologue*, XXVI (Spring 1994), 18.

zel, one that surely concerned the early days of the Native Guards when they were briefly under the general's command guarding the Opelousas Railroad.

Basically, Daniels was worn down. He was anxious to leave for the north. Resignation was the only way out. Brown was somehow able to negotiate for Daniels with General Banks. Why was the spy's involvement necessary? What was the agreement?

New Orleans, Louisiana

Wednesday April 29th 1863

Embarked aboard U.S. Steamer Gen'l Banks and came to New Orleans, arrived safely after a tedious trip of twelve hours—Saw Lt Col Hall of my Regiment and three of my companies at Fort Pike—

Found them in good condition though somewhat dissatisfied with the conduct of Col Hall—It seems that he has an unfortunate failing of getting intoxicated, & they charge him with being drunk—beastly so—for three days—during which he was entirely unable to attend to his command—I informed the gentleman that should I hear of the occurrence again—a court martial would investigate the same—He is not reliable and the soldiers will not I am afraid rely upon him in any event of emergency—

Thursday April 30th 1863

Put up at The St Charles Hotel[29]—city dead in business and appearance.—

Find all my old friends well & are glad to see me.—The beautiful Miss Victoria, like the Lily of The Valley, as chastely superb and as refreshingly charming as Eleanora's fairest offspring—

---

29. New Orleans' St. Charles Hotel became the headquarters for the invading Federals in May 1862 and remained an important boarding house for visiting Union military. It was on the corner of St. Charles and Common Streets in the center of the city. Capers, *Occupied City*, 61; "Norman's Plan of New Orleans & Environs, 1854," Fillmore Map Collection, No. 29, LC.

Friday, May 1st 1863

Called upon Brig Gen'l Sherman and Reported. Had a long and very pleasant interview with the General—

Genl Banks carrying everything before him in The "Teche" Country[30]—and why shouldn't he—He has a vastly superior force, and can drive them like chaff before the wind. Port Hudson will prove his masterpiece—I only trust he may be equal to the emergency—

Made the acquaintance of Frank Reynolds, Capt Manton's friend, find him a curious fellow—Saw Dr Wells of U.S. Steamer Tennessee—

Margaret in rooms on Rampart St. Must Divest myself of that encumbrance. There is danger in her connection—and she must be content with what I have already done for her—I can do no more—

Saturday, May 2d 1863

Went out yesterday with Madame Gur[hose?]—had a very pleasant drive.—Heard from Miss Annie—Strange that she can find consolation in her course—The Demon of Secessionism will rob the fairest flower of its beauty—sacrifice all to the demoniac passion—How she can reconcile her present actions with her past promise I can not understand—She has changed—oh so greatly changed—

Would that her heart was the same as when I left her the beauteous innocent joyous maiden some two years ago—but Destiny otherwise decrees—Time may question what circumstances has broken, but I doubt very much the reestablishment of those principles that gave her such character, such purity—such goodness and such affection as existed in the days of "Auld Lang Syne."—

Sunday, May 3d 1863

Learned this morning that Lt Palfrey, Engineer Officer at Ship Island, has preferred charges against me for taking some 15^{000} feet of lumber at The Post for the construction of The Batteries there[31]—I am surprised—

---

30. Banks's army pressed through the Teche district in a continuing campaign April 19–May 14. His army had a limited supply line and lived off the land as much as possible. Though ordered against "private foraging," his troops ignored the directive. Banks left for New Orleans April 25 on department business, returning to the field on April 30. Winters, *Civil War in Louisiana*, 218, 234.

31. No details of the charges were found in the arrest issued in Special Order No. 241, Def. of N.O. May 3, 1863. MSR of Nathan W. Daniels, 74th USCI [2nd LaNG], RG 94, NA.

as it was clearly a military necessity—and the Island would not today be in our possession had I not have done so—I shall call for a Court martial on the same—and can clearly prove that my services & that of my Regiment has not only saved the Post—but benefitted the Gov't thousands of dollars when the inactivity of The Engineer Dept—and its officers, would have lost the place and all it contained—I am very happy that the occasion has been given me to prove the great services of my command, and am astonished that Palfrey would dare to comment himself, when the facts, when they are produced will prove his inefficiency and incompetency—The Gentleman has raised the issue and he must meet it now—& it will not ride here. I intend to make him show at Washington an explanation of his course & the reason why he has not availed himself of the vast amount of material that has been furnished him to put the Island long ago in a good state of defence—

Monday, June 22^d 1863

Have been in the city some time, perfecting the matters of my Reg't. Gen'l Banks is at Port Hudson besieging the place but I much doubt the success of his plans.—The Guerillas came into Plaquemine yesterday & burnt a large number of our Transports, & today have captured Thibodauxville with its garrison of two companies.[32] Lt Col Hall is in command of my Rgt at Ship Island—I hope Gen'l Banks will order me to Plaquemine or to Port Hudson—as I can hold Plaquemine easily with my command.—The negro troops have demonstrated their ability to fight, and that successfully—at Port Hudson where in the commencement of the siege The 1st & 3^d Rgts stormed the works, doing the best fighting—according to undoubted authority—that was done in the field—losing 600 out of 900, and acting most like veterans than amateurs—[33]

32. Three Texas regiments of cavalry under Colonel J. P. Major surprised a Federal detachment at Plaquemine on the morning of June 18 and proceeded to capture and destroy three steamboats. On June 20, Brigadier General W. P. Lane's Confederates cut the railroad and telegraph lines at Thibodaux, ran the Yankees out of town, and feasted on raided military stores and whiskey rations. Winters, *Civil War in Louisiana*, 284–86.

33. Daniels' Port Hudson information was a bit exaggerated. The total casualties came to 180 (killed, wounded, and missing), or roughly 18 percent of the combined forces of the 1st and 3rd LaNG Regiments, numbering just over 1,000. Approximately 500 men saw combat, mostly from the 1st LaNG. The 3rd Regiment barely saw action. *OR*, Ser. I, Vol. XXVI, Pt. 1, p. 68; Glatthaar, *Forged in Battle*, 124–29; Winters, *Civil War in Louisiana*, 254; Hollandsworth, *Louisiana Native Guards*, 57–58.

Friday, July 17th 1863

Aleck Wible came into house yesterday morning No 6 Euterpe St. Rented the same June 24th of Quartermaster at $30 per month.—

Lost last week $1000, suppose it was taken by my boy Monroe, have him now under arrest.—

Have excellent news of the capture of Vicksburgh, Port Hudson and victory over Lee in Pennsylvania—a grand avalanche of success.—The Rebellion is over I think effectually squelched—Richmond is said to be besieged by Dix & will eventually fall.—[34]

I am here still in the city awaiting Gen'l Banks action. If he can afford the entertainment I certainly can—allthough it has already cost me some $3200.

Purchased new horse Black Hawk of Mr Brub for $350 last week. Commenced keeping horse some time the middle of last month at Gravis stables.

Wednesday, August 19th 1863
[Cross-written]

I have within the last week had some strange experience in the Philosophy of Dreams, having in two instances distinctly dreamed of events that have within a short time after happened. As I dreamed that I was walking through the forest when a hideous copperhead sprang out of the bushes and fastened its fangs in my foot.—I immediately sought for alcoholic drink or stimulant, but finding none experienced all the horrors of death from poison. I could feel my blood becoming chilled as the deadly poison gradually worked its way through my veins, & awoke only as I was about passing into unconsciousness. That same day I learned that an enemy had done me a great injury, but eventually I recovered entirely from the same—Shortly after I dreamed that I had a terrible battle with Aleck Wible and today sure enough we had a severe contest with language only, but had I not have been forwarned in my dream, it might have led to an essay with arms.—I also dreamed day before yesterday that I had a very

---

34. The successes of Vicksburg (with Port Hudson) and Gettysburg did, in fact, begin to turn the tide of the war. Union major general John A. Dix (1798–1879), aged sixty-three at the outbreak of hostilities, was considered too old for field duty. He commanded various departments over the course of the war, including the Department of Virginia from June to July 1863. Warner, *Generals in Blue*, 125–26.

pleasant and agreeable interview with Gen'l Banks and sure enough yesterday I rec'd instruction that he was to do me a favor. Last night I appeared to be upon the banks of The Mississippi River with my Regiment and suddenly saw an attack made upon a steamboat coming down by The Guerillas. I dreamed that we sallied forth, and dispersed them after a severe fight.—

Have Adjutant Prouty placed under arrest for insulting a Gentleman and Lady the other night. He has been dismissed the service, but the order was rescinded upon my representation to Gen'l Banks, and he is now in close confinement undergoing an investigation of the matter. He richly deserves dismissal as he is a low disgusting intriguant with no honor, intelligence or any virtue that would redeem his character.[35]

He has been very active endeavoring to impune me the one who can leave his position, & took leave from the ranks—but now he finds the reward of ingratitude and will if I am not mistaken suffer the full penalty of his crime—

Thursday, August 20th 1863
[Cross-written]

I am still here in New Orleans awaiting the settlement of my matters. I feel that great injustice has been done me by The Commanding General, in detaining me so long from my command by such frivolous charges as have been preferred—Meanwhile my Major has resigned and the rest of my line officers & The Regiment is fast becoming demoralized.[36] The Lt Col is entirely incompetent & will if allowed to remain disgrace the Regiment.—It is within my power to bring order out of chaos, but through the ill will of certain controlling persons I am kept [unjustly?] away, and not allowed an opportunity to prove myself or my command. Yet all must result well. Though suffering now infinitely I feel that my day will yet come and that my reward will equal my suffering. I have seen one after another whom I have befriended turn against me shruging the hand that gave them food until I have lost nearly all confidence in human race, true—

35. Although Daniels does not mention it, he too was charged in the incident in question. See n. 23 above, n. 37 below, and the discussion of the case in the Conclusion.

36. Major Francis E. Dumas wrote his resignation to Lieutenant Colonel Hall at Ship Island July 3, 1863. It was accepted by Dept. of the Gulf, Special Order No. 169, July 13, 1863. MSR of Francis E. Dumas, 74th USCI [2nd LaNG], RG 94, NA.

These serpents are below the brutes, but I have cast my bread freely upon the waters, and will patiently await its return. Their injustice would not rectify such acts of manhood. Dreamed last night that women unknown to me—followed me and could not get rid of them—scene changed and I was in some Post office looking over letters but found none for myself—scene changed and those everlasting women again haunted me until I awoke—

Weather cool and stormy. Equinoctial storm at hand—Ordered Mr Aleck Wible to find other premises. After doing what I have done for him, and then to have him endeavoring to injure me is enough of the depravity of human nature for me. I want nothing more to do with such a brute. Philanthropy in his case would be sin.—

Friday, August 21st 1863

Adjt Prouty's case came up today before Court Martial. Think it will go hard with him—but I hope he may get off. I have no ill will against him although I am conscious that he has done much, in fact all in his power to affect me.[37] Mr. [George M.] Chapman called up to see me and informed me of the loss of his Steamboat, The Lafourche by a snag below Donaldsonville. Is a total loss. Tis a pity, as he has worked hard for the small amount of money that he has put in her. They all come to me when they get into trouble, but are very apt to forget their debts when they are out of them. A large force of Gen'l Grants *Corps de Armee* landed this morning at Carrolton, probably intending a movement against Mobile or Galveston.[38] Mrs. [?] Turner called upon Gen'l Banks for a Pass out the lines, but failed to obtain one, she told the Gen'l that she wished him to order my Reg't to Bayou Sara. I wish the Gods he would. I could

---

37. Lieutenant Prouty was found guilty on two counts and sentenced to dismissal. Proceedings of General Court Martial, Trial of Elijah K. Prouty, August 21, 1863, MM 878, RG 153, Records of the Office of the Judge Advocate, NA.

38. Grant began redeploying his army after the Vicksburg victory, returning several divisions to Missouri and Kentucky and sending a strong force to occupy Natchez, Mississippi. Army general-in-chief Henry W. Halleck, in Washington, disapproved of a plan to take Mobile and on August 7 ordered Grant's 13th Corps to General Banks at New Orleans with instructions to cooperate with Banks in movements west of the Mississippi River into Texas. Ulysses S. Grant, *Personal Memoirs* (2 vols.; New York, 1885), I, 579–81.

sift that Sodom & Gohmorrah of it's secessionism—as I know every inch of the people & country for miles around.—[39]

Saturday, August 22ᵈ 1863

Called down to see Mr. E. Bischoff, an old acquaintance in Ohio, did not find him at home.—Sent Summons yesterday to witnesses at Ship Island. Called upon Commodore Bell aboard The Pensacola[40] relative to Capt Adams of The Vincennes Gave Deposition of Capt Manton of The Relief taken before Col Dwight, [Willis?], to Judge Advocate at Col Cahill's office. Rec'd copy of extra charges.—[41]

Dreamed last evening that I was again with my Reg't marching through the city.—Had a long conversation with one of Gen'l Ullman's Colonels last night. They all think that This Department are striving to break up *The Corps De Afrique* as most of the Colonels of the same are under arrest and that upon frivolous charges[42]—and they stand a very poor chance to obtain Justice in their complaint. Well come what may, if it be the policy of The Gov't we shall be sustained in our colored organization, but if not, we must go down. I believe it to be *the policy*, and have no

---

39. Daniels lived near Bayou Sara in Pointe Coupee Parish before the war. It was an important riverport and a strategic landing spot for troops in the Port Hudson assault. Damaged in a Federal gunboat attack in May, it remained occupied by the Federal army after the fall of Port Hudson. Winters, *Civil War in Louisiana*, 240–41.

40. Commodore Bell, who left for Galveston on the *Brooklyn* on May 18, returned to New Orleans to join the *Pensacola* and temporarily take command of the West Gulf Blockading Squadron. Extracts from the private diary of Commodore H. H. Bell, 1863, No. 6, *ORN*, Ser. I, Vol. XX, 763.

41. Colonel Charles S. Dwight, Maj. [surgeon] Samuel Willis, and Colonel Thomas W. Cahill of 9th Connecticut Volunteer Regiment, commanding 2nd brigade, 2nd division with Def. of N.O. Additional unspecified charges were forwarded by Lieutenant Colonel W. D. Smith, assistant inspector, against Colonel Daniels on August 19, 1863. MSR, Nathan W. Daniels, 74th USCI [2nd LaNG], RG 94, NA.

42. Colonel Stafford of the 1st LaNG was arrested August 1, 1863, at Port Hudson on charges preferred by Captain J. P. Garland of the 21st Maine Volunteers based on Stafford's improper conduct at a Baton Rouge picket line on May 14, 1863. Colonel John A. Nelson of the 3rd LaNG was placed under arrest at Port Hudson for conduct unbecoming an officer in "appropriating to himself and his own use the property of a widow lady." MSR's of Spencer H. Stafford and John A. Nelson, 73rd and 75th USCI [1st and 3rd LaNG], RG 94, NA. See related text of n. 24 above.

fears of the future—*It is right,* and must prevail. It matters little what color a man has to his skin if his brains are right, mind stamps the man, not race.—

Sunday, August 23ᵈ 1863

Mr. E. Bischoff called up to see me yesterday. He has been over in The Attakapas Country[43] during the Rebellion, having had some rather bitter experience in Rebeldom. Came very near being hung because he would not enter the army but finally escaped, and came down when Col Chickering brought down the rear guard of our army.[44] Says that he is sick of the South, and will go north very soon. He is a magnificent musician, and is now engaged in the concert rooms here at a high salary—

Went out Riding on my black horse "Beauty" who is a perfect devil in the horseflesh line—tried his best to dismount me, but that is an impossibility.—He succeeded in breaking up a buggy, though for me, last week.—Intend taking him home to my baby boy—Home, what sweetness in the name, but when shall I have the pleasure of enjoying its many blessings again, when shall I look upon the loved ones who are dearer to me far than life, or aught else—Tis now over a year since I left that home, perhaps many may intervene ere I shall look upon it again.—This terrible war desolates many hearthstones, takes away the dear and loved ones ne'er to gladden their home again, scarce a family but have some friend to mourn—some dear one lost in the strife of devilism against the best Institutions that this material sphere e'er witnessed.

Monday, August 24ᵗʰ 1863

Reported at Col Cahill's this morning, but witnesses had not arrived from Ship Island, therefore matters could not be attended to.—

Have the blues like Lucifer today. If there is any truth in Presentiments then have I one now, an oppressive feeling, as though some great calamity was suspended over me, affects me.—

43. Attakapas country was the present-day St. Martinville, Louisiana, area near Bayou Teche.

44. Colonel Thomas E. Chickering, 41st Massachusetts Infantry, was commander of the post at Baton Rouge with seven regiments under him, including the 3rd LaNG. *OR,* Ser. I, Vol. XV, 1114–15; Special Orders No. 64, Mar. 5, 1863, Ser. 1767, Dept. of the Gulf, RG 393, NA.

Part II, New Orleans

Some of my negro soldiers came up to see me, and it is really gratifying to witness the true affection these beings have for me. I can rest assured of one thing, that my soldiers almost worship me & that come what may, I have the hearts of my Regiment.—It is amusing to hear them talk of what they are going to do when I make my appearance on The Island. They say they have a chair constructed—as they call it a triumphal car, in which they are going to bear their beloved Colonel to his Quarters when he lands. True hearted and affectionate men, God grant that I may be restored again to them.—

Tuesday, August 25th 1863
Court Adjourned today on account of sickness of Judge Advocate.— Rec'd letter from mother with good news. All well at home and happy. Answered the same, and also wrote baby—
Dreamed last night that Lt Palfrey the originator of charges, came to me in the most friendly manner, and withdrew all that he had said and done. God knows such dream would be only right should it happen as there is not a vestige of truth in what he has said and preferred—
Steamer came up from Ship Island but did not bring my witnesses.
Some of my soldiers called upon me, are all very anxious that I should return to the command. Do not like Lt Col Hall, and nothing will do but I must come.—Well it depends entirely upon the Dept. I know that I can command that Regt better than any living man, & that it is only persecution that prevents my now being with them.—

Wednesday, August 26th & Thursday August 27th 1863
Reported at Court this morning. Witnesses not here, could not accordingly get my matter in.
Court Adjourned *sine die*[45]—so that my case will not be tried until another court is convened—It would seem as though the fates were not yet tired of persecuting me. Now I suppose I shall have to wait another month 'ere the [exc-----] could again be reached. Well, if Gov't can afford to lose

---

45. There was a lack of a quorum due to the absence of the 26th Massachusetts Volunteers officers. Court could not continue until the places were filled. Colonel T. W. Cahill, Def. of N. O., to Captain Duncan S. Walker, AAG, August 26, 1863. MSR of Nathan W. Daniels, 74th USCI [2nd LaNG], RG 94, NA.

my services, I can well afford to be idle, but it is a great injustice to me to be kept here from my command upon charges so frivolous, as are those that are made the basis of my persecution.

Capt Adams one of my witnesses came up, he says his testimony will be the fullest that he can give in my favor, and that he thinks I am the worst abused man that he knows of.—Has returned again to his Post to turn his command over to his successor, after which he will return here and await the examination.[46]

Dr. Willis came up on the Steamer, called and took dinner.

Dreamed last night that I had an interesting interview with Genls Grant & Banks, perhaps a favorable augury—maybe not—I shall not endure this state of things much longer—Shall send in my resignation if I do not get Justice very soon.—[47]

Wrote mother and baby today, also sent Newspaper to friends in Ohio.—

Friday, August 28th 1863

Weather for the first time for seven months cool & pleasant. Ree'd letter from Dicky Bray filled with good news from home.—Mother & my little baby boy all well.—Saw Col Cahill this morning relative to my charges He tells me that Capt Manton's Deposition is not admissable on account of the absence of the Prosecutor.—A damned pretty kettle of fish, when it is taken by Genl Banks own order, well if the Dep't don't know their business it is none of my fault, they cannot take advantage of their own mistake. Paymaster has been down and paid my Reg't, but only $7.00 per month. I cannot see why black soldiers, who are acknowledged by all to be equal to any whites, should not receive the same compensation for the same labor.[48]

---

46. Lieutenant Commander Henry A. Adams was relieved by Commander William H. Macomb the end of August 1863. Lieutenant Commander H. A. Adams to Hon. Gideon Welles, Sec. of the Navy, September 25, 1863, *ORN*, Ser. I, Vol. XX, 603.

47. Officers were allowed to resign their commissions at their discretion; enlisted men were required to serve three years.

48. White soldiers received $10 a month plus a $3 clothing allowance. However, "All persons of African descent enlisted as soldiers are to be paid 7 dollars a month as pay with a clothing allowance of $3 a month which will be settled in the same manner as with white volunteers. This rate of pay and clothing allowance applies in cases of colored non-commissioned officers as well as privates. White non-commissioned officers are to be paid

Part II, New Orleans

"Man's inhumanity to man makes countless millions mourn." Rec'd news of death of Brig Gen'l Strong at the storming of Fort Wagner at Charleston—Poor George was a noble fellow and beloved by all who knew him when here. "None knew him but to love him, none saw him but to bless."[49]

Saturday, August 29th 1863

Spent the evening last night with Maggie—had delightful time—Wrote Aleck Wible letter of Recommendation to Mr. Dennison, Cmsr of Internal Revenue recommending him for a clerkship—News recd yesterday of Gilmore's attack upon Charleston. He had his huge siege guns in position, and had already knocked some mighty holes in Fort Sumpter, besides giving the city a last of hot lead.—[50]

Gen'l Emory ordered into the field, and Col Beckwith the Commissary of The Dept, takes Command of The Defences of the Gulf, a good change, and one that will be very beneficial.[51]—It is said that Genl Emory is a slaveholder and altogether too proslavery to suit these times.—I only

---

as if serving in white Regiments." Colonel T. P. Andrews, Paymaster General, to Major H. O. Brigham, Paymaster, Dept. of the Gulf, July 24, 1863, LR, Ser. 1756, RG 393, Pt. 1, NA. See also n. 34 and related text in Pt. 1 of this book.

49. Brigadier General George C. Strong (1832–1863) served under General Butler in the Dept. of the Gulf as AAG of volunteers. Later, during Daniels' early days with the 2nd LaNG (September to December 1862), he was Butler's chief of staff and chief of ordnance. Warner, *Generals in Blue*, 483–84; General Correspondence, LR, Ser. 1756, Dept. of the Gulf, RG 393, Pt. 1, NA.

50. George Denison was a cousin and personal appointee of Salmon P. Chase, secretary of the treasury, who, in addition to the customs and tax business, helped spread his cousin's political influence in the area. John Nevin, *Salmon P. Chase: A Biography* (New York, 1995), 316. Union major general Quincy A. Gillmore (1825–1888) became commander of the 10th Corps and of the Department of the South June 12, 1863. After a failed attempt in July to subdue Fort Wagner outside of Charleston en route to retaking Fort Sumter in the harbor, Gillmore settled into siege operations, bombarding Sumter with eighteen heavy guns and firing briefly on the city with the "Swamp Angel," a powerful 8-inch rifled Parrott gun that found its mark from more than a mile and a half away. Warner, *Generals in Blue*, 176–77; *OR*, Ser. I, Vol. XXVIII, Pt. 1, p. 3; Johnson and Buel, eds., *Battles and Leaders*, IV, 13; Foote, *Fredericksburg to Meridian*, 698–99.

51. Colonel Edward G. Beckwith, Chief of Commissary, relieved Brigadier General William H. Emory (1811–1887) at Def. of N. O. by Special Orders No. 210, August 25, 1863. Special Orders, Ser. 1767, Dept. of the Gulf, RG 393, NA.

wish that the Anti-slavery men of this Dept were as thorough in their principles as are the proslavery ones—then we should not hear of the officers of The Colored Rgts being persecuted and the poor negroes made to suffer for what they cannot help—

Went up and saw Madam Rosa, she told me many things of the past that were true, said that for the next six months I should have plenty of trouble, but that after that period, matters would take a favorable turn—

Sunday, August 30th 1863
[Cross-written]
[continued from Aug. 29th]
... That between the ages of 28 and 30 I would be very successful, both in money and other matters, that during such years I would again marry. That I should succeed in all my present affairs though with much difficulty. That between the ages of 30 and 40 success would attend me, after that to 41 would meet with heavy losses which I would again recover from, and live to the advanced age of 70   humbugging, all of it.—Her timeletting has become a Profession and every one who can find nothing else to do takes a hand at it. Dreamed last night that I was in trouble again about an arrest, and then again that I was at a champagne party with my military friends.—Went up to Madam Rosa's last evening with Miss Bertine who had her future portrayed in glowing colors.—See by the Hotel Register that Capt Adams, Commdg U.S. Sloop of War Vincennes was at "The St Charles"   Have sent down an invitation for him to come up and see me. Want to see about his evidence.—Mrs. Turner & The Wibles are expecting to move out into their own house tomorrow. I hope the Lord they will as I am heartily tired of so large a family. Then I shall hope to have a little peace and quiet, as it is now tis a perfect bedlam.—Had a spiritual circle.[52] The Spirits of my Father, wife, and sister came. Upon spelling out the name it purported to be my sister Susan, who said she died some three weeks ago at home of fever, that she had come to communicate to me that I should get through with my matters in three weeks then take command

---

52. Spiritualists tried to communicate with spirits of the dead through gatherings of believers in a circle, or séance, often using a "medium" through whom the voices of the departed spoke. Ann Braude, *Radical Spirits: Spiritualism and Women's Rights in Nineteenth-Century America* (Boston, 1989), 20–25.

of my Regiment, be ordered to Baton Rouge & Port Hudson where I should have a fight with the enemy, be badly wounded, get a furlough, and go home to get cured of my wound. That I should be promoted the earlier part of next year. That Mr Lincoln would be the next President and a long communication relative to my affairs in general. That I should get a letter from home within three weeks containing an account of her death. Now we will see if the communication turns out to be true. If so it will be an astonishing test of the truth of Spiritualism. I most thoroughly believe in the doctrine, but know that evil spirits often give us mistruths, that is the stumbling block to my perfect beliefs—In fact the majority of Spiritual Communications and particularly those that come through a lower order of mediumship turn out to be false, the sport of a class of spirits who cannot get away from this earth sphere and who gratify their evil propensities in their befogging and bewildering the class who are constantly seeking physical transportation.—I care not for these Communications, they prove nothing to me—I know from the knowledge of my own senses that the doctrines are true and God almighty himself could not make me disbelieve my own senses.—I have had evidence which is incontrovertible and which gives me a perfect knowledge—not a faith—If no manifestation should ever occur again on earth twould make no difference with my knowledge—But I candidly believe that the time will soon come when we in our perfected development will be enabled to hold converse and intercourse with the spiritual world the same as we now do with each other upon earth—but it will require a far more perfect humanity than the earth now possesses—but it must eventually come—

Monday, August 31st 1863
[Cross-written]

Weather quite cool & very pleasant. Trust that this month may prove the last of my difficulties—

Capt Adams came up to see me. Told me that he would write me a letter which I could enclose to Gen' Banks and thus be enabled to get the weight of his testimony before Headquarters. Told me about Col Hall's operations on Ship Island, does not like Hall at all, says he is drunk the most of his time. That the soldiers detest him and know him thoroughly.—

Miss Maggie came up with Maria to make a call. Promised to go down and make them a visit tomorrow evening. Mr and Mrs [Masters?] up to spend the evening. Also Misses Mary and Bertine Schaeffer.[53] Had a delightful party and a very pleasant time. The Ladies dressed themselves up in my uniforms and cut a gay swell, made a call upon their friends across the street as Col's Black and White.

They went home about 12 o'clock. Mrs. Turner says this is her last night in New Orleans therefore she wants a grand time.—

New Orleans is not the same appearance that it was previous to this unholy Rebellion—then all was bustle business and money making—now the Boulevards that once teemed with wealth and activity are dead and deserted. In truth is the grass growing in many of the former business streets of this city. But another day is ahead. When this cursed system of slavery shall have been eradicated, when Just labor shall have been established and the colored man given all his rights, then shall we see a representation here—a growth with which its former prosperity cannot be at all compared—then will New Orleans [begin?] to rival New York and become the great metropolis of the south—but it must undergo first a severe discipline—the rich must become poor and old classes change their character—

Tuesday, September 1st 1863
[Cross-written]

Wrote long letter to Gen'l Banks in which I made the following points to wit: That I had been under arrest for four months upon frivolous charges, Preferred more through personal prejudice than through any interest to the Gov't—That I could establish by the evidence of the army & navy such position—That through the delay and the continued putting off I had lost some of my best witnesses—That his Judge Advocate authorization and The Major Gen'l order has been meted out in deposition of witnesses taken within the south. That I desired to take the testimony of other witnesses who were going north but could not on account of such ruling.[54]—That under Article 77 of War, an officer under arrest could not be confined to his quarters more than 8 days or until a Court martial could be assembled—whereas I has been restricted in my limits twice that pe-

---

53. This is the first of several different spellings for Schaeffer. Daniels also used Chaffer, Shaffer, Sheffer, and Cheffer.

54. A ruling concerning depositions of witnesses leaving to go north may have been imposed on Daniels by his particular court-martial.

riod, and a Court martial had meanwhile assembled & been dissolved without reaching my case. That I therefore Petitioned an immediate release from such order and an immediate trial before the proper tribunal.[55]—Mrs Turner & Mrs Wible with baby left this evening for Baton Rouge where they expect to procure a pass to go home to Bayou Sara—I very much doubt their success.—Yet I am glad they have gone as I am heartily sick of the crowd.—

I have no confidence in General Banks. I believe him to be a thorough Demogogue and only intent upon reaching the Presidential chair and little does he care by what means. The opposition accuse Butler of all manner of wrong deeds—but let him be ever so guilty (—and I do not believe him as he is anything but an honest man—or his administration here to have been anything else but an honest one) still has he the consciousness of doing his duty towards the poor enslaved race that he found in getting here upon his arrival—He had no half way measures—one knew immediately what he would or would not do, where Banks will forever promise but never inform unless it will result in his personal favor and benefit—

Wednesday, September 2^d 1863
[Cross-written]
Dreamed last night that I saw my mother and brother—and that they told me of my being in arrest. That it has been published in the northern papers.

Sent notices of the taking of Depositions of witness not in the Line or Staff of The United States Army, to Major Lieber Judge Advocate of The Gulf Dept. and to Capt Palfrey, US Engineer. The Prosecutor wrote my Quartermaster.

Wrote to Dicky Bray to day. Capt Adams sent me word that he would be on hand tomorrow morning. Aleck Wible came and took things of Mrs Turner. Hope this is the last that I shall have to do with the gang—

Gen'l Grant came down to day on Steamboat from Vicksburgh, is quartered at St. Charles Hotel. Adjt Gen'l Thomas of War Dept is with him.

---

55. Banks responded the next day ordering an immediate trial "with the least possible delay." Major General Norman Lieber, AAG to Colonel E. G. Beckwith, September 2, 1863. MSR of Nathan W. Daniels, 74th USCI [2nd LaNG], RG 94, NA.

They were seranaded by the city band this evening. Gen'l Grant showed himself, but did not make any speech. Will receive the citizens at Gen'l Banks Headquarters tomorrow evening. He is the Hero of the day & one every way deserving.—

General Grant is not only the hero of Vicksburgh but he is also that of Port Hudson, as that place surrendered immediately upon hearing the fall of Vicksburgh—and not to the prowess of Banks or the Army he commanded, six hours did not pass by after the news was received by them [and?] the stronghold was [occupied?] I do not think it right to give the embecile Gen'l Banks the credit, when the only thing that he did do was to hurl his forces against the ramparts when there was no earthly chance of victory and thereby lose some two thousand men—[56]

Thursday, September 3^d 1863
[Cross-written]

Maj. Gen'l Grant Reviews one of his Corps de Armee at Carrollton this afternoon. Sent mother large Photograph of Dr. [?] Smith, Capt [?] Brevont, Dr. Ceise Pierucci U.S. Navy & myself by mail.—William my body servant goes north to day via Cairo.—In Gen'l Grants case do we see how one may be traduced and persecuted and yet in the end come out triumphant. After the battle of Shiloh, Grant was ignored, deprived of his command, persecuted by all, yet now see where he stands.—Merit and Justice will in the end prevail.—I can take courage from this bright example and await the equity of the future.

Took Deposition of H A Adams Jr Lt Comdr US Navy before Justice of The Peace. Gave a splendid Deposition and one that will tell if it can only be introduced in evidence.—

Wrote long letter to Gen'l Banks in which I enclosed copy of Adams

---

56. Three months later, Daniels added "cross-writing" over this entry: "This dream I have since my arrival at the north found to be true as my arrest was falsely stated in a New York paper whose managers were opposed to all negro soldiers and their officers." Daniels Diary, December 25, 1863. Major General Norman Lieber, AAG, Dept. of Gulf, and now Captain John C. Palfrey. Grant and his staff arrived in New Orleans to talk with General Banks about carrying the war into Texas. Grant, *Personal Memoirs*, I, 581; Winters, *Civil War in Louisiana*, 294; Major General N. P. Banks to his wife, September 5, 1863, in Family Correspondence, Box 5, N. P. Banks Collection, LC. For Port Hudson's surrender, see related text for n. 16 above.

Deposition, his letter, and a copy of charges—Petitioning for an immediate hearing to an impartial tribunal or to have the matter submitted entirely to himself. I would be willing to accept his judgement, though it might be adverse as I am anxious to get out of the Department—Could I get a furlough and go to Washington I could obtain the agency of The Internal Revenue for Mobile an office equal to that of Major General—

Rec'd letter from mother, all well at home, so the spirit Communication that we rec'd was a humbug.—

Friday, September 4th 1863
[Cross-written]

It is five years to day since my darling Etta left the cares and troubles of this earth to put on the golden robes of another existence[57]—departed from those who loved her better than life to go to other scenes and brighter, fairer realms.—Mourned deeply as she had been loved fondly, her departure left a blank in the existence of those who still find misery in her absence but happiness in the knowledge of her beatitudes. Believing, yet knowing, that her bright spirit comes to me oft at "dewy morn & starry eve" to comfort and cheer my lonely wanderings, how can I wish her to leave those happy realms & put on again the trials and miseries of this mundane sphere. No! darling one, it is my wish to come to thee now, to live in perpetual bliss in thy dear companionship to bask in the sunshine of thy existence & learn from thy pured heart the secrets, the Joys, the knowledge of "that home from when bourne no traveler e'er returns."[58]— Our darling baby boy is yet left to me in whose features I behold thine, in whose affection I enjoy thy precious love.—Watch over and protect him, keep him from all evil, develop his daring intellect for good and noble purposes so that he may in future years become the champion of the true, the beautiful, the Progressive and The Good,—a bright scion of a noble house, teach him that nobility consists of humanity and all earnest dedication of one's self, to the doing of good and the enlightment of Ignorance and the removal of evil—

57. Etta was Daniels' wife. She died in 1858, leaving him with their baby boy, Waldo. Daniels Diary.

58. Daniels' quotation of Shakespeare should read, "The undiscover'd country from whose bourn / No traveler returns" (*Hamlet*, III, i).

Saturday, September 5th 1863
[Cross-written]

Believer [Coquetty?] says "I cannot believe that earth is man's abiding place. It can't be that our life, cast up by the ocean of eternity, is to float a moment upon its waves and sink into nothingness. Else why is it that the glorious aspirations, which peep like angels from the temple of our heart, are forever wandering about unsatisfied.—Why is it that the rainbow and clouds come over us with a beauty that is not of earth and then pass off and leave us to muse upon their faded loveliness—Why is it that the stars who hold their festival around the midnight throne are forever mocking us with their unapproachable glory. And finally why is it that bright forms of human beauty are presented to our mind and then taken from us leaving the thousand strands of our affection to flow back in: [Aeluni?] torments upon our hearts. We are born for a higher destiny than that of earth: there is a realm where the rainbow never fades, where the stars will be spread before us like Islands that slumber on the ocean and where the beings that pass before us live in our presence forever."—

Rec'd an order from Headquarters Defences of New Orleans—No 45—convening a Court Martial for my trial Sept 10, 1863 at 12 o'c yesterday.[59] Immediately notified Capt A. [Almon] L. Varney 13th Me Rgt & Judge Advocate that I would take Capt Adams testimony which I proceded to do last evening, all witnesses being present. Adams left this morning for New York—The Misses Chaffer & Madam Rosa spent the evening with me last evening—had a very pleasant little party at cards et cetera.—

Mr. Brown just released from Ship Island where he has been confined by order of Genl Butler for a long while—called up and saw me this morning, said that Gen'l Banks was very much opposed to me.—Also gave me a history of Gen'l Butlers private affairs here as he was his Private secretary consequently knowing to many things of that period.—[60]

Gen'l Grant & Banks Reviewed Grants corps de armee yesterday

---

59. Special Orders No. 45 for Daniels' court-martial was written September 4, 1863, two days after Banks's request. It specified the detail for the court to include eight officers: three from the 9th Conn., two from the 13th Maine, one from the 12th Maine, and one from the 4th Regt. Corps d'Afrique. Military Papers, Box 80, Miscellaneous Reports 1861–1864, N. P. Banks Collection, LC.

60. See text associated with nn. 27, 28 above.

morning, grand times—In returning from the Review, Gen'l Grant's horse undertook to run away and ran against a carriage throwing horse and rider to the ground, and severely injuring the General—so much so that he will be confined to his bed for a month.—Very unfortunate, as he was Just ready to start on his grand expedition.—[61]

Sunday, September 6th 1863
[Cross-written]

John T Barrett, New Orleans La. from Hadley Mass, nephew of Emory Hooker related to Gen'l Joe Hooker wishes me to see fighting Joe for him when I go to Washington.[62] It appears by the northern papers that Admiral Farragut has arrived safely in New York with The old Hartford and is now receiving the orations of the people as he richly merits. Capt Adams went north in the Steamer Evening Star yesterday, so they go, most of my fellow officers at Ship Island have already gone home. When will it be my turn.—Am now keeping house all by myself, a magnificent large house with only my colored boy Levi and cook Martha—but I enjoy the quiet and peace of the situation, and shall continue my bachelor existence. News rec'd that Gen'l Gilmore has succeeded in capturing Fort Sumter Battery, Wagner and all the outer works, and had notified the citizens that in 24 hours he should open his guns upon Charleston. Report says that Gilmore has hoisted the same old flag that was flying at the fort when Captured from Anderson[63]—Restitution is fast o'ertaking the disdain of this

---

61. There are many versions of this famous incident. General Thomas, riding with Grant, said a passing carryall struck Grant's horse in the shoulder. Grant himself thought the horse shied at a locomotive. General Banks, who was also there, stated, "I am frightened when I think he is a drunkard. His accident was caused by this, which was too manifest to all who saw him. . . . [He] prides himself on his horsemanship. We were splendidly mounted both of us on my own horses, the general having the fleetest and best." *OR*, Ser. III, Vol. III, 770; Grant, *Personal Memoirs*, I, 581; Major General N. P. Banks to his wife, September 4, 1863, in Family Correspondence, Box 5, N. P. Banks Collection, LC.

62. Union major general Joseph Hooker (1814–1879) received the "Fighting Joe" nom de guerre through a press report during the Peninsula campaign after the Battle of Williamsburg, May 5, 1862. The news release, meant to be, "Fighting — Joe Hooker," appeared in the newspapers minus the dash. Warner, *Generals in Blue*, 233–34.

63. Major (later Major General) Robert Anderson (1805–1871), the "hero of Fort Sumter," was in command of the fort during the thirty-four-hour opening bombardment of the war, April 12–13, 1861. "The old flag which floated from its parapet when the brave General

infernal nest of Rebellion.—That not one stone may be left [a------] in the place is the earnest prayer of all loyal hearts. Dreamed last night that I was in company with Major Dumas & Mr Victor, and that I was about starting on a journey—also that I saw my mother. By the late northern advices it appears that Gen'l Jim Lane has succeeding in dispatching the most of the Quantrill villains who lately sacked the town of and murdered the inhabitants of Lawrence Kansas.[64]—It is to be hoped that he will not spare one of the miscreants. Learned yesterday that Adjt Prouty had been dismissed the service by the Court Martial but recommended to the mercy of the Commanding General. I hope he may be retried and prosecuted to atone for his misconduct.[65] The weather now is beautiful, nights are cool and days pleasant, this evening as the Bright faced moon reflects her soft light upon the rushing Mississippi, she makes a bridge of golden [----tely] looking a shower of diamonds upon the quiet water, would that the human fortune of realm was as quiet and serene as are the grand attributes—then should we have peace and happiness, instead of war and misery.—

Capt Adams informed me when here last week that The U.S. Ship Relief Commanded by my friend Manton had gone home, and that upon stopping at Key West she had taken the yellow fever aboard, with which nearly her entire crew were taken. Lucky for the Captain that he took pas-

---

Anderson was forced to surrender to the Charleston devils, has been planted on the ruins of the fort by General Gillmore." Brigadier General Clinton B. Fisk to Major Samuel Montgomery, August 27, 1863. *OR*, Ser. I, Vol. XXIII, 481.

64. In the sack of Lawrence on August 21, 1863, 182 buildings were burned, and 183 bodies were buried afterward; the remains of 7 more were found later. U.S. senator and Union brigadier general James H. Lane of Kansas reported that 41 of Quantrill's men had been killed five days after the raid, and that he had organized his forces to follow the scattered enemy into Missouri. Quantrill, evading capture, continued raids until October 1863, when he and his men left for Texas. *OR*, Ser. I, Vol. XXII, Pt. 2, p. 487; Foote, *Fredericksburg to Meridian*, 706.

65. Lieutenant Prouty's status is confusing based on existing records. Although he supposedly was dismissed August 11 under Special Orders No. 196, his court-martial took place August 21. General Banks endorsed the court's ruling September 11, stating that the lieutenant was "out of the service." Special Orders No. 196, Dept. of the Gulf, August 11, 1863, Adjutant's Regimental Papers, 74th USCI [2nd LaNG], RG 94, NA; Proceedings of General Court Martial, Trial of Elijah K. Prouty, August 21, 1863, MM 878, RG 153, NA.

sage in a Steamship[66]—The old Relief has many pleasant associations connected with her—lying off Ship Island as she did all the time during my command of the Post—and commanded by one of the most glorious fellows that ever walked the deck of a ship. Many were the social gatherings that we enjoyed in her old cabin and lay well the memories there awakened remain buried in my heart—as there was a truth an earnestness and a reliability in this glorious Manton—which influenced all who came within his pleasant circle—none knew him but to love him, none sought him but to bless—When I first met the Captain he was disposed to be prejudiced on account of my being in command of colored troops—and in fact this prejudice extended to all of the Officers both in the army and navy at first and was very discouraging to those brave and earnest men who had taken the noble work in hand—but a short time for discord or change in the Captain. He saw the calm of the Colored organization and his prejudice vanished speedily—and ever afterward he was one of the strongest advocates that we had. His personal friendship was to me very valuable and I shall never forget the pleasant scenes that the old Island and Ship have afforded us together—When I forget my [---------] then will the name of Benjamin Manton be buried in Oblivion

Monday, September 7th 1863

Dreamed last night that I was at school with the first teacher I ever had Mr Arbity and that I also was with The Benton family of Syracuse. Sent papers to Dickie Bray and my friend C D Childs.

Additional charges preferred by Lt Jones of the 13th Maine relative to their charge. Have pretty much made up my mind to send in my resignation as I am informed through good and reliable sources that I can obtain the internal Revenue of the Alabama Department if I go to Washington that will be a position of some value. An officer in the colored organization, no matter what his rank stands no chance of obtaining Justice in this Department. As to Gen'l Banks Lieutenants I believe him to be well inclined, but he has bad influence around him that will not permit him to

66. The *Relief* went home to New York City. Acting Volunteer Lieutenant Benjamin D. Manton resigned at home in Providence, Rhode Island, on September 10, 1863, due to his wife's illness. RG 45, U.S. Navy, Volumes of Officer Records, Resignation of Officers, 1863, NA.

see the Just side of the case—however, these matters will all come out for the best, they are brought about for some good purpose of that I am well satisfied. In this respect Gen'l Butler was the best man of the time, as he would not permit a man to be persecuted when he knew such a man was right, but now t'is a different thing, a different power has the [be----].—

Tuesday, September 8th 1863
Rec'd letters yesterday from my friend Miss May Searles & from one P. G. Smith of Montpelier [Vermont] relative to his Nephew George H Holms, arrived the latter this morning.—

Rec'd Circutus from Washington through the Gulf Dep't [neutralizing?] the last order of Gen'l Banks relative to my arrest—et cetera.

Had an interview with Major Gen'l Banks this morning relative to my affairs. He told me still to consider myself under arrest and to await the action at Washington of his second order. That he could not take other action in the matter. Called upon Major Lieber, A. A. General of Gulf Dept. and he informed me that the second order had been sent on to Washington. Therefore shall be obliged to await the action of such, and be compelled to remain in the city when I had hoped to get away north soon.— Rec'd additional charge from Capt Varney of The 13th Maine—Learned particulars relative to Genl Weitzels intent in my affairs. Let the matters go on, they will do themselves more harm than they can do with me.

Wednesday, September 9th and Thursday, September 10th 1863
Wrote a letter to Col Cahill this Thursday morning asking him to inform me whether I should attend the Court Martial that was to convene this morning—at his Headquarters for my trial.—Learned unofficially however, from Adjt Prouty that such Court had been dissolved so that my matters have become still more complicated.[67]—Called upon Major [?] Vedder U.S. Paymaster and rec'd my pay for last four months—Rec'd visit from Mr Brown, a former Political Prisoner upon Ship Island, who is now again in The U.S. service. He informed me of considerable of Gen'l Butlers affairs, and is determined to bring the Gen'l if possible to Justice—

---

67. The court met, read the previous day's proceedings, and adjourned. Proceedings of a General Court-Martial for the trial of Colonel N. W. Daniels, September 10, 1863, Military Papers, Box 80, Misc. Reports 1861–1864, N. P. Banks Collection, LC.

Part II, New Orleans

Has Gen'l Banks assistance in the same. Wrote letter to The Gen'l relative to the same.[68] Rec'd calls from Cap't Belley & Capt Dauchy who has Just been promoted to a Captaincy in my Regiment upon my recommendation. Rec'd letter and private secretary from Col Hall at Ship Island. Gave Aleck Wible the letter from Gen'l Shepley[69] to Gen'l Banks having in the same endorsed the authority to act, relative to the [Levees?] in St. Charles Parish, La.—Am informed of the contemplated treachery of Adjt Prouty and shall take measures to head the gentleman off.—Paid Phil Livery keeper for my horse expenses, $50 on a/c.—Received visitors Mr & Mrs. [Masters?], Mrs [Pallisin?] and Mr Crumpton this evening. Had a delightful game of cards, broke up about midnight—Was informed by Aleck Thible in the presence of Levi that he never told Adjt Prouty that I said I had gained my point in his dismissal from service and that his wife never said anything of the kind—

Friday, September 11th 1863

Capt Villevert called upon me and informed me relative to matters in my Regiment. Mr Brown also called and finished his letter to Gen'l Banks stating that he would be willing to go through the Confederacy to Richmond, & then Washington, and asking a personal interview[70]—Livery man informed me that Major Vedder had my order for $50.—

Learned through a friend this morning that Capt Dauchy was writing a letter for the benefit of the Adjutant stating that I had said that I should make my point out of the Adjutant. In fact he has written the letter and I have seen it but thank God it will not succeed in effecting anything, fortunately I have too many friends and too much influence to permit such

---

68. Brown described his past service to the U.S. government, his connections in England, in Washington, with the Confederacy, and with General Butler's past affairs in New Orleans. James George Brown to Major General N. P. Banks, August 24, 1863, in General Correspondence, 1839–1893, Box 28, N. P. Banks Collections, LC.

69. Brigadier General George F. Shepley (1819–1878) was appointed Military Governor of Louisiana in mid-June 1862. Edwin M. Stanton to Major General B. F. Butler, June 10, 1862, *OR*, Ser. I, Vol. XV, 471.

70. Brown spelled out the route he would take through the Confederacy reporting all fortifications and military "particulars" to the Federal government. He stated he was the only one who could "check" Butler, thereby helping Banks politically. James G. Brown to Major General N. P. Banks, September 11, 1863, in General Correspondence, Box 28, N. P. Banks Collection, LC.

trifles to have any effect. It is a trifle & still a falsehood and comes from one [against] whom I have always been pitted.

Saturday, September 12th 1863

Went down to The U.S. Barracks this morning. Had a delightful drive. Saw Chapman relative to my going north, shall have my matter with him.—Brown saw Gen'l Banks, everything favorable to a happy *denoument*.—Will meet him in Washington. Mr. Wible saw Gen'l Banks who referred his documents to Col Clark who told him that they were all right & would be endorsed & the a/c paid Monday morning.[71] Thus everything is coming out all right as I predicted they would—now it only remains for my resignation to be accepted, if the Department can dispense with my services, and then I am off for Washington where I hope to be able to take a position in the civil department of The Government which will afford me some satisfaction for the troubles and trials that have beset me thus far in this Rebellion

Sunday, September 13th 1863

Mr Brown called down to see me. Went and saw Gen'l Banks who promised that my Resignation should be immediately accepted, that he had not intended doing so, but that he now would. Brown proposes going to Washington via of the Confederacy. Will go to Mobile, thence to Augusta, thence to Richmond, and then take his chances of getting through the Confederate lines. Tis a desperate task but one that I am confident he can accomplish if anyone can—As Gen'l Banks said to him should he succeed, his position is made at Washington and he can take almost any place that he may desire—should he fail death of course must be the consequence.—He will be sent out of our lines as a Registered enemy, for the purpose of giving heroic eclat with the Confederates, & will then gradually work his way to Richmond, taking notes of all troops, fortifications and other matters that may be of importance to our government.[72] I hope to be able to meet him in Washington in two weeks at least—News from

71. Colonel John S. Clark, aide-de-camp to General Banks.

72. A "registered enemy" was one who refused to take the oath of allegiance to the Union. He was allowed to cross enemy lines with only personal clothes and $50 but could not return to the military department. Winters, *Civil War in Louisiana*, 136.

the north that Sumpter has not yet fallen, Charleston is therefore as yet in Confederate territory, but I hope not for any length of time.—

Went up with Brown and saw Madam Rosa, she told him some important things relative to his future—Called upon Mrs Wallis on Magazine St.

It would be strange if I should succeed in doing as great a favor for B[rown]—as he has for me—and then ultimately conjointly with him, accomplish what we have so well planned—

Monday, September 14th 1863

Sent to Maj Lieber A. A. Genl of Gulf Dept a copy of my original Resignation. Brown will see him and get the same through to Gen'l Banks. Sergeant Lemicus Warren Cre called to see about claim of his mother and children to confiscated estate of his father. He has a good claim and I shall take care to bring it to the attention of the proper authorities at Washington. The names are Mrs. Mary Williams Lemicus Cre, Janesetta Cre, & Angeline [Leon?], lives at Carr, 34 Perdido St. New Orleans La.—

Dreamed last night that Brown was shot in my presence, but not killed.—

Music in Coliseum square very fine, great crowd of ladies & gentlemen. Gen'l Banks present with Gen'l Bowen & others.[73] Called up in the evening to see Miss Annie in company with Brown. She was very glad to see me and my resignation seemed to give her great pleasure and made a great difference in her reception. Asked me for the Portrait that Mrs. Wible gave me—I think this is the end of our intimacy.—

Tuesday, September 15th 1863

Dreamed last night that I was stung by some insect, also that I had taken a subordinate position in the army, also that Mr Vance had returned.—[74]

Called upon Phil Liver[y] & learned that Bay horse had been sold by

---

73. Brigadier General James Bowen (1810–1886) was provost marshal of the Department of the Gulf. Warner, *Generals in Blue*, 39.

74. Hamilton McNeil Vance was the Confederate cotton merchant whose vacated New Orleans house Daniels entered on November 3, 1862, and in whose diary he was now writing.

Buell—Mr Brown saw Major Lieber who told him that he would attend to the Resignation and call the attention of The Commanding Gen'l to the same.—Mr Wible did not succeed in getting his a/c through the Provost Department, must now try the Quartermaster. Called upon Misses Schaffer with B—had a very pleasant evening.

Maj Genl's Grant and Brig Gen'l Thomas started for Vicksburgh yesterday. The General has mostly recovered from the severe bruises that he rec'd last week from the fall from his horse—It has since transpired that Grant, Banks, Stone, and a lot of the high authorities were having a gay race & that Grant was ahead when the accident occurred.—[75]

Wednesday, September 16*th* 1863

Dreamed last night that I saw President Lincoln and his wife—hope it may be a favorable augury.[76] Wrote Lt Noyes to take charge of my effects at Ship Island and send the same to Mr George M Chapman. Wrote a letter of Introduction to the Officer Commdg Fort Banks for Miss Scheffer.—I trust that another forty eight hours may not transpire 'ere my matters will be arranged and myself on the way to Washington.—When once there I cannot fail to succeed in attaining the position that I desire.—

Another expedition has gone into The Teche Country under Gen'ls Franklin and Weitzel. I hope it will not be as miserable a failure as the last.[77]

---

75. The horse race included Banks's chief of staff, General Charles P. Stone. Grant, accompanied by Brigadier General Lorenzo Thomas, was carried on a stretcher to a Vicksburg-bound steamer. Two days after the accident, Banks issued an order prohibiting all military personnel from riding faster than a trot in the streets of New Orleans. Grant, *Personal Memoirs*, I, 582; Special Orders No. 223, September 7, 1863, LR, Ser. 1844, Provost Marshal Office, Dept. of the Gulf, RG 393, Pt. 1, NA.

76. Daniels later wrote over this entry that "the dream was realized in the months November & December 1863." He met with President Lincoln, who told him that he could have "the appointment of Internal Revenue in Louisiana if Sec'y [of the Treasury] Chase would recommend him." Daniels Diary, November 9, 1863. See also n. 89 below.

77. Major General William B. Franklin (1823–1903) and General Weitzel set off September 5 on an abortive, disorganized Texas expedition into Sabine Pass, which ended in retreat after losing two gunboats and several hundred men. Reports varied on the number captured (from more than 200 to as many as 400) and killed (42 to 50), with no losses to the Confederates. Banks, still needing to gain ground in Texas, then sent the two generals

Mr. Brown here with me during the day. If I am not very much mistaken, we shall accomplish all that we desire by the 1st November. Went with Miss Bertine Sheffer down to see spiritual medium—Could not find the one we were directed to, but saw an old colored man who prescribed well in Miss B's disease.—

Thursday, September 17*th* 1863

Went down to the Lake with Miss Bertine last evening, had a delightful time. She made me her confidant and told me her history which is a strange one. It seems that her father & mother died here in New Orleans of yellow fever when she was an infant. That an old lady who has since gone to Germany of the name of Miller took her and gave her to Mr. Chaffer, by whom she was adopted and has since been brought up as a daughter. That her relations are in Germany, and said to be wealthy, mayhaps of noble blood—she knows nothing of them and it seems to have been the policy of her adopted father to keep her as much in the dark as possible relative to her family affairs—She has an Uncle who is wealthy in South Carolina, but does not know his name or place of residence—her true name is Albertine Thaler. She has the appearance of gentle blood, does not resemble in any particulars the family with whom she is domociled. I should like to investigate her [genealogy?].[78] I think she would be found of a high family. Property affairs have probably prevented her being found out & acknowledged.—Her history is highly romantic and will eventually prove a strange one.—We went down to the old clairvoyant, who told her of her ill health & a remedy for the same—then drove down to the Lake, having a very pleasant time.—

Friday, September 18*th* 1863

Brown & myself went yesterday to see The Spiritualist [---], called upon Mr. [?] Train who took us to a spiritual circle where it was predicted that in two months blood would flow in the streets of New Orleans like

---

north up the Teche and west overland. *OR*, Ser. I, Vol. XXVI, Pt. 2, pp. 286, 288–92, 294–310; Winters, *Civil War in Louisiana*, 296–98; McPherson, *Battle Cry of Freedom*, 683.

78. Daniels crossed out several letters in struggling with what is obviously meant to be "genealogy."

water, that the French Citizens were in secret conclave of war preparing for an uprising, that a great encounter was shortly to result between the French and our army in the Rio Grande[79]—Went up and saw the spiritual medium Norwood, who told me that I should be entirely successful in my undertakings, that I should return to this place by November, and that I must go immediately to Washington—that Gen'l Banks would [die Inefected?] and That both Brown and myself would be successful.—The Misses Cheffer over here, at a service society.

Went with Mr Brown down to see about getting things for his intended trip. Bought and presented him a Pistol, Locket et cetera.—Called to see Maria, had a pleasant interview, shall accept of her very polite Invitation.

Took letters from Gen'l Banks to Brown for safe keeping for him to take to Washington. Gen'l Banks playing a big strike for the Presidency. He and Seward are together against Chase, Butler and Stanton.—[80]

Saturday, September 19th 1863

No news as yet from Gen'l Banks relative to my Resignation, although he explicitly promised Brown that it should be accepted.—The Steamer Morning Star came in this morning from New York and I expect the Gen'l has been awaiting advices from Washington, and that now my affairs will be speedily settled. Shall wait until Monday Morning and then if not rec'd will call again upon The General—this uncertainty is worse than defeat. This waiting the beck and nod of the self assured functionaires.—If he does not take action in the matter then I shall go to Washington by the Steamer Tuesday and effect my objects at The War Department.—

Brown left this evening on The Steamer assigned him by Commodore Bell, which will take him to Pensacola, or as near Mobile as possible from whence he will make his way as speedily as possible to Richmond, there procure some foreign position (which he undoubtedly can with his influ-

---

79. There was concern that the French, who succeeded in capturing Mexico City with 35,000 troops in June 1863, would enter the U.S. in support of the Confederacy.

80. William H. Seward, Salmon P. Chase, Benjamin F. Butler, and Edwin M. Stanton. Banks, a politician before the war, aligned himself with more moderate Republicans, such as Seward, against the War Democrats—Butler and Stanton—who had ties to Radical Republicans, such as Chase. James M. McPherson, *Ordeal By Fire: The Civil War and Reconstruction* (New York, 1982), 272–73, 306, 404, 406; Nevin, *Salmon P. Chase*, 315.

ences in the Confederacy) from Jeff Davis, & then he will make his way to Washington and show up his information—et cetera to The Sect'y of State.—

Sunday, September 20th 1863
Mr. [?] Read up to see about my house. I concluded to leave it with him whilst I am gone and then take it upon my return.—Gave Mrs [?] Waiters official recommendation for Teacher in the Public schools.—Rec'd Communication from Commission of Freedmen N. G. relative to condition of African people under my command, & any information that I may possess relative to the race.—Shall address Robert Dale Owen upon the same.—[81]

Went out riding on "Beauty" through the suburbs of the city. Had a glorious canter. Stopped and called upon the old negro medium near the basin who has such astonishing healing mediumistic powers. He told me not to place any confidence in Gen'l Banks, that he was not reliable, that all that he cared for was The Presidency, not the country. He also said that I should not go as soon as I anticipated, that I would go by the sea, and would return by November.—Called down to see Delia, spent the evening had a pleasant visit, indeed passed a delightful night. She is the wife of a gentleman who is now in the Confederate Army and accordingly takes a fancy to blue coats and brass buttons. Oh woman, what a mystery thou art; how true the saying of Shakespeare . . . "Oh God that we can call the lovely creatures ours but not their passions."[82]—Probably the poor Confed soldier is thinking of his wife and dear ones with fondness, trusting in their fidelity and love, finding consolation in their faith when, lo and behold she is playing truant to his bed, and taking another into the heart that should remain loyal to her first love.—The ammoral would say, why do you then contribute to her transgression, why not, chide and check her disloyalty. I can simply answer, another would take my place should I refuse to

---

81. Robert Dale Owen was one of three men appointed as the American Freedmen's Inquiry Commission by Edwin Stanton in March, 1863. The commission issued a preliminary report June 30, 1863, and a final report May 15, 1864. *OR*, Ser. III, Vol. III, 430–54; Ser. III, Vol. IV, 289–382.

82. Again misremembering Shakespeare: "O curse of marriage! / That we can call these delicate creatures ours, / And not their appetites" (*Othello*, III, iii).

contribute to her enjoyment, and I should get no thanks for yielding the exquisite pleasure that her society *et cetera* affords me—*sid [sufficits?].*—[83]

Monday, September 21st 1863
Mr. & Mrs. Read up to [fire?] up house. They will occupy it during my absence. Intend leaving tomorrow evening on The Steamer Morning Star if Gen'l Banks attends to my business as he promised.—

Called to see Gen'l Banks had a very pleasant interview with him. He said that he told Brown that he would do all that he could to further my interests—but that he could not take any action until the documents that had been forwarded to Washington came back, that he expected them every day, & that then he would attend to the matter.[84] Invited me to call upon him often, was very pleasant and agreeable. He probably is aware that it lies within my power to do him much good or harm politically as I may choose to act, and therefore wishes to retain me on his side. Adjt Prouty up to see me about his affairs—I feel sorry for the poor fellow and will do all in my power to have him reinstated although he as heretofore done me much injury.—

Tuesday, September 22d 1863
[Cross-written]
Had a strange dream last night. Me thought I was on the water and that a steamboat came rushing into us capsizing our craft and submerging us all, but that we finally succeeded in escaping. It seemed as though my mother was with me. Then again I appeared to be in a room with my cousin Lucie Hutchinson—now dead—and my mother and little son came into see us, then again that we were all upon a high balcony when we heard guns firing in the distance & upon looking on the water in front of the house I discovered a Privateer chasing a steamer.—Mr. Read moved into house with his family & a very pleasant one they are. Called upon

---

83. Possibly intending "sed sufficit" (but enough) or even "satis quod sufficit" (what suffices is enough).

84. Daniels wrote this same day to the departmental adjutant's office inquiring when Banks's Special Orders were sent to Washington. The response indicated that there was no way to determine when. Colonel N. W. Daniels to Dept. of the Gulf, September 21, 1863, LR, III, Ser. 1747, Dept. of the Gulf, RG 393, Pt. 1, NA.

Part II, New Orleans

Miss Albertine, and Miss Cheffer gave me important papers to have translated relative to Miss Albertine, they will throw some light upon her parentage. Soldiers of my Reg't called to see me and informed me of some of my Lt Col Hall's movements on the Island since I had left—that he had been guilty of selling passes to his soldiers, had been drunk the most of the time, and was generally disliked by all upon The Island. Went down and saw Capt Henry Rey who was excellent spiritual medium and gave me some good test communication.[85] I was told that my future mission was in the Civil department of the Government & that I should succeed in all my contemplated maneuvers, that they controlled and directed my actions far more than I had any idea of.—

Spent last night with Delia, the charming young Creole grass widow[86]—Had to keep a strong guard in picket duty to look out for attacks from the enemy—She is a sweet creature as lovely as she is passionate, as fond as she is impulsive—Two bright eyed children are the gems of her household—and if she is not careful of your humble servant, another jewel will ere long adorn her hearthstone [c---net]. When two such passionate beings come together *something* must happen or nature will prove sadly untrue to herself. What a *mystery* is woman—seeming most cold when most her heart is burning. Hiding the melting passions within her breast and scarce returning one glance on him for whom her proud soul's yearning—

Wednesday, September 23^d 1863
[Cross-written]
Met Col Stafford and Lt Col Finnegas last evening on Esplanade St.[87]

---

85. Captain Henry L. Rey, a black officer, resigned April 6, 1863, from the First Louisiana Native Guards.

86. *Grass widow* was a derogatory term at the time, its various applications considered "vulgar" by 1860 standards. It could mean a divorced woman, a woman with a child out of wedlock, or in this case, a woman living alone apart from her husband.

87. Lieutenant Colonel Henry Finnegass was second in command under Colonel John Nelson of the 3rd LaNG. Finnegass was charged with "disobedience of orders on the field of battle" at Port Hudson for refusing Nelson's commands. He was supposed to be court-martialed, but complications arose because Colonel Nelson, himself recently dismissed, was not present to testify about the incident. Finnegass was on his way to Washington to see about his affairs after the commander of Port Hudson, Brigadier General George L. Andrew, pressed for his removal. Although a dishonorable dismissal dated March 19, 1864, ap-

They go to Washington by the Steamer Gen'l Washington next Saturday. I think I shall go with them. Stafford says that Col Nelson of the 3ᵈ was deeply implicated in cotton speculation and was compelled to resign and that he is accused of using disrespectful language toward The President of The United States. It appears that Gen'l Banks is determined to get rid of the organization of Native Guards because they were established by Gen'l Butler, & of course are opposed to him politically, but he has made a great mistake, he had much better have kept the influence of such organization in this Dept—and that he will discover 'ere long.—

News brought by last steamer that Rosencrantz had captured Chattanooga the center of the Confederate lines, & Burnside Knoxville—thus clearing Tennessee entirely of Rebels, a glorious Commendation. Fort Wagner has also succumbed to Gen'l Gilmore's admirable strategy[88]— Steamboats are being constantly fired upon on The Mississippi so it seems the banks are not yet clear.—A new paper started here last Sunday, called "The N. O. Times" evidently Secretary Chase's organ—& it starts off well.[89] I hope it may succeed. [L-----] Delta out with advices through Mobile forces of the opponent. Charleston not yet taken—Lincoln has suspended The Habeas Corpus Act in all cases a good action, & one that will

---

pears on Finnegass' MSR, he was on duty in General Butler's Department of the James that summer. Hollandsworth, *Louisiana Native Guards*, 81–82; Daniels Diary, August 24, 1864.

88. Major General William S. Rosecrans (1819–1898), commanding the Army of the Cumberland, forced the Confederates to withdraw from middle Tennessee and occupied Chattanooga September 9, 1863, after feinting above and crossing below on the Tennessee River. Burnside with his Army of the Ohio outmaneuvered Rebel defenders of east Tennessee and entered Knoxville September 3. Major General Quincy A. Gillmore directed a severe barrage on Fort Wagner, September 5–7, that caused Rebel forces to abandon the fort; they moved unnoticed during the night to batteries nearer Charleston. "The whole island is ours," Gillmore commented, "but the enemy have escaped us." Warner, *Generals in Blue*, 58, 159–60, 176–77, 411; Johnson and Buel, eds., *Battles and Leaders*, III, 680, and IV, 18, 20; McPherson, *Battle Cry of Freedom*, 669–70.

89. Salmon P. Chase, secretary of the treasury, spread his political influence in New Orleans and Louisiana beyond his personally appointed department agents and tax collectors for the Union. Anticipating his candidacy for president the following year, he hoped to outmaneuver Lincoln's more conservative approach on the state's reconstruction by attempting to establish himself as leader of a Republican coalition in New Orleans that welcomed blacks in the political arena. He created an "organization" through ties with groups and newspapers to promote his more radical views. Nevin, *Salmon P. Chase*, 213, 315–20.

strike terror into Copperheadism.[90] Mr. Aleck Wible has gone this morning to Baton Rouge on business for Mr. Chapman. The Col [S. M.?] Mansfield of the 17th Corps de Afrique called to see me this P.M.—

Thursday, September 24th 1863
[Cross-written]
I Yesterday rec'd a spiritual communication through an old negro who is ignorant and scarcely capable of reading or writing. T'is strange. He wrote this under influence and very rapidly—Then give a copy.—

"To Col Daniels. God in his wisdom has ordained Progress a law of nature. Men can by their false theories suspend the effects of such law for a brief period, but no opposition, no barrier, can delay it's ultimate enforcement. It must & shall have continuous [aggression?] through coming ages. The will of the Deity that Governs all of us must command the entire universe. Men will be destroyed in resisting such mighty power such an eternal will based as it is upon The Infinite. Then our dear friend, Go forward, be not delayed by any consideration of false interpretation of the laws that Progress inculcate—They are impervious—they may stop for a moment, but they cannot be overcome. Forward then man—thy heart & intellect are strong and thy voice shall express what thy heart doth feel. Forward, thy body must follow the spirit that [---] it and express with energy the teachings that are given to it by those who follow thee of our world.—We have made this difference between you and us, brother, & you will readily understand the contest between those who are in material bondage and those who freed from it have come to you through the medium.—Forward! Forward we will be with you and God who is with us will Protect you, the Representative of Progress Union & Freedom for all and ever.—Washington and others."—

Went down and saw old Valmour,[91] he told me that I should succeed in my undertakings to the civil department of The Gov't

---

90. Lincoln's suspension of the writ of habeas corpus created martial law and made possible the arrests of "all persons discouraging volunteers enlistments, resisting militia drafts, or guilty of any disloyal practice affording aid and comfort to the rebels"—in other words, of "copperheads," who opposed the Union's policy of total war. McPherson, *Battle Cry of Freedom*, 493–94.

91. J. B. Valmour was a free black long renowned in New Orleans as a spiritualist medium with healing powers. In 1858, pressure from the city's Catholic clergy had caused Valmour to curtail the most overt of his spiritualist activities, which he conducted at his black-

Maj. Gen'l Banks undoubtedly thinks that we miserable petty Colonels of negro Regiments are imbeciles and not to be feared in his grand intro for the Presidential sweepstakes.

> "He doth bestride the narrow world
> Like a Colossus and we petty men—
> Walk under his huge legs and peep about
> To find ourselves dishonorable graves"

but Imagine that he will discover the truth of the old saying *"Mons parturiens nascitur mus."*[92]—If his Presidential spasms produce anything more than vapor I shall be sadly mistaken, and will acknowledge the cur. I will admit defeat when it comes, never before.—Gen'l Banks is too conservative. He has more Policy than Principle, is too much opposed to Progress. Looks to The Executive seat instead of his countries welfare— In fact I almost believe he would be willing to permit these southern states to retain their institution of Slavery.—

I can support no such man. The one who will be my choice must be radically opposed to slavery of all kinds, social, moral and religious—one who will fight the good fight of Progress and further the advancement of Civilization & Humanity. We want no laggards now to lead the people. They must be practical living men—Those who have the Principle to guide and the firmness to enforce such Principles. Slavery can never be allowed another foothold upon this Continent. The iron foot of Civilization must awake it to action and from its ruins shall arise a noble structure whose base shall be eternal liberty and whose crest shall reach to Heaven itself.—

Friday, September 25th 1863
Wrote the following Poem this morning to our Glorious old stars & stripes.

---

smith shop. See, for example, Caryn Cossé Bell, *Revolution, Romanticism, and the Afro-Creole Protest Tradition in Louisiana, 1718–1868* (Baton Rouge, 1997), 187–88, 206–207, 213, 214.

92. Daniels again misfires on Horace's "Parturient montes, nascetur ridiculus mus." See Pt. 1, n. 97.

Part II, New Orleans

1.
 From tyrannical oppression—
 From fanatical transgression,
Was Columbia's stars and stripes, born in famous days of yore.—
  Cradled in the lap of Freedom,
  Nurtured by the blood of Freemen,
Proudly throw her pennant heavenward, o'er America's realms to soar.—

2.
 Heavenward her folds extending
  Peace, and Truth, and Freedom blending.
Near a century unsullied, blessed the land she floated o'er
  When with hands of foul pollution
  Demons siezed [sic] her constitution,
And besought them to submerge it madly in fraternal gore.—

3.
 Then her Isles of Light retreating
  Blending with the paled stripes weeping,
O'er Columbia's fearful struggle, sadly did her fate deplore.
  Through the lurid battle shining,
  Faintly as the Night cloud's lining
Piercing through war's leaden mantle freedom's beacon opes the door.—

4.
 Then from out fraternal ruin
  Like the Light of Bethlehem,
Blushes forth in heaven orbed beauty, the recreant stars with those of yore.
  Freedom seizes now the sceptre,
  Wisdom wields the pale faced spectre.
With one huge throe, the Proclamation, Liberty comes forever more.—

5.
 Again anew to Freedom plighted,
  All in holy faith united.
With Peace and Truth and Progress blending, their cloud of radiance [now?] pour,
  From Maine's highest hills extending
  O'er our fairest plains expending
Southward, Westward—onward ever, glory's blazeth golden shore.—

6.
Then unfurl our glorious banner,
Proudly to the heavens fling her.
O'er Union sail, let Union banner, in the Union's cause now soar,
And by our sires who fought before us,
By the gentle ones who bore us,
We swear allegiance to those colors, and our fealty evermore.—

Was foolish enough to try my hand at a game of Faro last evening by which I lost some Five hundred dollars, oh the horror of gaming, this is the first and the last time that I shall ever suffer myself to be thus led astray, the suffering of one such transgression is sufficient punishment for me for all my life.—

Saturday, September 26th 1863

Capt Kilborne City Prvt Marshall gave me a Pass to the city of New York yesterday.[93] Chapman Gave me $300. Left Horse saddle & other things with him until I return which I hope will be within four weeks—considerable is yet due me from Chapman. Engaged passage on Steamboat Minnehaha for Cairo—Lt [?] Gordon of Genl Ullmans Corps de Afrique a friend introduced by Mr. Read accompanies me—Saw my Quartermaster Lt Souvinet on the steamer—sent word by him to Capt Dauchy relative to personal effects on Ship Island. Bid Miss Albertine & sister goodbye Well I leave The Gulf Department a little over a year after I arrived thoroughly disgusted with the present administration of the same. I hope to return very soon with power that Genl Banks cannot disturb then we will see what courses he will take That he has acted very unjustly towards all officers connected with Genl Butler in any shape none can deny and that he will as soon as [heaven?] receive his reward none doubt—Steamboat left wharf at five oclock steamed across the River where we are at this time 12 oclock M taking in wood—

93. Captain Curtis W. Killborn gave Daniels the pass after requesting information on the colonel's status from Colonel E. G. Beckwith. Captain C. W. Killborn to Colonel E. G. Beckwith, Provost Marshal General, September 25, 1863, MSR of Nathan W. Daniels, 74th USCI [2nd LaNG], RG 94, NA.

Conclusion

By August 1863, public opinion had changed over whether to arm black troops to assist the Union war effort. Skeptics who questioned blacks' ability to fight were enlightened by the Native Guards' aggressive attack on Port Hudson the previous May and subsequent action by other black units in a desperate hand-to-hand battle at Milliken's Bend, Louisiana, on June 7. The movement gained momentum July 17 with battle actions of the 1st Kansas Colored Infantry at Honey Springs, Indian Territory, and on July 18 with the hailed assault on South Carolina's Fort Wagner by the Massachusetts 54th Infantry. Newspaper reports, especially those published after the latter engagement, were instrumental in spreading the word to a doubting public, who now paid attention, along with President Lincoln. Recruiting began in earnest in the North, while in the South, General Lorenzo Thomas, sent from Washington, signed up men in the Mississippi Valley, and General Banks's Corps d'Afrique continued to encourage enlistment in Louisiana, assisted by General Ullmann from the War Department. The experiment of tapping black manpower for Union forces would eventually prove its validity with the total enlistment of U.S. Colored Troops reaching nearly 180,000.

The use of black commissioned officers for these troops was limited at first to General Butler's corps of seventy-six free blacks in the Louisiana Native Guards. After they were replaced by whites during 1863, it took until January 1865 before a small group—only eleven—new black officers appeared in comparable infantry and artillery units. Although the early leaders did not last long in their regiments, they helped establish the Native Guards as pioneers who advanced the cause of the black man's equal place in military service. The officers fought prejudice in the form of denied promotion, the insulting examining boards, ever-present abuse from white soldiers, and unequal pay (even after leaving their regiments, they continued to pressure authorities for a retroactive parity of their monthly pay with that of whites).[1]

At the time, the most sensitive situations were those where black and white troops and officers were assigned to the same duty. The military environment demanded discipline and cohesiveness, but northern white soldiers were continually disruptive when exposed to black leaders. Men from the 13th Maine Regiment reportedly "could not acknowledge a negro their superior, by any virtue of shoulder straps he might wear."[2] Before their assignment in the Department of the Gulf, Yankee troops had no experience with the color line, the "free" versus "freed," as it applied to the local black population. They had no appreciation or understanding of the "free colored" soldiers' distinction between themselves and newly freed, darker slaves. To those cultured, educated free blacks of varying shades, light and dark, there was a vast difference.

Nowhere was the problem of coexistence more pronounced than with the 2nd Regiment under Colonel Daniels. There had been minor racial incidents in the fall of 1862 while the 2nd was guarding the Opelousas Railroad with white troops. However, the major upheaval that more than likely snapped General Banks to attention took place on Ship Island when Daniels arrested the privates and commissioned officers of the 13th Maine detachment for refusing to drill with his men. This wholesale arrest of white soldiers was the most dramatic event involving the Louisiana Native Guards and their black officers. It was both a supportive and a defensive measure for the colonel, who wanted respect for all his men. Yet,

---

1. The money issue would not begin to be resolved until mid-June 1864 when Congress allowed the same pay for blacks who were already free by April 19, 1861. Other freed men denied equal pay under the latter authorization had to wait until March 1865 for approval of a new law to settle the stalemate. Glatthaar, *Forged in Battle*, 174–75, 179; Captain P. B. S. Pinchback and ten officers of 2nd LaNG, to Edwin M. Stanton, October 1863, LR, Ser. 360, Colored Troops Division, RG 94, NA, found in Berlin et al., eds., *Black Military Experience*, 381–82.

2. David C. Rankin, "The Forgotten People: Free People of Color in New Orleans, 1850–1870" (Ph.D. dissertation, Johns Hopkins University, 1976), 182, found in Hollandsworth, *Louisiana Native Guards*, 43.

even for a commanding officer with abolitionist proclivities, his reaction to the Maine men's refusal was perhaps extreme for the times, for the attitude of the majority in the military department was surely represented by the Maine regiment's colonel, Henry Rust, with his "nigger on the brain" remarks.[3]

The disciplinary crisis, coming as it did a few weeks after Banks's arrival in New Orleans, probably alarmed and possibly embarrassed the new commanding general, drawing attention to a touchy situation he had not yet addressed. With Banks already disposed against the black officers, Daniels' performance may have acted as the immediate catalyst in the general's decision to oust Butler's troublesome appointments. The colonel's move, albeit supportive of the men, inadvertently laid the groundwork for their officers' removal, as well as his own.

General Butler seems to have used no particular criteria in choosing his white commanding officers for the Native Guards. During a conversation between the two generals after the change of command in December 1862, Banks inquired about the three regiments' colonels. Butler described his choices for the positions: 1st Regiment, Colonel Stafford, "not the best"; 2nd Regiment, Colonel Daniels, "a Southern man"; and 3rd Regiment, Colonel Nelson, "a good soldier."[4]

Of the three, Stafford, in spite of Butler's remark, appears to have been the strongest, most active leader and the most popular with the men. In December 1862, a few months after the regiments' organization, two petitions, one from the 1st and 2nd Louisiana Native Guards together and a separate one from the 3rd Regiment, requested that all the colored troops be brigaded as one under the command of Stafford. They wanted him because they trusted him, had confidence in him, and wished to reward his efforts in recruiting for them. Two-thirds of the 2nd Regiment's officers signed. (Where did this leave Daniels in the minds of his men?) Stafford's letters on his men's behalf were always strongly worded, for pay, arms, equipment, equal attention, less labor. His efforts, however, brought only

---

3. Upon taking his new command at Fort Jackson, Colonel Rust learned there were to be black troops under him who had not yet arrived. He promptly left for New Orleans "to see if the nigger question could not be settled another way, either by allowing myself or them to take the field anytime to get rid of them." Rust Diary, January 21, 1863, MOLLUS.

4. Official memo of Banks conversation with General Butler, December 18, 1862, Military Papers, Box 79, N. P. Banks Collection, LC.

a series of complaints against him from white officers not partial to black troops. Most of the charges lodged against him ensued from his outbursts of frustration in defense of his men's needs and rights. For Banks, he must have been a continuing irritant.[5]

Colonel Nelson of the 3rd Regiment, the "good soldier," had little support from his men. On February 19, 1863, nearly a month after Daniels' arrest of the 13th Maine men, all sixteen of Nelson's black officers signed a mass resignation in a petition to General Banks citing numerous prejudicial situations: "even our own Regimental commander has abused us, under cover of his authority." Nelson had been warned earlier against impressment of blacks during recruitment, but he paid little attention and even continued his roughshod methods later while on a new assignment; he was also thought to be speculating on the side. On June 1, 1863, during the siege at Port Hudson, the colonel arrested his own lieutenant colonel, Henry Finnegass, for improper conduct "on the eve of an engagement," an act that cannot have denoted harmony in front of their black soldiers.[6] With his less than stellar record and for various other reasons, Nelson too must have caused Banks problems.

And what of Nathan W. Daniels, the "Southern man?" After his arrest of the 13th Maine men, he was surely being monitored by superior officers and others in the department not enlightened to the use of black soldiers, let alone black officers. Any little slip in Daniels' performance could be used against him—and was.

General Banks, together with Brigadier General Thomas W. Sherman from the Defenses of New Orleans, may have been grasping at straws to find a reason to remove Colonel Daniels. The charges preferred against him by Lieutenant Palfrey for using 15,000 board feet of lumber on batteries at Ship Island were a concern, but evidently not sufficient for removal. Palfrey had asked Washington for an estimated $100,000 appropriation for fiscal 1863 to repair and finish the fort, yet by December of 1862 he knew he was already running out of money. The first tier of the

---

5. Petition of 3rd LaNG and 1st and 2nd LaNG to Major General N. P. Banks, received December 31, 1862, LR, II, Ser. 1747, Dept. of the Gulf, RG 393, Pt. 1, NA.

6. Captain J. A. Gla et al. to Major N. P. Banks, February 19, 1863, MSR of Leon G. Forstall, 75th USCI [3rd LaNG], RG 94, NA, found in Berlin et al., eds., *Black Military Experience*, 317. Finnegass refused orders to ready his men for what he considered to be another futile, most likely suicidal, attack on the enemy. Hollandsworth, *Louisiana Native Guards*, 56.

Conclusion

fort was finished by mid-February 1863, when his increasing duties in the department required more of his time back in New Orleans.[7] The engineer was aware of finances, but Daniels' lumber requisition was based on necessity, not cost, reflecting his feeling of responsibility in strengthening the military post. Was it too much, given Palfrey's budgetary restraints? Did he not follow correct procedure? Earlier, the department had received many large bills for lumber and a "great quantity of materials had been seized and issued without a very strict or careful accountability."[8] Was "accountability" the problem? The colonel collected witnesses and depositions from friends on the island. Then the department stalled the court-martial; charges issued in May were still not resolved by August. It was more than likely the second part of Palfrey's accusations, concerning Daniels' conduct on the island, that carried more weight.

A Bostonian from a refined family and a graduate of the U.S. Military Academy at West Point, Palfrey disapproved of the "riff-raff" filling the service. He considered himself a "pretty good abolitionist" and an officer not overly concerned with rank, but he was not pleased, after his military education and following nine years of experience, that black officers in the Native Guards now outranked him. From Palfrey's perspective, Daniels and the black officers represented all that was wrong with the black troops. Writing to his father from Ship Island two days before sending the charges against the colonel to headquarters, the engineer confided: "My men complain of great annoyance and interference from the Colonel commanding. He is an unprincipled man, and in a position to do a great deal of harm. He does not restrain his men, and they follow his bad example. It is a pity they should only have for commanders of black troops men who are not considered fit for any other command.... I believe I shall try what I can do in getting this Colonel transferred to Fort Pike, and have his Lt. Col., a modest and sensible young man, put in command here."[9]

---

7. Bearss, *Historic Structure Report*, 104, 117.

8. Colonel S. B. Holabird, Chief Quartermaster, to Major General N. P. Banks, January 15, 1863, LR, Ser. 1756, Dept. of the Gulf, RG 393, Pt. 1, NA.

9. Lieutenant John Carver Palfrey to John Gorham Palfrey, November 9, December 28, 1862, April 19, August 16, 1863, in John Gorham Palfrey Papers, bMS Am 1704 (608), Houghton Library, Harvard University, published by permission of Houghton Library, Harvard University. Palfrey considered the black regiments good soldiers who performed well, but only if they had good officers—white officers.

Incriminating as the engineer's feelings were when woven into a formal complaint, they evidently were not strong enough to eject the colonel. On August 7, 1863, however, General Banks got what he needed. Lieutenant Commander George Perkins preferred charges not only against Daniels' adjutant, Lieutenant Elijah Prouty, *but also against the colonel* for indecent language in conduct unbecoming an officer and a gentleman in the presence of a lady. Almost a year and a half earlier, after the Federal fleet anchored in front of New Orleans, then-lieutenant Perkins and Captain Theodorus Bailey, acting as envoys for the navy, had walked alone through a menacing mob to present civil authorities with a demand for the city's surrender.[10] Now captain of the gunboat *Sciota*, Perkins was appalled at his encounter with Prouty and Daniels and reported it immediately to Banks. In the diary, Daniels mentions Prouty's involvement, but not his own, and writes as if totally detached from the situation. It is understandable that he did not document the incident, as it certainly reflected upon his behavior. Perkins to Banks:

> I have the honor to make the following report.
>
> On the evening of the 7th inst. while riding on horse back with Captain Cooks wife of the Navy,[11] I was over taken by two Officers of the Army, driving in a buggy, who drove so near us as to force us from the road and commenced bantering us about fast horses; at first I made no reply, but seeing that it was not their intention to drive on, or to let me pass, I replied that I was riding with a Lady and hoped they would leave me. As this had no effect, I rode along side of the buggy and asked them if they wanted anything of me, and repeated that I was riding with a Lady, and asked them if they would drive on or let me pass, and if they were Gentlemen they would do so, when the one driving wanted to know if I knew who I was talking to, and who are you anyway. I told them, Captain Perkins of the "Sciota," and then joined Mrs Cook. One of them remarked that I was a damned upstart. I replied by saying, I see you are Officers of the Army and are sadly disgracing your Uniform to night, when the one on the left of the buggy said I was a damned Shit-arse, and a damned fool. I again told him I was with a Lady

---

10. Johnson and Buel, eds., *Battles and Leaders,* II, 91.

11. Lieutenant Commander Augustus P. Cooke, captain of the *Estrella,* left the day before with his ship under orders to proceed, with the *Genessee,* to assist at Ship Island in case of an anticipated attack there. *ORN,* Ser. I, Vol. XX, 435.

Conclusion

and hoped he would have some regard for her if he did not for me, and if they would tell me their names the matter could be better arranged in town than on the road. The one on the left replied by saying, you say you are riding with a Lady, but I say you are riding with a damned whore, and you are a damned Shit arse, and I room at 122 St. Charles Hotel, and will repeat the same thing tomorrow morning. I remarked that he was an ungentlemanly puppy—when the one on the right and driving asked me what I said—I told him that I said he was not a Gentleman—He replied that I was a damned fool, and that his name was Colonel Daniels, and then drew his whip and commenced striking at me; just then coming to a cross street, I turned and left them. I am very Respectfully, Your Obt. Servt, G. H. Perkins, Lieut. Comdr. U.S.N.[12]

Those looking to remove the colonel latched onto this report. Daniels certainly was aware of the charges against him because he received a copy of the complaint the next day with a request for an "immediate report and explanation." According to existing records, *four days later*, on August 11, Colonel Daniels, based on the navy officer's charge, was "dishonorably dismissed" from the service, along with Lieutenant Prouty, by Special Orders No. 196, Department of the Gulf.[13]

Daniels immediately appealed to General Banks. The general must have listened, for he countermanded the dismissal order, but at the same time, in order not to lose the seriousness of the charges, requested a second court-martial.[14] During all this, the colonel's diary entries still

---

12. Lieutenant Commander George H. Perkins to Major General N. P. Banks, August 7, 1863, LR, Ser. 1756, Dept. of the Gulf, RG 393, Pt. 1, NA.

13. LR, III, Ser. 1747, *ibid.;* MSR of Nathan W. Daniels, 74th USCI [2nd LaNG], RG 94, NA. According to Prouty, Daniels had asked the lieutenant to drive with him to town and then to the lake, where they met a party of "disrespectful character." Later, on the road, Prouty mistook Perkins and Mrs. Cooke for that party. He apologized afterward for his thoughtless language and explained the circumstances. Testifying in his own defense during court proceedings, Prouty admitted to "a breach of military etiquette in being in company with an officer under arrest" and stated that Daniels only took him riding "for the purpose of making his point, what he meant by it I am not able to state since the affair occurred." A character reference for Prouty stated: "I fear the company in which he [Prouty] was found at the time of his offense, had more to do with his improper conduct, than any evil disposition on his part." Proceedings of General Court Martial, Trial of Elijah K. Prouty, August 21, 1863, MM 878, RG 183, NA.

14. MSR of Nathan W. Daniels, 74th USCI [2nd LaNG], RG 94, NA.

focused on the original Ship Island lumber charge, with no mention of his role in the Perkins-Prouty incident. Petty charges from other individuals, especially from the 13th Maine Regiment, continued to come at him as late as August 22 and September 7 and 8, after his alleged dismissal.

It took five long months for the colonel's matters to be resolved. Part of the delay may have been due to Daniels' desire to prove himself innocent of the engineer Palfrey's charge—to challenge his accuser with witnesses and depositions in a court-martial. At first the colonel did not mention resigning, but then the military legal process stalled. Banks may have contributed to the lack of progress; he was known to be a weak disciplinarian who often reversed his decisions and rarely followed through.[15] It was only later, after prolonged confusion and additional charges, that Daniels mentioned resignation in the diary. It was the intervention of the spy, James George Brown, however, that finalized the move.

No resignation was found in surviving records. Given that there seems to have been a deal of some kind between General Banks and Daniels involving the spy Brown, perhaps this is understandable. It is interesting that documents relating to the colonel's never-held court-martial on the Ship Island charge were found in General Banks's personal papers, not in Department of the Gulf records, regimental records, or Daniels' Military Service Record. The latter contains statements in a September 25 correspondence between Captain C. W. Killborn and Colonel E. G. Beckwith of the Provost Marshal's Office in New Orleans that exemplify the confusion regarding Daniels' status. Captain Killborn:

> Col. Daniels of the 2nd Reg't Corps d'Afrique has applied to me for a pass to NY. This Col. was dismissed from the Service. The order was afterwards countermanded by Gen'l Banks and ordered to be tried by Court Martial and as I do not know the decision of the court, I am unable to act in the premises. Please instruct me what to do.

Colonel Beckwith's reply:

> Col. Daniels was dismissed from the service by the President before the court ordered by me met for his trial. He is therefore, out of service.[16]

15. Harrington, *Fighting Politician*, 63.
16. Captain C. W. Killborn to Colonel E. G. Beckwith, Pro Mar Gen, September 25, 1863, MSR of Nathan W. Daniels, 74th USCI [2nd LaNG], RG 94, NA.

Conclusion

"Dishonorable dismissal" is the final documented remark amid confusing, conflicting military records on Nathan W. Daniels. However, none of it applied as far as the colonel was concerned, because the commanding general had allowed a resignation and he left the Department of the Gulf with that understanding. The day after the exchange between Killborn and Beckwith, a bitter and disgusted Daniels was on a Mississippi River steamboat headed north.

It is obvious that the Department of the Gulf was not ready to recognize the black man of varying skin colors, free or freed, enlisted or officer, at the colonel's level of acceptance. Politics entered Daniels' final thoughts on the matter, for although he understood General Banks to be opposed to the Native Guards with their black officers and to him personally, he thought that the general removed all three colonels simply because they were recruited by General Butler, a man for whom Banks had little regard.

Banks the general needed the best men to lead his troops. But Banks the politician was less concerned for the black soldiers and their pride in a well-trained regiment than for how that regiment would reflect upon his reputation. He needed "good officers" to make it all work. His ejection of Butler's appointments was a personal move with political undertones, not so much to remove the latter's influence as to define his own image.

In August 1863, one of Banks's subordinates met with Lincoln in Washington and later conveyed to the general the president's thoughts spelling out the future for black troops in the Department of the Gulf. The letter also indirectly supported the removal of Daniels. Already a marked man under arrest, the colonel was now an even more likely target, given Banks's eagerness to please the president. Lincoln, according to Banks's informant,

> seemed particularly anxious that the "Corps d'Afrique" should be filled up and that the greatest possible number of black troops should be put into the field—It was evident that he preferred to be called upon for anything rather than men.— . . . No one any longer doubts the wisdom of creating black soldiers, but everywhere there is a doubt as to how far the work will be efficiently done. The "Corps d'Afrique" must be the best drilled, best instructed, and best officered body of black troops in the country; they must be purely soldiers, regiments of negro laborers must be distinct from them, then they will clearly prove their quality and merit. . . . There are going to

be so many badly officered negro Rgts that your exception will be more marked and noted—[17]

After the removal of their original three colonels, the Louisiana Native Guard Volunteers continued under a succession of commanding officers in General Banks's Corps d'Afrique and, after April 1864, as the 73rd, 74th, and 75th Regiments of the United States Colored Infantry (USCI).

Colonel Spencer H. Stafford of the 1st Louisiana Native Guards was dismissed from the service on September 8, 1863, by Special Orders No. 224. However, in the spring of 1864, General Benjamin Butler reinstated him with an assignment to the 10th Regiment U.S. Colored Infantry in the general's Department of Virginia and North Carolina. Together with other black units, the colonel's troops were part of the 1st Brigade of the 3rd Division, under Brigadier General Edward W. Hincks, and saw duty in the Petersburg campaign. In 1871 a War Department order, following a request from his Native Guards, who appreciated all he had done for them, revoked Stafford's original "dismissal" order and substituted "honorable discharge," retroactive to August 15, 1863.[18]

Records for Colonel John A. Nelson of the 3rd Regiment indicate he was discharged August 14, 1863, under Special Orders No. 199, although he had written a resignation on August 8. Whatever the circumstances, after leaving his command he created further troubles as described by Daniels, then in Washington, in a January 15, 1864, diary entry:

> See by this evening's paper that Col. Jack Nelson formerly Colonel of the 3rd Native Guards but lately of the 10th colored troops has been Dismissed the service by Maj. Gen'l Butler on account of having impressed by force colored men into the service. This is bad business for him as he resigned in Louisiana to escape Dismissal, came north and as Col. Stafford informed me, through false reference representation to Gen'l Butler obtained the General's influence in the command of the 10th. The General was duly informed of all this by Stafford and I can readily see that Butler has taken the

17. Brigadier General William Dwight to Major General N. P. Banks, August 20, 1863, in General Correspondence, Box 28, N. P. Banks Collection, LC.

18. Butler became commander of the Department of Virginia and North Carolina, later called the Department (and Army) of the James, in December 1863. OR, Ser. I, Vol. XL, 152, 555; Daniels Diary II, August 26, 1864; MSR of Spencer H. Stafford, 73rd USCI [1st LaNG], RG 94, NA.

Conclusion

first opportunity to get rid of him. I cannot say that I am sorry for him as he was not fit to command the color'd troops.[19]

The 2nd Louisiana Native Guards basically served out its existence in oblivion on Ship Island and at Fort Pike. The regiment's numbers dropped from a high of 995 men at muster in the fall of 1862 to 976 men in February 1863, to 716 in June, and 612 by October 1863. Loss of the black officers, resulting low morale, sickness, and desertion contributed to the drop in numbers. Colonel William M. Grosvenor relieved Lieutenant Colonel Alfred Hall in November 1863 but was dismissed in May 1864 for keeping a woman in his quarters on the island. Colonel Ernest W. Homstedt took command in June under the new 74th USCI designation. The next month the regiment merged with the 91st USCI to bring the numbers up to authorized strength. The companies were then reshuffled: five companies, F, G, H (the latter had been at Fort Pike), I, and K were assigned to Ship Island; Company A remained at Fort Pike, now joined by B and C from the island; Companies D (from the island) and E (from Fort Pike), moved to Fort Macomb, which like Fort Pike guarded the pass connecting Lake Pontchartrain and the Gulf of Mexico. There was a brief deployment from August into September for three companies from Ship Island to Mobile Point, Alabama, to help with the assault on Fort Morgan, but they arrived only just before the Confederates surrendered. Once back at Ship Island, the regiment remained with its split detachments until it mustered out in October 1865.[20]

The 2nd Regiment's black officers, who were removed or resigned, returned to New Orleans and their families. A few of them rallied in the summer of 1863 when General Banks, in an about-face based on a pressing manpower shortage, planned to raise two sixty-day black regiments,

---

19. MSR of John A. Nelson, 75th USCI [2nd LaNG], RG 94, NA; Colonel Nelson was dismissed from the 10th Regiment USCT March 15, 1864. *Official Army Register of the Volunteer Force of the United States Army for the Years 1861–1865* (Washington, D.C., 1865), Pt. 8, p. 180. Colonel Stafford replaced him as commander of the 10th.

20. Regimental Papers, 74th USCI [2nd LaNG], RG 94, NA; Bearss, *Historic Study*, 212, 223, 224; Hollandsworth, *Louisiana Native Guards*, 80, 99–100; *Official Army Register*, Pt. 8. Records kept during Daniels' tour of duty were sporadic and often incomplete, at first at least partly because of both the rush from muster to the field and a lack of books, and later because of the problems created by a divided regiment.

offering the ex-officers a chance at recommission if they were successful in gathering new recruits.[21]

Of the seventy-six black officers who served in the Native Guards, the majority of those politically active in pursuit of their civil rights after the war were from Colonel Daniels' regiment. Former major Francis E. Dumas, a rich planter before the war who had recruited a company of his own slaves, became the wealthiest black in the state afterward. "A gentleman of fine tact and ability," he came within two votes of being nominated for governor of Louisiana in 1868 during the Radical Reconstruction. When offered the number two spot behind Henry Clay Warmoth, the Radical white nominee, Dumas declined, leaving the appointment to another free man of color, Oscar J. Dunn.[22]

Ex-captain P. B. S. Pinchback raised a company of black cavalry for Banks the summer after he left the 2nd Louisiana Native Guards, but he never received a recommission. A few months later, in a November 6 mass meeting of free blacks, he pressed for "political rights for the free community," declaring that as soldiers who fought, and as citizens, they should have the right to vote. This light-skinned free black also argued that in order to advance the free blacks' cause, lighter people of color should distance themselves from the darker ex-slaves. Society, he claimed, made a grievous error when "prejudice weighed equally against all those who had African blood in their veins, no matter how small the amount."

After the war, Pinchback purchased a newspaper and through it launched into politics, concerned over which blacks would make decisions for the diverse colored population. Following the sudden death of Lieutenant Governor Dunn, Governor Warmoth appointed Pinchback to fill the position. When Warmoth himself was removed from office in early December 1872 after accusations of rampant corruption, Pinchback took over as governor for the slightly more than a month that remained of Warmoth's term.[23]

Lieutenant Robert Isabelle, who passed the Department of the Gulf's

21. Berlin *et al.*, eds., *Black Military Experience*, 307.

22. Blassingame, *Black New Orleans*, 72, 212; Everett, "Ben Butler and the Louisiana Native Guards," 211; Hollandsworth, *Louisiana Native Guards*, 110–11.

23. Blassingame, *Black New Orleans*, 36; Tunnell, *Crucible of Reconstruction*, 77; Foner, *Short History of Reconstruction*, 22; Hollandsworth, *Louisiana Native Guards*, 82, 111.

Conclusion

examining board in February 1863 but resigned afterward in frustration, also raised recruits for Banks's sixty-day regiments that summer. He became captain of the 7th Louisiana Regiment in July and mustered out August 6. In 1867–1868 he was a delegate to the Radical Republican convention, and as a legislator in February 1870 he pressed for the education of black children through integration with white schools. He later became a pension agent and earned a law degree, practicing in New Orleans.[24]

In March 1864, former captain Arnold Bertonneau and Jean-Baptiste Roudanez, brother of the owner of the black French newspaper *L'Union*, traveled to Washington to deliver a petition to President Lincoln on the eve of Louisiana's state constitutional convention. Signed by approximately one thousand New Orleans free blacks, the document requested the right to vote that had been denied them in an earlier election. The two men continued their quest in Boston, where they met with well-known abolitionists including Frederick Douglass, Wendell Phillips, and William Lloyd Garrison. Bertonneau, a wine merchant, pursued his civil rights through politics and was elected a delegate from New Orleans to the constitutional convention of 1867–1868. Pressing for equality in education like his fellow soldier Robert Isabelle, he unsuccessfully sued the city of New Orleans in 1877 for denying his children entrance to the public schools.[25]

Former captain Samuel Ringgold personified the ever-present difficulties facing the black population when in late 1864 he found himself swept up in an impressment of contrabands collected to work on a levee. He requested that he be treated differently from the others and given the respect due a member of a different "social scale" and an educated, property-owning taxpayer.[26]

Other black officers from the 2nd Regiment who pressed for their rights in the political arena often serving in civic positions were William

---

24. Lieutenant R. H. Isabelle to Brigadier General Daniel Ullmann, June 12, 1863, in Berlin *et al.*, eds., *Black Military Experience*, 330; *Official Army Register*, Pt. 8, p. 318; Tunnell, *Crucible of Reconstruction*, 232, 240; Hollandsworth, *Louisiana Native Guards*, 109.

25. Blassingame, *Black New Orleans*, 212; McPherson, *Negro's Civil War*, 272–73; Tunnell, *Crucible of Reconstruction*, 231; Joshi and Reidy, "'To Come Forward and Aid,'" 337; Hollandsworth, *Louisiana Native Guards*, 94–95, 109.

26. Joshi and Reidy, "'To Come Forward and Aid,'" 340.

Barrett, Ernest Morphy, Octave Rey, and the multilingual translator and former quartermaster, Charles S. Sauvinet.[27]

Lieutenant John C. Palfrey, the engineer officer who was the first to prefer charges against Colonel Daniels, confided to his father when Daniels was under arrest, "General Banks wanted to make me Colonel of the 2nd La N. Guards (black) stationed here [Ship Island], and put me in command of the Island—I refused because it was simply Infantry, and because they had black officers.... One objection was I did not like the looks of taking Col. Daniels Regiment after being instrumental in discharging him." Palfrey knew that Banks was purging the Native Guards of black officers. He himself was later offered other black infantry regiments but still said no, as he was committed to the engineers.[28] He remained in the Department of the Gulf for the duration of the war, responsible for the fortifications around New Orleans and those involved in the Red River and Mobile campaigns. Resigning from the army as a brigadier general in 1866, he later joined the Engineering School at Dartmouth College.

Lieutenant Elijah K. Prouty, the adjutant dismissed in August on the charges brought by Lieutenant Commander Perkins, applied for reappointment in October 1863, but was denied approval by the Secretary of War.[29]

Lieutenant Colonel Alfred Hall remained in command at Ship Island for six months after having taken over from Daniels in May 1863. On his arrival at the post, he referred to the regiment as being in a "state of disorder." He stayed until November 1863, and as he declared later in an inter-

27. Hollandsworth, *Louisiana Native Guards*, 105, 110.

28. Lieutenant J. C. Palfrey to J. G. Palfrey, August 16, 1863, in Palfrey Papers, Houghton Library. In spite of Palfrey's strict allegiance to the engineers, it was actually his idea to combine the 2nd LaNG infantry and a black engineer regiment as suggested by Major D. C. Houston in a July 25, 1863, letter to headquarters (see n. 20 and related text, Pt. 2). Houston wanted Palfrey to take a command in subsequent black engineer units, but Palfrey vacillated. He was particular in his demands, wanting nothing to do with black officers, requesting specific men (Butler's "free men and mechanics") and additional "advantages." Superiors in the department were opposed to his shift to black troops, and by October 1863 he had said no to Houston: "all ideas of advancing me in the negro service have been given up" (J. C. Palfrey to J. G. Palfrey, October 18, 1863, in Palfrey Papers, Houghton Library).

29. C. W. Foster, AAG Vols., to Major General N. P. Banks, October 20, 1863, MSR of Elijah K. Prouty, 74th USCI [2nd LaNG], RG 94, NA.

Conclusion

view, "brought it up to the standing of a good Regiment" before the next commanding officer, Colonel Grosvenor, arrived. (A medical report issued on Hall that month described him as "suffering from congestion of the liver with a generally debilitated system.") He went to a temporary command with the 176th New York Volunteers in New Orleans, and in May 1864 returned to Fort Pike, where he remained until October 1865, when he was "dishonorably dismissed" for "neglect of duty"—having been absent from his command during its mustering out.[30]

The spy James George Brown never completed his mission as outlined in the diary. He got hung up in Mobile after Confederate authorities there, not quite trusting his purported motives, ordered him followed in hope of ensnaring other suspected Union spies with whom he associated. By December 1863, he had somehow landed in Chattanooga at headquarters for the Army of the Cumberland. Commanding major general George H. Thomas, wanting to use Brown's services himself but unsure of the spy's role for Banks, held him for questioning and then sent him to Washington for further interrogation. Both Daniels and Brown—the latter temporarily confined in the Old Capitol Prison—were in the city in January 1864, but no information has been found to indicate whether the two ever met, then or thereafter.[31]

Hamilton McNeil Vance, the original owner of the diary, returned to New Orleans after the war and continued with his cotton business, Byrne, Vance & Co., at 3 Carondelet in the city. He died January 10, 1870, of "apoplexy" at age forty-six.[32]

Colonel Nathan W. Daniels continued to write in the diary and in two additional diaries over the next four years. When he left the Department of the Gulf, he traveled north to visit his family in Ohio and by early November had arrived in Washington via New York City. He made the capital city his home off and on for the next year and a half and did not return immediately to Louisiana as he had expressed hope of doing in the diary. He met with various people, including President Lincoln, Robert Dale Owen of the American Freedmen's Inquiry Commission, General Butler, Colonel Stafford, and others.

---

30. MSR of Alfred G. Hall, 74th USCI [2nd LaNG], RG 94, NA.
31. Davis, "Curious Civil War Career of James George Brown," 20–21.
32. New Orleans *Picayune*, January 11, 1870.

While in the capital, Daniels worked diligently for the creation of what was to become the Bureau of Refugees, Freedmen, and Abandoned Lands, otherwise known as the Freedmen's Bureau.[33] His nonstop campaigning for the rights of the newly emancipated black race kept him active lobbying key politicians who could enact what was needed and just. He was in the city in July 1864 during the Confederates' brief two-day siege, which found the former colonel on the verge of becoming aide-de-camp to General [Charles?] Thomas before the crisis subsided and his services were no longer needed.[34]

Daniels remained active in spiritualism, attending séances and making friends with local believers. In March 1865, shortly after the presidential inauguration, Mrs. Lincoln—a devoted spiritualist herself—invited the "celebrated" spirit artist Mr. W. P. Anderson, visiting from New York City with his wife and accompanied by Daniels, to a séance in the Green Room of the White House. The president was occupied in his private apartment, but Mrs. Lincoln, with her son Tad and cousin General Todd, received them to try and communicate with Willie, Tad's brother, who had died in February 1862.[35]

Another spiritualist acquaintance was the striking and talented twenty-five-year-old Cora Hatch, a popular speaker of the day who would prove to be one of the most famous mediums and trance lecturers of the nineteenth century. She followed a lecture circuit through the northeastern cities, her physical appearance and speeches creating a lasting impression on her audiences.[36] The twenty-nine-year-old bachelor did not

---

33. The Freedmen's Bureau was created to dispense food, clothing, and some type of land to freed slaves, to aid both white and black refugees, and to administer lands confiscated by the military or abandoned during the war. The bill authorizing the agency was passed by both houses on March 3, 1865, "on the last hour of the last night of the session of Congress"; Daniels Diary II, March 5, 1865.

34. Daniels Diary II, July 11, 1864

35. *Ibid.*, March [7?], 1865. Union brigadier general John Blair Smith Todd (1814–72) was four years older than his cousin Mary Todd Lincoln. He had served in Florida, Mexico, and on the Dakota frontier before the war and commanded the North Missouri District and the 6th Division of the Army of the Tennessee in 1861 and 1862 before his commission expired. Active in Dakota Territory politics, he served several years as a delegate to Congress. Although recently defeated, he was still in Washington at the time of this White House séance. Warner, *Generals in Blue*, 507–508.

36. Braude, *Radical Spirits*, 29, 86, 87.

note in his diary when he first met Cora, but Daniels had at last found a woman who embodied all his ideals: a spirit believer and fellow abolitionist.

On June 24, 1865, President Andrew Johnson appointed the former colonel as collector of Internal Revenue for the Second District of Louisiana. On July 25, Daniels boarded a ship in New York bound for New Orleans, arriving there August 2. "Flaming notices" announced his arrival in the newspapers *Delta* and New Orleans *Times*, whereas the radical black New Orleans *Tribune* gave him "very complimentary" coverage. One of the first people he looked up was Francis Dumas. They made financial arrangements among various friends from earlier days, black and white, for the creation and sale of bonds in accordance with the duties of Daniels' new position. Some of these friends, fearing Daniels' sentiments too radical, refused the colonel's efforts, leaving him less than successful in his return to the city.[37]

It is not known when Daniels traveled back to Washington, but on December 8, 1865, he and Cora were married there in a spur-of-the-moment ceremony with only a handful of spiritualist friends in attendance. His son by his first wife, Etta, must have remained with Daniels' mother in Ohio, for there is no indication that the boy joined the newly married couple.

During their time in the capital, Daniels and Cora were popular and frequent speakers in the black community's churches and meeting places, often the only whites present. As ardent supporters of the Freedmen's Bureau, they worked tirelessly for the country's black population, now overwhelmed with the process called "reconstruction." Cora wrote in Daniels' diary of one occasion, February 23, 1866:

> This evening was set apart by . . . ourselves to address the Color'd people of this city in one of their churches [Asbury Methodist Church]—and it has proved an occasion of the deepest interest to all who were present—The church was crowded in every part, and doubtless many were unable to gain admittance.— . . . My darling husband addressed them on the "Rights, Qualifications and Injustices of the Color'd Freemen of America" relating his personal experience among them as citizen and soldier—declaring that their rights were the same as our own and their qualifications equal—or ca-

---

37. Daniels Scrapbook, unidentified newspaper article.

pable of becoming so thro' a full possession of their Rights.—depicted in glowing terms and words of praise the heroism of his regiment (color'd) upon the battlefield and recited many horrible instances of atrocities which have and are being daily committed upon these unfortunate people by the Reconstructed traitors and slave holders in the south.... His remarks were rec'd with great favor and applause by the audience most of whom were color'd.

Two weeks after this particular gathering, the couple bumped into General Banks at a reception for Speaker of the House Schuyler Colfax. The general was cordial enough toward the former colonel and his talented wife, although Daniels, who still harbored strong emotions about the man, felt that he was only trying to make up for his past "meanness and tyranny."

By mid-March 1866, Mr. and Mrs. Daniels had moved close to Cora's family, near Cuba in western New York. They lived the idyllic family life in a small cottage, planting a garden and enjoying the company of relatives. Earlier they had traveled her lecture circuit between Washington, Philadelphia, New York, and Boston; now, from June to August, they followed her "western tour" as far as St. Louis and the prairies of Missouri, returning to Cuba to await the birth of their child. In early September, Daniels attended the Southern Loyal Union Convention in Philadelphia as a delegate from Louisiana. While there, he was selected as a member of the Committee of Pilgrimage, a group of orators who would spread out to speak to audiences in various northern cities, before reuniting at Lincoln's tomb.[38] Daniels' activities, however, were cut short on September 27, 1866, for at 12:15 P.M. Cora gave birth to their baby girl.

After almost two months at home, the new father left for Washington in November and remained there into the spring, except for periodic visits to see his wife and child. By now, Daniels had become a prolific writer and knowledgeable newspaper correspondent for selected papers, including the *National Anti-Slavery Standard,* the *Religio-Philosophical Journal,* the Rochester (N.Y.) *Express,* and the black New Orleans *Tribune.* The radical readers followed every detailed move on the Reconstruction question through his observations in the House of Representatives and the Senate. President Andrew Johnson incurred more and more

---

38. *Ibid.,* unidentified newspaper article, September [6/7?], 1866.

Conclusion

of Daniels' wrath as being the main obstacle to progress for a healing nation, especially as related to his lack of support for the Freedmen's Bureau. According to the colonel, Congress knew what it had to do, but all efforts were futile with the uncompromising Johnson at the helm; impeachment was gaining momentum as the only answer.[39]

On his thirty-fifth birthday, May 10, 1867, Daniels received word that he had been confirmed as "Register under the Bankrupt Act for the 4th District of Louisiana." He quickly returned home to Cora and his eight-month-old baby and together they made hurried preparations for leaving. Five days later the three were off to New Orleans with high hopes for a new undertaking in the southern city.

> *May 29th 1867 New Orleans*
> Reached this city this evening at 5 o'clock. Came down the Mississippi on the steamboat—Ruth, and have had a delightful passage.—The weather is somewhat different from that of the north and we do not find their [-------] at all uncomfortable. Darling is delighted with the country and I trust now that health and prosperity may be accorded us.—Took rooms on Canal St.—and tomorrow shall proceed to business.

Politics consumed Daniels on his arrival, and for the next several months he pushed for greater Radical Republican influence in Louisiana's Reconstruction. He spoke "at considerable length and with characteristic eloquence" before black audiences in packed meeting halls and churches. He recalled the roles of blacks during the war, their "bravery in battle and integrity at home, their appreciation of the duties of entire citizenship, which have been so long and unjustly denied them." Conscious of their strength in numbers and feeling the urgency of the upcoming fall elections, he zealously pressed for the registration of black voters.[40]

In a June 19 article to the Rochester *Express*, Daniels commented on the new outbreak of cholera in the city, blaming the filthy conditions of the canals and the suburbs. He cautioned that the situation was ripe for an epidemic of that disease and of yellow fever, which would create a general exodus at a crucial time before the fall state constitutional convention. A column on September 6 mentioned that yellow fever was, in fact, at epi-

---

39. *Ibid.*, Rochester (N.Y) *Express*, January 27, 1867.
40. *Ibid.*, New Orleans *Republican*, n.d.

demic strength, although "of a milder type than ever before." Daniels casually wrote that many people had left the city but there was no panic; the disease responded well to treatment, and fatalities occurred only when victims ignored help or overindulged in food or drink.

Three and a half weeks later Daniels was dead. Undoubtedly he had lived through earlier outbreaks of yellow fever in his years in Louisiana, but this time he did not escape the dreaded killer he treated so lightly. Cora became ill but rallied where her husband could not. Sadly, their little girl also contracted the disease and died several weeks after her father.

An October 3 obituary from the New Orleans *Tribune* stated the following:

> Yesterday afternoon our noble and talented friend, Colonel Nathan W. Daniels, fell victim to the prevailing epidemic. Scarcely a greater loss could befall the liberal party at this time, and that loss will be sorely felt in the Convention, to which he had just been elected, and of which he would have been one of the ablest and trustiest leaders.
>
> Our readers are familiar with the record of the Colonel, since he entered the Union army in 1862. Hundreds of our friends served with him under his command, in the First [2nd] Native Guard Regiment, of which he was Colonel. They had an opportunity to become acquainted with his noble character and his perfect sense of the equality and rights of men. As a Federal officer, his record belongs to our national history, and will speak high for his military ability.
>
> Col. Daniels incurred the ill-will of Gen. Banks for his having taken part in behalf of his colored officers. He had then to retire from the field. But he continued making active service in the ranks of the Radical Republican party. During his stay at the National Capital in 1865 and 1866, he did a great deal to acquaint the Republican members of Congress with the true state of affairs in the South.
>
> Col. Daniels returned to Louisiana last spring, bringing with him his talented wife, Cora Hatch, well-known in the literary world, who is now afflicted with this great bereavement.
>
> Col. Daniels was only thirty-two [thirty-one] years of age. He was a native of Syracuse, N.Y. and recently a resident of Jefferson City. He was the presiding officer of the Central Executive Committee of the Republican party, for the parish of Jefferson, President of the Third Ward Club of Jef-

ferson City, and one of the delegates elected to the coming Convention. He had been identified with the life and welfare of our State for many years before the war, having been a resident of the parish of Point Coupee. He leaves a great many friends to deplore his untimely loss; and his name, his philanthropy, his good will to all men, will be long remembered by the colored population of Jefferson.

A dedicated advocate for the people of African descent, Daniels died at a peak of intensity and at a crucial time in history. His early abolitionist tendencies had ignited with his experience as commander of the 2nd Louisiana Native Guards. Though his leadership and character were in question, in the end what undid him as a military officer was his eagerness to bring the black race, in all its color variations, onto equal footing in a white world dominated by prejudice. His intimate exposure to inequities in the military environment helped propel him toward an ever deepening and maturing commitment to people of color. His own words, written in Washington on July 20, 1864, more than three years before his death, summarize his role in the ongoing struggle:

> If devotion to a principal [sic], the giving of one's entire being to the physical and religious advancement of an oppressed race be aught deserving of success, then shall I accomplish my hopes.—Then shall I beholding schemes for the Afric's improvement realized, then shall I see this ill starred race taking the place in the machinery of the world that their God given rights entitle them to. For long months have I been laboring here to inaugurate a system whereby the nation may extend to the negroes the protection and the education that is due them as citizens of their Great Republic....
>
> ... I have devoted my life to the successful solution of this great problem ... yet will the ultimatum be reached, the undertaking accomplished, and the status of the black man be placed on a full equality with that of his pale faced brother. It is right, it is holy, it is just.

Appendix 1
Officer Roster

2nd Regiment Louisiana Native Guard Volunteers Field, Staff, and Noncommissioned Officers, October 1862–August 1863

Regiment mustered October 12, 1862. Name changed June 1863 to 2nd Regiment Corps d'Afrique. Reorganized April 1864 as 74th Regiment United States Colored Infantry (USCI). Battle: April 9, 1863, East Pascagoula, Mississippi.

Field and Staff Officers
Col. Nathan W. Daniels.° Provost Marshal, St. Charles, St. John the Baptist, and St. James Parishes. Dismissed/resigned Aug./Sept. 1863.
Lt. Col. Alfred G. Hall.° Transferred from 9th Conn. Vols. Oct. 21, 1862.
Maj. Francis E. Dumas. Transferred from 1st La. Native Guards Oct. 23, 1862. Resigned July 13, 1863.
Adjutant: Lt. Elijah K. Prouty.° Transferred from 8th Vermont Vols. Dismissed Aug. 11, 1863.
Quartermaster: Lt. Charles S. Sauvinet.
Surgeon: Maj. Samuel M. Willis.° Transferred from 26th Mass. Vols. Oct. 23, 1863.
Chaplain: Stephen O. Hodgman.° Only southern white preacher to accept chaplaincy in a black regiment.

Noncommissioned Staff
Sgt. Maj. James Noyes.° Transferred from 8th Vt.
Quartermaster Sgt. Chas. F. Dauchy.° Transferred from 13th Conn.

Appendix 1

Commissary Sgt. Charles Bodman.
Drum Major Paul Belanson. Promoted from Company B, 2nd LaNG.

Line Officers
Ship Island, Mississippi, under Col. Nathan W. Daniels (Companies B, C, D, F, G, I, K)

Captains	*Company*	*Removed/Resigned in 1863*
William B. Barrett	B	July 20
Hannibal Carter	C	May 30
Edward P. Chase	D	May 30
Samuel W. Ringgold	F	July 20
Joseph Villeverd[e]	G	Continued (8/15/64)
William Belley	I	Continued (4/5/64)
Samuel J. Wilkinson	K	July 20
1st Lieutenants		
Joseph Jones	B	July 13
George F. Watson	C	May 30
Louis De Gray	D	May 30
Joseph Wellington	F	May 30
Alphonse Fleury	G	April 4
Ernest A. Hubeau	I	January 22
Calvin B. Glover	K	May 30
2nd Lieutenants		
Peter [Pierre] O. Da[e]premond[t]	B	July 17
Frank L. Trask	C	Continued (2/21/64)
John W. Latting	D	May 30
Solomon Hay[e]s	F	February 18
Theodore[ule] A. Martin	G	Continued (8/15/64)
Jules [Joseph] P. Lewis [Louis]	I	April 4
Jasper Thompson	K	May 30

Officer Roster

Fort Pike, Louisiana, under Lt. Col. Alfred G. Hall (Companies A, E, H)

Captains

P. B. S. Pinchback	A	September 11
Monro[s]e Mu[e]rillion	E	February 24
Arnold Bertonneau	H	March 5

1st Lieutenants

William F. Keeling	A	February 24
Ernest Morphy	E	March 5
Octave Rey	H	March 5

2nd Lieutenants

William Peabody°	A	Continued (8/18/64)
Lucien Scott	E	February 24
Robert H. Isabelle	H	March 5

Source: Names compiled from original muster rolls, October 12, 1862, signed by company captains, and roster of December 12, 1862. Spelling variations appear in brackets. Resignations and removal dates taken from *Official Army Register,* Pt. 8, p. 248, based on dates received, Department of the Gulf. May be different from dates in the diary, from date written, date accepted, or from Special Orders.

°White officer.

Appendix 2
Enlisted Roster with Company Officers

The following remarks are observations and not to be considered definitive conclusions.

French names on the roster might indicate free people of color, although this is scarcely a certainty. The original enlistment of eight out of ten companies individually contained up to a high of 40 percent of French names. Two companies had a notable *absence* of French names.

Companies thought to be free: B and G. Companies thought to be slave: C and K. Others thought to be a mixture, in varying proportions, of free blacks and ex-slaves, with contrabands outnumbering the free men.

Companies B and G fought at Pascagoula. Were *both* companies made up of free blacks? Company G, under forty-nine-year-old Captain Joseph Villeverd, contained the greatest proportion of French names in the regiment. Company B, under Captain William Barrett, although known to be free, had only twelve French names. Companies C and K, probably contrabands, had reputations as troublemakers and were singled out by Daniels as being "ignorant."

A random sample of Company D (Glatthaar, *Forged in Battle*, 273) broke down into the following occupations: blacksmith, bricklayer, brickmaker, carpenter, cigarmaker, clerk, cook, cooper, fisherman, gardener, mechanic, painter, plasterer, servant, shoemaker, steamboat hand, tailor, teamster, tinsmith, and wagoner. No laborers or field hands were listed. Were they free men? There were only one or two French names.

Listed here are 984 men plus 11 field, staff, and noncommissioned staff, for a total regiment of 995, of whom 8 were white. Ages (given in parentheses) often suggest fathers, sons, or brothers. Those over forty or under twenty combined for a quarter of the regiment. The oldest man listed was sixty-one.

Appendix 2

The names are taken from the original Company Muster Rolls, October 12, 1862. Uncertain or inaccurate spelling may often reflect the names' being given orally; some changes/corrections are obtained from later months' entries. *P* denotes a man killed or wounded in the battle at Pascagoula; an asterisk means white.

COMPANY A

Capt. P. B. S. Pinchback (25)
1st Lt. William Keeling (27)
2nd Lt. Samuel Lawrence (27)
  [then William Peabody*]

Sergeants
1st: Butler, William (27)
2nd: Midleton, Charles (22)
3rd: Brooks, George (30)
4th: Hardee, William (19)
5th: Spaulding, Theodore (22)

Corporals
1st: Theodore, Edmund (19)
2nd: Benedict, Peter (23)
3rd: Winslow, Miles (46)
4th: Landre, Clement (26)
5th: Thomas, William (28)
6th: White, Joseph (22)
7th: Thomas, David (24)
8th: Evans, Benjamin (33)

Musicians
Murray, Zachariah (28)
Williams, John (55)

Teamster
Brown, Emmanuel

Privates
Barber, Nicholas (28)
Barrow, Richard (22)
Black, Berry
Brooks, Charles (22)
Burton, John (20)
Clements, John (38)
Clinton, Coy (31)
Colburt, John (37)
Coleman, Daniel (21)
Coleman, William (32)
Congo, August (25)
Congo, Wimba (20)
Craigg, Joseph (31)
[Dapois?], Paul (23)
[Desioux?], Paul (22)
Edward, Prince (28)
Ferry, William (29)
Green, Dick (22)
Green, Richard (22)
Harrison, Benjamin (17)
Harrison, Edmund (40)
Hawthorne, James (22)
Hill, Alexandria (45)
Isaac, Eli (30)
Jacks, Joseph (57)
Jackson, Andrew
Jackson, Ephriam (45)
Jackson, John (22)
Jackson, John N. (27)
Jackson, Nelson (20)
James, Edward (27)
James, Riley (20)
Jones, Alfred (27)
Johnson, James (42)
Johnson, Matthew (30)
Johnson, Raspberry (22)
Johnson, Solomon
Joseph, [Passlido?] (50)
Landre, Edward
Lawrence, [Clemine?] (20)
Lewis, Francois (25)

Enlisted Roster with Company Officers

Levondois, Alfred (30)
Linsey, Moses
Lipscomb, Tony (30)
McJoseph, Kinney (30)
McKay, Aaron (22)
Malcomb, George (20)
Parker, Samuel (43)
Perry, Comodore (61)
[Pethxon?], David (41)
Quima, James (36)
Reddick, Isaiah (22)
Reels, Frederick (40)
Richerdson, William (23)
Richerson, Henry (32)
Ruffin, York (25)
Smith, Daniel (40)
Smith, Joseph (35)
Smith, Sandy (30)
Smith, Simmeon (22)
Sonzett, Henry (18)
Thomas, Charles (48)
Thomas, Foch (33)
Thomas, Henry (50)
Thompson, Lenard (46)
Tonls, Peter (48)
Washington, Maddison (45)
Waters, Henry (26)
Webster, James (38)
Whitehead, Buck (55)
William, Isaac (46)
Wilson, Daniel (29)
Winston, Frank (28)
Woods, Jerome (44)
[Illegible]
Williams, Charles (25)
Williams, [Save?]

COMPANY B

Capt. William Barrett
1st Lt. Joseph Jones
2nd Lt. P. O. Dapremont

Sergeants
1st: Baron, William (23), P
2nd: Campbell, Alfred (25)
3rd: Hill, Henry H. (27)
4th: Dunbar, Paul (21)
5th: Calhoun, John (20)

Corporals
1st: Manuel, John (21)
2nd: [Dubreuil?], John B. (27)
3rd: St. Amont, Raphael (26)
4th: Jordan, [Beryamaine?] (32)
5th: Kelly, John H. (20)
6th: Hottendorf, William (22)
7th: Joseph, Jones (27)
8th: Thomas, Scott (22), P

Musicians
[Belanson], Paul (26)
Reynolds, Charles (27)

Privates
[Alcorn?], Seymour (30)
Anderson, John (25)
Baptiste, Charles (20)
Barber, Stephen (18)
Bennette, Matthew (21)
Bolden, Frederick (18)
Brown, Philip (21)
Campbell, Peter (23)
Chafer, Moses (23)
Chalmers, Henry (24)
Chamblin, Thomas (40)
Chapman, Frank (23)
Charles, Estigneau (23)
Charmois, Joseph A. (27)
Chase, Samuel (27)
Clay, Edward (23)
Coleman, Monroe (27)
Cooper, Mathew (21)
Crawford, William (21)
Davis, Sandy (20)

Davis, Thomas #1 (33)
Davis, Thomas #2 (22)
Denson, George (39)
D'forsa, Paul (18)
Doughty, Willis (20)
Dozier, John (43)
Enoch, James (20)
Felix, Jordan (25)
Fisher, Nelson (26)
Flemmings, Anthony (29)
Fortune, Richard (22)
Francis, George (20)
Fransura, John (37), P
Green, Alexander (23), P
Harper, [Limas?] (27)
Hays, Francis (22)
Hicks, Nathan (30)
Hunter, Alan B. (20)
[Hurete?], George (31)
Jackson, Elijah (32)
Jackson, Manuel (18)
Jeanette, Henry (24)
Johnson, James (25)
Johnson, Laurel (25)
Johnson, Mark (20)
Johnson, [Mupon?] (40)
Johnson, Robert (25)
Joseph, John (18)
Joseph, Moses (34)
Kinslock, S. Zaccharia (22)
Labranche, Lucien (23)
Landre, Charles (20)
Lawrence, Benjamin (27)
Leonard, Joseph (19)
Lewis, Stephen (20)
Merritt, George (23)
Monroe, Henry (43)
Moore, James (24), P
Parker, John (35)
Posy, William (35)

Ransom, Peter (32)
Reid, Mitchell (25)
Roaster, Claiborne (27)
[Ross?], James (20)
Ruffin, Wiley (21)
Sampson, Harvey (36)
Sanders, Jacob (39)
Shaw, Jacob S. (30)
Smith, Westley (21)
Swan, Robert (20), P
Talbot, Patrick (28)
Turner, Joseph (20), P
Ward, Alfred (28)
Ware, John (32)
Washington, Elijah (34)
Williams, Frank (29)
Williams, Robert G. (22)
Williams, William (20)
Wilson, Charles (30)
Wilson, Ogeese (33)

Company C

Capt. Hannibal Carter (27)
1st Lt. George F. Watson (27)
2nd Lt. Frank S. Trask (24)

Sergeants
1st: Douse, Richard (26)
2nd: Mathews, George (24)
3rd: Washington, George (19)
4th: Winchester, William (18)
5th: Joseph, Henry (22)

Corporals
1st: Tuley, Edward (29)
2nd: Forkins, George (28)
3rd: Woods, John[son] (21)
4th: Davis, Gaskill (18)
5th: Stroud, Dennis (27)
6th: Thornton, Alfred (26)

Enlisted Roster with Company Officers

7th: Johnson, Leon (23)
8th: Black, William (25)

Musicians
Davis, Peter (25)
Green, William (19)

Teamster
Glassby, Israel (21)

Privates
Allen, Telemachus (42)
Ames, Henry (23)
Anderson, Robert (44)
Ase, Thomas (32)
Baam, Joseph (22)
Bell, Fred (33)
Bembee, Peter (20)
Bessicks, Charles (23)
Bosley, John (28)
Brown, Clifford (25)
Brown, Robert (30)
Butler, Thomas (40)
Cee, John (24)
Cephas, Joseph (45)
Chapman, John (24)
Chapman, William (29)
Coleman, Samuel (38)
Conley, Thomas (18)
Dumas, Alexander (26)
Fillman, Ben (20)
Givens, Henry (27)
Graham, Charles (28)
Grant, William (32)
Harrison, Samuel (30)
Henderson, Isaac (25)
Henderson, Robert (26)
Henry, John (27)
Hogan, George (28)
Jackson, Andrew (21)
Jackson, Robert (22)
Johnson, Edward (21)
Johnson, Gabriel (28)
Johnson, Manuel (33)
Kenan, Octave (22)
Landor, Lewis (19)
Levan, Lewis (19)
Lewis, Samuel (32)
Madison, Griffe (40)
Millandon, Jacob (39)
Nackir, Charles (23)
Noel, Joseph (40)
Norris, Lee (40)
Oliver, Scott (27)
Oneil, James (22)
Outler, Paul (29)
Page, Fielding (47)
Pleasance, William (45)
Porter, Peter (28)
Powell, William (42)
Pullam, Levi (31)
Ramsey, Major (27)
Raspberry, Edward (42)
Rice, Jack (40)
Richardson, Alfred (21)
Robinson, Obadiah (32)
Rose, John (32)
Royal, Philip (18)
Smith, Calvin (24)
Smith, John (25)
Smith, Lewis (28)
Stevenson, Garritt (28)
Taylor, Lewis (21)
Taylor, Robert (25)
Taylor, Van Meter (28)
Tellman, Perry (19)
Thomas, John (28)
Troutman, Charles (36)
Umfree, Tanko (20)
Valcour, Levi (41)
Victor, Isaac (22)

Walker, Robert (25)
Warrick, [C---sta?] (33)
Washington, James (30)
[Westery?], Lewis (39)
Wilkinson, Abraham (26)
Williams, Frank (28)
Williams, Nelson (23)
Williams, Thomas (23)
Woodley, Henry (42)
Woods, Johnson (20)
[Illegible]
Zelms, Solomon (25)

Company D

Capt. Edward Chase (28)
1st Lt. Louis DeGray (25)
2nd Lt. John W. Latting (30)

Sergeants
1st: Weeks, George W. (19)
2nd: Matthews, George H. (20)
3rd: Taylor, Charles (33)
4th: Thomas, Samuel (33)
5th: Newson, Edward (24)

Corporals
1st: Maning, Giles (48)
2nd: Pryor, George (31)
3rd: Johnson, John (32)
4th: Hill, John (22)
5th: Garner, Richard (45)
6th: Scott, David (29)
7th: Scott, Aleander (19)

Musicians
Fleming, David (21)
Johnson, Alfred (19)

Teamster
Henry, John (40)

Privates
Alcide, Joseph (21)
Alfred, Eugene (20)
Armistead, William (35)
Arnold, James (40)
Barlo, Thomos (32)
Bates, John (45)
Bell, Wesley (47)
Bennett, James (23)
Bentley, William (28)
Bond, Andrew (25)
Boway, Edward (21)
Boyer, Leonard (20)
Boyer, William (19)
Broaden, Robert (32)
Brooks, Daniel (46)
Brown, John (39)
Bush, Levy (35)
Caraway, Lewis (30)
Charleston, Lewis (26)
Colbreath, Henry (22)
Collins, Thomas (24)
Cyrus, Cruton (25)
Demoruelle, Felix (24)
Glenn, Archey (43)
Green, Beverly (27)
Green, John D. (44)
Green, Willis (24)
Hale, Nelson (33)
Harrison, Gilbert (21)
Henderson, Edward (42)
Henson, Alfred (21)
Hickey, Benjamin (39)
Hill, George (39)
Hill, Moses (25)
Holston, Charles (33)
Jefferson, Lewis (28)
Johnson, Lewis (25)
Jones, Henry (26)
Jordan, Alfred (24)

Enlisted Roster with Company Officers

Kent, Basile (27)
Key, Eanus (19)
Lane, Edward (21)
Lewis, John (48)
Louis, August (23)
Mankin, Frederick (38)
Martin, Alfred (36)
Moore, Madison (27)
Morton, Wilson (40)
Myers, Alexander (26)
Newby, Joshua (22)
Palmer, Peter (22)
Parker, James (22)
Parsly, Christmas (23)
Perkins, Robert (20)
Reed, Manuel (21)
Rice, George (27)
Richardson, Prince (34)
Ridly, Augustus (23)
Robert, William #1 (21)
Robert, William #2 (23)
Robinson, John (35)
Robinson, Thomas (24)
Rollins, Charles (28)
Sewell, Robert (33)
Simpkin, Crawford (28)
Smith, Charles (39)
Smith, Edward (25)
Smith, Henry
Smith, Robert (26)
Smith, William (23)
Spratly, Gilbert (30)
Swan, Simion (37)
Thomas, Edward (37)
Thunly, William (36)
Ware, James (42)
Washington, George (21)
Webb, Moses (42)
Westland, Rufus (30)
Williams, Kenian (30)

COMPANY E

Capt. Monrose Murillion
1st Lt. Ernest Morphy
2nd Lt. Lucien Scott

Sergeants

1st: Picou, Alexander (17)
2nd: Picou, Aristide (28)
3rd: Bernard, John (25)
4th: Herare, Manuel (23)

Corporals

1st: Chevalier, Armand (22)
2nd: Gronge, Numa (26)
3rd: Allaine, Emile (25)
4th: Picou, Dussuau (20)
5th: Desbordes, Francois (27)
6th: Rosario, Jules (44)
7th: Monde, Manuel (25)
8th: Lincoln, James (20)

Musician

Gale, John

Teamster

[None listed]

Privates

Adams, George (42)
Allain, Albert (18)
Auguste, Charles (26)
Baquet, Radolph (18)
Bosque, Eugene (38)
Brady, Henry (21)
Brown, Joe (32)
Bryan, Sam (35)
Celestin, John (45)
Chausel, Gabriel (40)
Clay, Henry (35)
Danford, Bennett (37)
Decomb, Charles (24)
Dixson, Oscar (28)

Appendix 2

Dix, Amade (19)
Doucet, Aristite (23)
[Dutel?], Eugene (28)
Edward, [Prier?] (22)
Eugene, Andre (24)
Felix, Joe (17)
Fogussen, Henry (22)
Garcond, Armond (17)
Godinse, Eugene (23)
Green, Louis (24)
Gronge, Everise (45)
Groun, Medilice (23)
Henry, Charles (19)
Henry, Joe (32)
Hollande, Joseph (21)
Homar, Charley (24)
Horay, Edward (18)
Hortaire, Zaman (21)
Jean, Baptiste M. (23)
Johnson, David (38)
Johnson, William (23)
Jones, Alfred (21)
Joseph, Paul (27)
Labastry, Eugene (42)
Lacoste, Fortune (45)
Lary, Daniel (17)
Lary, Thomas (22)
Lee, Washington (19)
Long, Thomas (32)
Loraine, John (40)
Louis, Erneste (24)
McDowl, George (22)
Manuel, Louis (26)
Michel, Jacob (20)
Monde, [H]Albert (19)
Moreau, Julien (18)
Nelson, Stafford (19)
Nicholson, George (28)
Octave, Pierre (20)
Peron, Francis (19)

Pierre, John (20)
Praker, John (26)
Princianes, John [Joseph] (18)
Prosper, Harry (39)
Randall, John (19)
Ranier, J. Baptiste (29)
Rene, [Casemare?] (45)
Richardson, John (44)
Robertson, Joe (20)
Ruby, Surrier (34)
Salamon, John (25)
Sanders, Daniel (26)
Scott, Anthony (43)
Shelby, John (19)
Silvain, Joseph (44)
Simon, Westly (23)
Smith, Jacob (28)
Thurner, Richard (19)
[Uchetkerion?], Alfred (19)
Victor, John (20)
Walker, Richard (25)
[Illegible]
Walton, Peter (42)
Watson, Alfred (44)
Watson, Peter (42)
White, John (37)
[Willembre?], William (37)
William, Julien Fouchet (25)
William, William (21)
Williams, Sam Robertson (38)
Wilson, Hippolite Raymond (44)
Wilson, Isaac (28)
Wilson, Jerry (24)
Young, Jerry (20)

COMPANY F

Capt. Samuel Ringgold
1st Lt. Joseph Wellington
2nd Lt. Solomon Hays

Enlisted Roster with Company Officers

Sergeants
1st: Sheppheard, Richard (37)
2nd: Warren, D. L. (20)
3rd: Pinckney, Samuel (26)
4th: Simmons, Thomas (22)
5th: Russell, Sanford (33)

Corporals
1st: Wilson, Henry
2nd: Baker, Thomas (22)
3rd: Richardson, Isaac (38)
4th: Bell, Syrus (35)
5th: Carry, John (44)
6th: Fuller, John (38)
7th: Armstrong, Alfred (35)
8th: Hogan, Samuel (45)

Musicians
Giles, William F. (31)
Smith, Joseph (25)

Teamster
Bibbins, Alfred (45)

Privates
[Adain?], James (27)
Alexander, Elijah (25)
Anderson, Robert (36)
Baley, John (36)
Baptiste, Jean (35)
[Baxley?], Isaac (35)
Beamon, James (34)
Bennett, [Moses?] (38)
Blackwell, John (33)
Butler, David (44)
Chester, John (25)
Claiborne, John (19)
Coleman, Archie (45)
Cook, Joshua (45)
[Crucell?], Charles (18)
Dennis, Alfred (40)
Dorsey, John (43)
Dudley, Elijah (44)
Duyon, Arain (27)
Edwards, Mingo (42)
Fil[l]more, Joseph (27)
Fisher, Joseph (23)
Fraiser [Frazier], Sim[m]on (20)
Gabriel, Joseph (28)
Gaunt, Charles (24)
Giles, Major (27)
Graves, London (27)
Green, Fenton (33)
Gross, Benjamin (40)
Harris, David (45)
Harris, Joseph (29)
Harrison, William (36)
Henry, John (21)
Hense, Jerry (45)
Holto[e]n, Robert (20)
Irwin, Alfred (19)
Irwin, Alphonse (19)
Johnson, Henry (40)
Jones, Nelson (39)
Kairo, Edward (23)
Levi, Thomas (45)
McKinney, Peter (23)
Mathew, Joseph #1 (35)
Mathew, Joseph #2 (21)
Mitchell, Berry (45)
Nelson, Williams (24)
Nicholson, Nathaniel (24)
Peter, Eli (22)
Peter, William (26)
Pierre, John (24)
Pollard, William (27)
Price, George (36)
Prior, Benjamin (25)
Raison, Giles (18)
Randolph, William (26)
Reynolds, Charles (36)
Riley, Nelson (28)

Robain, Octave (31)
Robertson, John (23)
Roe, Morgan (21)
Ross, David (45)
Rubin, Joseph (25)
Samuel, William (31)
Simmons, James (21)
Spencer, Edward (27)
Spencer, Rubin (23)
Sulivan, Samuel (23)
Sully, Elijah (22)
[Terry?], Samuel (24)
Thornton, William (32)
Walker, James (44)
Weakes, Frederick (26)
William, Daniel (25)
William, Henry (24)
William, Henry (36)
Young, Danbridge (33)

Company G

Capt. Joseph Villeverd[e] (49)
1st Lt. Alphonse Fleury (32)
2nd Lt. Theodule Martin (25)

Sergeants
1st: Martin, Thomas (19)
2nd: Duluc, Etienne (24)
3rd: Frilot, Arthur (20)
4th: Martin, Louis (21)
5th: Lavigney, J. B. (32)

Corporals
1st: Forestals, Martin (32)
2nd: Duval, Emile (22)
3rd: Ducre, Gustave (36)
4th: Naroce, Joseph (33)
5th: Polin, Poree (26)
6th: Alugas, Jerome (20)
7th: Boutin, Ernest (20)
8th: Signac, Pierre (30)

Musician
Thompson, George (22)

Teamster
Carriere, Arthur (28)

Privates
Alexis, Isadore (23)
Alfred, Joseph (22)
Berquier, Henry (28)
Bertonniere, Pierre (26)
Biani, Joseph (27)
Brooks, Henry (35)
Brown, John (23)
Butler, John (20)
Caniel, Sam (45)
Carey, Colman (32)
Carter, Hatcher (45)
Castille, Joseph (45)
Castin, Theophile (19)
Clay, Henry (26)
Collins, Thomas (35)
Delile, Antoine (24)
Dewson, Alexander (22)
Donbar, Isaac (26)
Donelson, Joseph (31)
Dorensbourg, Jacques (20)
Dorensbourg, Lorent (19)
Drew, Thomas (22)
Dufreine, Joseph (24)
Duval, Charles (22)
Edouard, Francois (25)
Edmond, Manuel (39)
Edward, William (19)
Fagot, Victor (23)
Fills, Columbus (26)
Fischer, Robin (35)
Fischer, William (26)
Fouret, Belfort (26)
Francis, [Jessy?] (33)
Franklin, Samuel (26)

Enlisted Roster with Company Officers

Fulton, Alfred (23)
Ginkens, J. Henry (23)
Gordon, Dick (40)
Grant, Brister (27)
Hambleton, Patrick (30)
Isidore, Francois (25)
Jackson, Andrew O. (24)
John, Henry (20)
John, Woodson (36)
Johnson, James (24)
Johnson, King (35)
Johnson, William (24)
Lamois, J. Baptiste (20)
Latrobe, Belmont (26)
Leche, Augustin (23)
Louis, Price (19)
Loyer, Francois (19)
[Lu?], Joseph (25)
Manuel, Oscar (29)
Martin, St. Victor (20)
Mason, Joseph (33)
Nash, Thompton (35)
Povee, Anthony (33)
Povee, Ernest (22)
Povee, Medard (19)
Price, Kater (25)
Ring, George (25)
Sedan, Robert (40)
Simon, Leon (26)
Smith, Smart (30)
Tchara, Touton (23)
Thompson, Cornelius (30)
Vargen, Joe (23)
Vest, George (21)
Victor, John (22)
Victor, Marseille (20)
Walker, John (34)
Washington, Colman (20), *P*
Williams, John (20)
Willian, Joseph (24)

Willis, Joseph (26)
Wilson, John (24)
Wood, George (23)
[Woodberry?], Algiers (20)
Woods, William (23)

COMPANY H

Capt. Arnold Bertonneau (28)
1st Lt. Elijah King Prouty* (26)
   [shortly Octave Rey]
2nd Lt. Octave Rey (25)
   [shortly Robert H. Isabelle]

Sergeants
1st: Johnson, [Sanely?] (35)
2nd: Defille, J. B. (27)
3rd: Thomas, Louis (28)
4th: Marshall, George (30)
5th: Jones, Anthony F. (28)

Corporals
1st: Jailliot, Jules (27)
2nd: Hamot, Anatole S. (20)
3rd: Jackson, Baptiste (20)
4th: Williams, Spenser (45)
5th: Owens, Harrison (20)
6th: Gravier, Brenard, Sr. (47)
7th: Gravier, Brenard, Jr. (20)
8th: Williams, Henry (27)

Musicians
Franklin, Charles (27)
Turner, John (31)

Teamster
Shinks, Henry (35)

Privates
Akins, Tim (19)
Allen, John (40)
Anderson, James (23)
Anderson, Moses (24)

Appendix 2

Bentley, Charles (25)
Boston, Lucien (24)
Bowman, Wallace (28)
Bryant, Edouard (21)
Burch, Peter (27)
Camell, Joseph (18)
Castre, Felil (27)
Cizer, Charley (27)
Cook, Gilford (18)
Cook, Thomas (24)
Cooper, [Paul?] (24)
Cornish, Joseph (36)
Daniel, Augustin (18)
Denis, John (31)
Dunn, George (26)
Edmund, William G. (20)
Edouards, Silas (21)
Ellis, John (33)
Enlow, George (30)
[Fritor?], George
Gaines, Robert (24)
Gaskin, Oscar (26)
Gibins, Edouard (27)
Grein, Henry (39)
Hanson, Ned (38)
Henry, John (22)
Herbert, Peet (18)
Ige, Henry (18)
Jackson, Andrew (25)
Jones, David (35)
Jones, Paul (24)
Jones, Samuel (25)
Johnson, Elijah (27)
Johnson, Jefferson (29)
Julien, Edouard (30)
Kind, Henry (24)
Larcer, Charles (20)
McCann, Anatol (20)
Madison, George (24)
[Meach?], Eli (20)
Miller, Ferdinand (18)

Mitchell, Caro (27)
Mitchell, Simon (31)
Mosby, Alfred (19)
Newton, John (22)
Pauche, Julian (20)
Payne, Calvin (30)
Peters, Stephen (23)
Pierson, William (44)
Prosper, Louis (21)
Reed, Moses (23)
Redick, Alfred (30)
Richardson, George (35)
Robertson, Stephen (30)
Rubin, Henry (24)
Smith, Alexander (21)
Smith, John (26)
Sova, Sedic (22)
Spot, Alexandria (42)
Stanislas, Victor (30)
Strange, John (21)
Thomas, George (25)
Thomas, Louis (24)
Thompson, John [29?]
Trotter, Alex (30)
Vincent, Charles (25)
Washington, George (23)
Washington, Isaac (27)
William, Madison (25)
Williams, Isrill (26)
Williams, James (30)
Woods, Robert (22)

Company I

Capt. William Belley
1st Lt. Ernest Hubeau
2nd Lt. Jules P. Louis

Sergeants
1st: Bordeaux, J. A. (25)
2nd: Vida, Adrien (20)
3rd: Bellevue, Joseph (25)

Enlisted Roster with Company Officers

4th: Martin, Louis (30)
5th: Mainduburg, Estene (19)

Corporals
1st: Wallace, [Jessy?] (28)
2nd: Bonne, Paul (42)
3rd: William, Thomas (24)
4th: Labaud, Joseph (23)
5th: Toolmar, Joseph (30)
6th: Ford, Louis (37)
7th: Flemming, Peter (31)
8th: Carro, Joseph (27)

Musicians
Cizard, Philip (43)
Harrison, Harry (19)

Teamster
Bodley, York (44)

Privates
Adbair, John (23)
Alexander, Leon (21)
Anderson, Robert (21)
Antoine, August (44)
Antoine, Paul (22)
Ardie, Joseph (38)
Baker, Jefferson (21)
Bellevue, Thomas (17)
Biamie, Jules (48)
Blanchard, Felix (21)
Brien, Alexander (21)
Brown, Paul (22)
Camille, Paul (30)
Carter, Samuel (22)
Cheller, John (23)
Charpanter, Eugene (21)
Chata, Philip (18)
Clay, Victor (18)
Clofa, Tousin (20)
Daboval, George (42)
Davis, Edward (22)
Delasize, Charles (20)

Doliole, Gaspard (42)
Edward, Harchie (24)
Eigley, Alfred (25)
Fisherman, Sam (27)
Fostaine, John (28)
Frank, Alcide (19)
Grandin, March (26)
Grims, George (22)
Guino, Etienne (19)
Hays, Bobby (21)
Hegman, Charles (31)
Henry, James (27)
Herman, Anderson (22)
Jackson, Garland (21)
Jackson, Henry I. (24)
John, Cornelius (19)
Johnson, Alfred (43)
Joseph, Edward (26)
Joseph, Henry (23)
Jourdon, Alphonse (22)
Julien, Narcisse (25)
Landre, Pierre (20)
Lawrence, William (18)
Lee, John (23)
Lewis, Joseph (42)
Mackinney, Louis (42)
McQuilty, Enoch (21)
Marcelin, William (22)
Morico, Joseph (21)
Nadore, Felly (21)
Nichols, Henry (24)
Nunan, John (26)
Oubry, Ayenor M. (20)
Padat, August (20)
Pascale, Edmand (37)
Peter, John (24)
Philip, Hiler (25)
Pierre, Harmogene (32)
Polfat, John (23)
Powell, Thomas (22)
Roben, George (45)

Appendix 2

Robe[r]tson, Harvey (29)
Rovira, Alexis (22)
[Sanneselle?], Victor (20)
Small, Peter (27)
Smith, Allendo (22)
Smith, Celasten (21)
Smith, Grefen (25)
Smith, Milton (22)
Thomas, William H. (21)
Valsin, Thomas (20)
Vinet, Joseph (21)
Webster, William (25)
Wells, Henry (21)
William, Charles (19)
William, John (27)
Wilson, Julien (25)

COMPANY K

Capt. Samuel J. Wilkinson (28)
1st Lt. Calvin Glover (22)
2nd Lt. Jasper Thompson (34)

Sergeants
1st: Holmes, George (19)
2nd: Campbell, Charles (18)
3rd: Steptoe, William (31)
4th: Johnson, Richard (31)
5th: Jones, Henry (28)

Corporals
1st: Brown, Edward (35)
2nd: Sheppard, Moses (24)
3rd: Santiago, St. Tlisse (23)
4th: Anora, John (38)
5th: Parker, George (25)
6th: Holmes, Richard (24)
7th: Draper, William (26)
8th: Mack, Thomas (24)

Musician
Welsh, Joseph (45)

Teamster
Preston, Hector (45)

Privates
Abram, Isaac (22)
Adam, John (39)
Alfred, Robert[s?] (21)
Allemar, Francis (24)
Amadie, St. Louis (18)
Azoff, Clement (21)
Baptiste, George (25)
Baptiste, John (32)
Baseau, Julien (35)
[Boss?], William (32)
Boswell, Major (25)
Bowman, Peter (25)
Boyd, Harrison (32)
Brook, Zachariah (35)
Brooks, George (20)
Brooks, Samuel (25)
Brown, Preston (28)
Burns, Samuel (41)
Butler, George (21)
[Ceason?], Spenser (26)
Charles, Clement (26)
Cleo, Celestine (21)
Criven, James (31)
Davis, Amos (25)
Dennis, Reymor (35)
Draco, David (20)
Edwards, Joseph (20)
Estare, Louis (26)
Ettienne, Frevoll (22)
Fister, Louis (21)
Francis, Oscar (25)
Godley, Joseph (25)
Graham, Fricker (44)
Graham, Samuel (24)
Hamilton, Isaac (21)
Harrison, Edmond (30)

Enlisted Roster with Company Officers

Henry, John (37)
Hickman, John (44)
Johnason, Harry (19)
Johnson, Allen (34)
Johnson, Samuel (22)
Johnson, William #1 (23)
Johnson, William #2 (39)
Jones, Henry (43)
Jones, Nathan (28)
Jones, William (28)
Joseph, Augustine (24)
Joseph, Eugene (23)
Joseph, Gabriel (28)
Lumbert, Andrew (22)
Lumsey, Charles (39)
McLaine, William[s] (25)
Mitchell, Eli (30)
Parker, Jessie (27)
Parraway, Robert (27)
Pauzey, John (38)
Phillips, Brice (25)
Pope, Gibson (40)

Proudfoot, Manuel (45)
Reed, Charles (21)
Robertson, Alexander (25)
Rube, Brill (22)
Saunders, Ephrihim (31)
Short, William (21)
Simmons, Frank (25)
Smith, David (26)
Smith, Dred (43)
Smith, Robert (18)
Staton, Mansfield (40)
Taylor, William (19)
Tollvier, William (43)
Turner, Louis (25)
Undley, Samuel (35)
Voltaire, Henry (31)
Watson, Joshua (22)
West, Roberts (22)
William, John (26)
Wilson, Joseph (20)
Wilson, Robert (21)
Young, Caesar (20)

Appendix 3
Ships and Captains

The following vessels called at Ship Island during the period of January 12 to April 29, 1863; the names of the captains are given if known. *Source: ORN*, Ser. I, Vol. XIX, pp. xv, xvi, 477, 595, Vol. XX, p. xiii; Daniels Diary.

Antona. Screw steamer, 565 tons, 56 crew, 4 guns.
Belle. Sloop.
Belle of Mobile. Schooner.
Brooklyn. Screw steamer, 2,070 tons, 259 crew, 25 guns. Commodore H. H. Bell.
Circassian. Supply steamer, 1,750 tons, 142 crew, 6 guns. Acting Volunteer Lt. William B. Eaton.
Clifton. Gunboat/side-wheel steamer, 892 tons, 121 crew, 8 guns. Lt. Comdr. Richard L. Law.
Eastern Queen. Steamer, U.S. Army transport, 881 tons. Capt. [?] Collins.
Eliza Anne. Schooner.
General Banks. Steamer, U.S. Army transport.
Ann Houghton. Bark, 326 tons, 27 crew, 2 guns. Acting Master N. Graham.
John P. Jackson. Gunboat/side-wheel steamer, 787 tons, 99 crew, 6 guns. Lt. Comdr. Henry A. Adams, then Acting Master N. D'Oyly.
Mississippi. Side-wheel steamer, U.S. transport, 1,692 tons, 229 crew, 12 guns. Capt. M. Smith/Capt. [?] Baxter.
Morning Star. U.S. mail steamer.
Nassau. Gunboat/side-wheel steamer.
New Brunswick. Steamer, U.S. Army transport, 909 tons.
New England. Gov't ship/War Dept. quartermaster's vessel (carried coal), 439 tons. Capt. [?] Edgerlady.

Appendix 3

Pinola. Gunboat, 507 tons, 75 crew, 4 guns. Lt. Comdr. James Stillwell.

Relief. Store ship, 468 tons, 51 crew, 3 guns. Acting Volunteer Lt. Benjamin D. Manton.

Rocky Hill. Schooner.

Tennessee. Side-wheel steamer, U.S. transport, 1,275 tons, 217 crew, 5 guns. Lt. Comdr. P. C. Johnson, then Acting Master J. D. Childs.

Union. Supply ship, screw steamer, 1,114 tons.

Vincennes. Sloop of war, 700 tons, 162 crew, 19 guns. Lt. Comdr. John Madigan, then Lt. Comdr. Henry A. Adams.

Venturi. Schooner.

William Hunter. Schooner. Tim Baker.

Bibliography

COLLECTIONS, DIARIES

Houghton Library, Harvard University, Cambridge
Palfrey, John Gorham. Papers.

In possession of C. P. Weaver
Daniels, Nathan W. Diary II (May 16, 1864–December 8, 1865).
Daniels, Nathan W. Diary III (January 4, 1865–May 29, 1867).
Daniels, Nathan W. Scrapbook (Newspaper articles).

Library of Congress, Washington, D.C.
Banks, Nathaniel P. Collection.
Butler, Benjamin F. Collection.

The Historic New Orleans Collection, New Orleans
Rust, Henry. Diary (September 4, 1863–December 26, 1864). Manuscript Division, MSS 261.

University of Maryland
Freedmen and Southern Society Project.

United States Army Military History Institute, Carlisle Barracks, Pennsylvania
Rust, Henry. Diary (July 11, 1862–January 21, 1863). Commandery Collection, Military Order of the Loyal Legion of the United States.

GOVERNMENT DOCUMENTS

General Services Administration. "Tabular Analysis of the Records of the U.S. Colored Troops and Their Predecessor Units in the National Archives of the

United States." National Archives and Records Service. 1973; rpr. Washington, D.C., 1985.

National Archives, Washington, D.C.
Compiled Records Showing Service of Military Units in Volunteer Union Organizations, M-594.
Record Group 24: Records of Bureau of Naval Personnel.
Record Group 45: U.S. Navy, Volumes of Officer Records, Resignation of Officers, 1863.
Record Group 77: Records of the Office of the Chief of Engineers.
Record Group 94: Records of the Adjutant General's Office, 1780s–1917.
    8th Vermont Volunteer Infantry.
        Regimental Orders, Descriptive Records. 4 vols.
    74th U.S. Colored Infantry [USCI].
        Carded Military Service Records, Volunteer Organizations, Civil War.
        Office of Adjutant's Regimental Papers.
        Returns, Muster Rolls, Regimental Papers.
        Regimental Books, Adjutant General's Office. 2 vols.
Record Group 153: Records of the Office of the Judge Advocate General.
Record Group 393: Records of the U.S. Army Continental Commands, 1821–1920, Department of the Gulf, Part 1.
    Series 1741. Copies of Letters Sent, 1862–1863.
    Series 1747. Register of Letters Received, 1863.
    Series 1752. Register of Letters Received, January 1863–December 1864.
    Series 1756. Letters Received, 1863, Boxes 1–6.
    Series 1763. General Orders, March 1862–December 1863.
    Series 1767. Special Orders, October 1861–August 1866.
    Series 1770. Miscellaneous Orders Received, 1862–1865.
    Series 1818. Letters Sent and Orders Issued by Engineer Office, January–December 1863.
    Series 1842. Provost Marshal Office, General Records, Register of Letters Received, January–May 1863.
    Series 1844. Provost Marshal Office, Letters Received, March–December 1863.
    Series 1918. Civil Affairs, Register of Letters Received, Vol. I, January 1863–December 1864.

National Park Service, Technical Information Center, Denver, Colorado.
Bearss, Edwin, C. *Historic Resource Study, Ship Island, Harrison County, Mississippi: Gulf Islands National Seashore, Florida/Mississippi.* July, 1984.

———. *Historic Structure Report, Administrative and Historical Data Section, Fort Massachusetts, Ship Island, Harrison County, Mississippi, 1857–1935: Gulf Islands National Seashore, Florida/Mississippi.* January 1984.

Other Official Publications

Official Army Register of the Volunteer Force of the United States Army for the Years 1861–1865. Washington, D.C., 1865–1867, Pt. 8.

Official Records of the Union and Confederate Navies in the War of the Rebellion. 30 vols. Washington, D.C., 1894–1922.

Revised U.S. Army Regulations of 1861. Washington, D.C., 1867.

The War of the Rebellion: A Compilation of the Official Records of the Union and Confederate Armies. 128 vols. Washington, D.C., 1880–1901.

Books

Primary

Berlin, Ira, et al., eds. *Freedom: A Documentary History of Emancipation 1861–1867.*
    Ser. 1, Vol. I, *The Destruction of Slavery.* New York, 1985.
    Ser. 1, Vol. III, *The Wartime Genesis of Free Labor: The Lower South.* New York, 1990.
    Ser. 2, *The Black Military Experience.* New York, 1982.

Carpenter, George. *History of the Eighth Regiment Vermont Volunteers, 1861–1865.* Boston, 1886.

Hepworth, George Hughes. *The Whip, Hoe, and Sword; or, The Gulf-Department in '63.* 1864; rpr. Baton Rouge, 1979.

Higginson, Thomas Wentworth. *Army Life in a Black Regiment.* 1869; rpr. New York, 1984.

Irwin, Richard B. *History of the Nineteenth Army Corps.* New York, 1892.

Johnson, Robert U., and Clarence C. Buel, eds. *Battles and Leaders of the Civil War.* 4 vols. New York, 1887.

Lufkin, Edwin B. *History of the Thirteenth Maine Regiment from Its Organization in 1861 to Its Muster-Out in 1865.* Bridgton, Maine, 1898.

Secondary

Bell, Caryn Cossé. *Revolution, Romanticism, and the Afro-Creole Protest Tradition in Louisiana, 1718–1868.* Baton Rouge, 1997.

Berlin, Ira. *Slaves Without Masters: The Free Negro in the Antebellum South.* New York, 1974.

Berlin, Ira, et al. *Slaves No More: Three Essays on Emancipation and the Civil War.* New York, 1992.

Bibliography

Blassingame, John W. *Black New Orleans, 1860–1880*. Chicago, 1973.
Boatner, Mark M. III. *The Civil War Dictionary.* 1959; rpr. New York, 1991.
Braude, Ann. *Radical Spirits: Spiritualism and Women's Rights in Nineteenth-Century America.* Boston, 1989.
Capers, Gerald M. *Occupied City: New Orleans Under the Federals, 1862–1865.* Lexington, Ky., 1965.
Catton, Bruce. *Grant Takes Command.* Boston, 1969.
Cornish, Dudley. *The Sable Arm: Negro Troops in the Union Army, 1861–1865.* New York, 1966.
Donald, David. *Divided We Fought.* New York, 1952.
Dyer, Frederick H. *A Compendium of the War of the Rebellion.* 1908; rpr. Dayton, 1978.
Foner, Eric. *A Short History of Reconstruction, 1863–1877.* New York, 1990.
Foote, Shelby. *Fredericksburg to Meridian.* 1963; rpr. New York, 1986. Vol. II of Foote, *The Civil War: A Narrative.* 3 vols.
Gehman, Mary. *The Free People of Color of New Orleans.* New Orleans, 1994.
Glatthaar, Joseph T. *Forged in Battle: The Civil War Alliance of Black Soldiers and White Officers.* New York, 1990.
Grant, Ulysses S. *Personal Memoirs.* Vol. I of 2 vols. New York, 1885.
Guernsey, Alfred H., and Howard M. Alden. *Harper's Pictorial History of the Great Rebellion,* Pt. 1. Chicago, 1866.
Harrington, Fred Harvey. *Fighting Politician: Major General N. P. Banks.* Philadelphia, 1948.
Hollandsworth, James G. *The Louisiana Native Guards: The Black Military Experience During the Civil War.* Baton Rouge, 1995.
Horan, James D. *Mathew Brady: Historian with a Camera.* New York, 1955.
Mays, Joe H. *Black Americans and Their Contributions Toward Union Victory in the American Civil War, 1861–1865.* Lanham, Md., 1984.
McPherson, James M. *Battle Cry of Freedom: The Civil War Era.* New York, 1989.
———. *The Negro's Civil War: How American Negroes Felt and Acted During the War for the Union.* New York, 1965.
———. *Ordeal By Fire: The Civil War and Reconstruction.* New York, 1982.
———. *What They Fought For, 1861–1865.* Baton Rouge, 1994.
Nevin, John. *Salmon P. Chase: A Biography.* New York, 1995.
Parton, James. *General Butler in New Orleans: History of the Administration of the Department of the Gulf in the Year 1862.* Boston, 1868.
Phillips, Charles, and Alan Axelrod. *My Brother's Face: Portraits of the Civil War.* San Francisco, 1993.

Quarles, Benjamin. *The Negro in the Civil War*. Boston, 1953.
Redkey, Edwin S. *A Grand Army of Black Men: Letters from African-American Soldiers in the Union Army, 1861–1865*. New York, 1992.
Stern, Philip Van Doren. *The Confederate Navy: A Pictorial History*. Garden City, N.Y., 1962.
Taylor, Joe Gray. *Louisiana Reconstructed, 1863–1877*. Baton Rouge, 1974.
Tunnell, Ted. *Crucible of Reconstruction: War, Radicalism, and Race in Louisiana*. Baton Rouge, 1984.
Warner, Ezra J. *Generals in Blue: Lives of the Union Commanders*. Baton Rouge, 1964.
———. *Generals in Gray: Lives of the Confederate Commanders*. Baton Rouge, 1959.
Westwood, Howard C. *Black Troops, White Commanders, and Freedmen During the Civil War*. Carbondale, Ill., 1992.
Wilson, Joseph T. *The Black Phalanx: A History of the Negro Soldiers of the United States Wars of 1775–1812 and 1861–1865*. 1890; rpr. New York, 1994.
Winters, John D. *The Civil War in Louisiana*. 1963; rpr. Baton Rouge, 1991.

ARTICLES, PAMPHLETS

Berry, Mary F. "Negro Troops in Blue and Gray: The Louisiana Native Guards, 1861–1863." *Louisiana History*, VIII (Spring 1967), 165–90.
Blassingame, John W. "The Selection of Officers and Non-Commissioned Officers of Negro Troops in the Union Army, 1863–1865." *Negro History Bulletin* (January 1967), 8–11.
Burns, Zed H. "Ship Island: An Annotated Bibliography." *Journal of Mississippi History*, XXXII (May 1990), 147–51.
Everett, Donald E. "Ben Butler and the Louisiana Native Guards, 1861–1862." *Journal of Southern History*, XXIV (May 1958), 202–17.
Gardner's Business Directory. New Orleans, 1861. The Historic New Orleans Collection, New Orleans.
Joshi, Manoj K., and Joseph P. Reidy. "'To Come Forward and Aid in Putting Down This Unholy Rebellion': The Officers of Louisiana's Free Black Native Guard During the Civil War Era." *Southern Studies*, XXI (Fall 1982), 326–42.
Scott, Robert Davis. "The Curious Civil War Career of James George Brown, Spy." *Prologue*, XXVI (spring 1994), 17–31.
Weinert, Richard P. "The Neglected Key to the Gulf Coast." *Journal of Mississippi History*, XXXI (November 1969), 269–301.
Westwood, Howard C. "Benjamin Butler's Enlistment of Black Troops in New Orleans in 1862." *Louisiana History*, XXVI (Winter 1985), 5–22.

Newpapers

Boston *Daily Transcript*
New Orleans *Era*
New Orleans *Picayune*
New Orleans *Tribune*
New York *Daily Tribune*
New York *Herald*

Index

Adams, Henry A., 30, 38, 39, 41, 50, 54, 56, 58, 61, 65, 70, 74, 83, 99, 127, 135, 139, 140; testimony for Daniels, 130, 132, 133, 136, 138
Alabama River, 56, 72
Alabama (ship), 48
Albatross (ship), 59 n. 50
Alcide, Joseph, 51
Alexander, Dr. [?], 95
Algiers, La., 17, 20
American Freedmen's Inquiry Commission, 109, 149 n. 81, 171
Anderson, Robert, 139–40 n. 63
Anderson, W. P., 172
Atchafalaya River, 65 n. 61

Bailey, Theodorus, 162
Baker, Timothy, 91
Banks, Nathaniel P., xvi–xvii, 30, 32; examination board, 33; views on black officers, 35–36, 110, 116; raising 4th LaNG, 45, 46; Port Hudson campaign, 45, 53, 54, 59, 62, 64, 73, 112–14, 123; at Bayou Teche and western Louisiana, 45, 88, 89, 90n, 103, 108, 111–12, 122; on Native Guards, 75, 152, 165; rule of New Orleans, 107–108; establishes Corps d'Afrique, 110–11; political activity, 119–20, 135, 148, 152, 165; use of spy Brown, 120, 142–43, 144, 148, 164, 171; in Daniels' dismissal, 138, 142, 144, 148, 150, 160, 162–63, 164, 170; on 13th Maine, 158–59; sixty-day regiments, 167–68, 169; in Washington, 174; mentioned, 31, 61, 79, 85, 108 n. 3, 125, 126
Baron, William, 84n
Barrett, William, 44, 61, 79, 91, 114–15, 169–70
Bassett, Chauncey, 11–12 n. 15, 118
Baton Rouge, La., 9, 45, 112, 118, 135
Bayou Sara, La. 126–27, 127 n. 39, 135
Bayou Teche, La., 16, 45, 88, 111, 146
Beckwith, Edward G., 131, 164
Bell, Henry H., 38, 98, 99; mentioned, 148
Belley, William, 143
Bertonneau, Arnold, 33, 63, 169; mentioned 52 n. 42, 61 n. 56, 94–95 n. 88
Berwick Bay, La., 16, 64, 110
Biloxi, Miss., 76, 77; mentioned, 71, 72
Bischoff, E., 127, 128
Bisland, La., 88 n. 82, 90n
Black officers. *See* Louisiana Native Guards
Black troops, xv–xvi, xix–xx, 7–8, 109, 110–11, 157–58
Blas family. *See* Ship Island, Miss.: Refugees

Index

Bodman, Charles, 93
Bond, Andrew, 51
Boston *Liberator*, 100
Boston *Transcript*, 51
Boutte Station, La., 17, 28 n. 6
Brady, Mathew, xviii–xix
Bowen, James, 145
Bragg, Braxton, 58
Brashear City, La., 17, 19, 31, 48, 110
Bray, James Forter, 94
Brooklyn (ship), 38, 39, 98, 99, 101, 104, 127 n. 40
Brown, James George, 120, 121, 138, 142–49 *passim*, 164, 171
Buckner, Simon B., 48
Buell, Don Carlos, 71
Bureau of Colored Troops, 111
Bureau of Refugees, Freedmen, and Abandoned Lands. *See* Freedmen's Bureau
Burnside, Ambrose, 59, 152 n. 88
Butler, Andrew, 20
Butler, Benjamin F.: raising Louisiana Native Guards, xvi, 9–15, 96, 109, 115, 157, 159; on Ship Island, 1; in New Orleans, 5–6, 7, 20, 21; and contrabands, 6, 7; and Phelps controversy, 8–9; on Baton Rouge, 9; and Godfrey Weitzel protest, 18; discipline of 8th Vermont Volunteer Infantry, 28 n. 6; opposition to, 20, 135; political ties of, 148 n. 80; as commander Department of the James, 166 n. 18; mentioned, 46, 97, 107, 120, 138, 142, 171
Byrne, Vance & Co., 171

Cahill, Thomas W., 127 n. 41, 128, 130, 142
Cailloux, Andre, 115n
Calhoun, John, 70 n. 64
Camp Moore, La., 5
Camp Parapet, La., 8
Camp Strong Station, La., 15

Carter, Hannibal, 19, 61, 79, 80, 99, 102 n. 100
Cat Island, Miss., 52, 75
Chapman, George M., 126, 144, 146, 156; mentioned, 153
Charleston, S. C.: battle of, 98, 101, 131, 139, 152 n. 88; mentioned, 40, 53, 59, 77, 89, 103, 104n
Chase, Salmon P., 131 n. 50, 148 n. 80, 152 n. 89
Chickering, Thomas, 128
Clark, John S., 144
Clifton (ship), 32, 50–51, 58, 64–65
[Cline?], James. *See* Ship Island, Miss.: Refugees
Colfax, Schuyler, 174
Committee of Pilgrimage, 174
Confiscation Acts, 7
Congo, Augusta and Wimba, 12 n. 16
9th Connecticut Volunteer Infantry, 14, 127 n. 41, 138 n. 59
Conscription Act (Confederate), 65 n. 62
Contrabands, 6–7, 11, 169. *See also* Ship Island, Miss.: Contrabands
Cooke, Augustus P., 162 n. 11
Corps d'Afrique, 110, 111, 117, 127, 165; 4th Regiment, 138 n. 59; mentioned, 115, 153, 157, 164. *See also* Louisiana Native Guards; United States Colored Infantry (USCI)
Corps d'Armée, 126, 136, 138
Cre, Lemicus Warren and family, 145

Daniels, Cora Hatch, xxi, 172–74, 175, 176
Daniels, Etta and Waldo, 137, 173
Daniels, Nathan W.: diary background, xx–xxi; early years, duty, 14, 17, 71, 107; recruitment by Butler, 14; with 13th Maine Volunteer Infantry, 26–27, 28–29, 31, 47, 48, 51, 92–93, 94, 96, 97, 138 n. 59, 158–59, 164; takes command of Ship Island, 26–27, 32, 47–48; and ra-

Index

cial problems, 28, 39–40, 42, 48 n. 40, 57–58, 92–93, 158–59; improves island's defenses, 29–31, 49–50; regimental/post daily business, 32, 47–104 *passim;* on Lt. Col. Hall, 33, 108, 125, 129, 133; on black troops, his men, his officers, 34, 41, 54, 63, 64, 68–69, 78, 90, 92, 97, 102, 123, 127–28, 132; discipline of men, 36, 43–44, 60, 70, 98, 100, 116; personal and social life on Ship Island, 37, 38, 39, 66, 68, 70, 97, 141; and women friends, 38, 75, 88, 91, 100, 122, 131, 145, 149, 151; on battle at Pascagoula, Miss., 40–42, 79–87, 88, 89, 91, 95; and charges against officers, 91, 99, 102; and pay issue, 94 n. 88, 130; life in New Orleans, 107–108, 117, 121, 124, 128, 133–34, 138, 145, 149; on spiritualism, 117, 132–33, 137, 147–48, 149, 151, 153, 172–73; on Lt. Prouty and charges, 117–18, 125, 126, 140, 143–44, 150; and Lt. Palfrey's charge, 108–109, 122–23, 129, 160–61, 164; court-martial preparations, frustrations, 118, 123, 127, 128, 129, 130, 134–35, 136, 138, 142; dismissal/resignation of, 120, 130, 141, 144, 145, 146, 148, 163, 164, 165; on Banks, 122, 124, 125, 134–35, 136, 138, 141–42, 150, 154, 156, 165, 174; dreams of, 124–30 *passim,* 135, 140, 141, 145, 146, 150; morale of, 125, 128; and additional charges, 127, 141, 142, 164; on Department of the Gulf, 127, 141, 156, 165; on Butler, 135, 142; marriage and family, 137, 173–74; and Lt. Comdr. Perkins' charge, 162–63; as speaker, journalist, activist, 172, 173–77; death and obituary, 176–77. *See also* Louisiana Native Guards: 2nd Regiment

Dauchy, Charles, 62, 75, 143, 156
Dauphin Island, Ala., 48 n. 41, 66n
Davis, Jefferson, 2, 71; mentioned, 119, 149
Deer Island, Miss., 77
Defenses of New Orleans, 52 n. 43, 107, 112; mentioned, 22, 138, 160
Delany, Martin, xviii n, 15 n. 21
Denison, George, 131 n. 50
Department of the Gulf, 21–22, 46, 109–10, 111, 117, 164, 165
Diana (ship), 65 n. 61, 89, 90n
Dix, John A., 124n
Dog (Escatawpa) River, 72n
Douglass, Frederick, 169
D'Oyly, N. See *J. P. Jackson* (ship)
[Dubreuil?], John, 70 n. 64
Dumas, Francis E., xviii, 14–15, 34–35, 40, 41, 80, 83, 88, 115, 125 n. 36, 168, 173; mentioned, 37, 63 n. 60, 75, 79, 140
Dunbar, Paul, 70
Dunham, Robert H., 31, 32
Dunn, Oscar J., 168
Dupont, Samuel F., 77
Dwight, Charles S., 127 n. 41
Dyer, Isaac, 99

Edgerlady, Capt. "Edge," 39, 62; mentioned, 58, 97
Emory, William H., 112, 131
Escatawpa (Dog) River, 72n
Estrella (ship), 162 n. 11
Evening Star (ship), 139

Farragut, David G., 1, 30, 59, 62, 64, 73, 89–90, 139
Finnegass, Henry, 151–52, 160
Fleury, Alphonse, 70
Fort Gaines, 48, 66n
Fort Jackson, 1, 5, 27, 31, 47, 48
Fort Macomb, 167
Fort Massachusetts. *See* Ship Island, Miss.
Fort Morgan, 48, 75, 167
Fort Pemberton, 59 n. 51

Index

Fort Pike, 22, 63, 65. *See also* 2nd Louisiana Native Guards
Fort St. Leon, 61 n. 57
Fort St. Philip, 1, 5, 27, 31, 47, 48
Fort Sumter, 131, 139; mentioned, 4
Fort Wagner, 131 n. 50, 152 n. 88
Fortress Monroe, 6
Fox, Gustave V., 77n
Franklin, William B., 146 n. 77
Fransura, John, 84n
Freedmen's Bureau, 172, 173, 175

Gallagher, William, 62
Galveston, Tex., 56; mentioned, 38, 126
Garland, J. P., 127 n. 42
Garrison, William Lloyd, 169
General Washington (ship), 152
Genessee (ship), 162 n. 11
Gens de couleur, 2
Giddings, G. R., 11–12 n. 15
Gihon, Dr. [?], 62
Gillmore, Quincy A., 131, 139, 152
Glover, Calvin, 99, 102 n. 100
Gordon, Lt. [?], 156
[Gracien?], Andrew. *See* Ship Island, Miss.: Refugees
Grant, Ulysses S., 101 n. 97, 111, 112, 113, 135–36, 138–39, 146; mentioned, 21, 45, 114
Grant, William, 60
Grants Pass, 30, 31; mentioned, 51, 52, 62, 75
Green, Alexander, 84n
Grosvenor, William M., 167; mentioned, 171

Habeas corpus, 152
Hall, Alfred G., 14, 20, 22, 26, 47; replacing black officers, examination boards, 33, 109; conduct of, 44, 108, 121, 151; at Fort Pike, 44, 171; at Ship Island, 109, 114, 116, 117, 123, 133, 167, 170–71; and loss of officers, 114–15, 116; men's dislike of, 129, 133; medical report on, 171; dismissal of, 171; mentioned, 56, 57, 61, 66, 70. *See also* Louisiana Native Guards: 2nd Regiment
Halleck, Henry W., 112; mentioned, 10, 17, 18, 20, 32
Hanby, Augustus P., 94
Hartford (ship), 59, 64, 73, 139
Hatteras (ship), 48 n. 39, 56 n. 46
Havana, Cuba, 16, 51
Higginson, Thomas W., xix, 8
Hincks, Edward W., 166
Hitchcock, Robert B., 29
Hodgman, Stephen, 14, 97–98, 116
Holabird, Samuel B., 22, 60 n. 53, 66
Holmstedt, Ernest W., 167
Honey Springs, Indian Terr., 157
Hooker, "Fighting Joe," 139 n. 62
Horn Island, Miss., 55, 79
Houston, D. C., 30, 116–17, 170 n. 28
Hubeau, Ernest, 32
Hugo, Victor, 68n
Hunter, David, 7–8, 77

Irish Bend (Nerson's Woods), La., 88 n. 82, 90n
Irwin, Richard B., 31
Isabelle, Robert, 33, 61 n. 56, 169; mentioned 34, 52 n. 42
Island Mound, Mo., 8

J. P. Jackson (ship), 65–66 n. 62, 72–73, 75; racial troubles involving, 39–40, 41–42, 58 n. 48; at Pascagoula, 79–84 *passim*, 88, 101; mentioned, 30, 38 n. 29, 50, 51, 58, 65
Jacques, Eugene. *See* Ship Island, Miss.: Refugees
Jenkins, Thornton A., 29
Johnson, Andrew, 173, 174–75
Johnson, Laurel (Orrill), 70 n. 64, 103
Jones, Joseph, 43–44, 79, 80, 83, 98, 100

Index

1st Kansas Colored Infantry, 8, 157
Keeling, William F., 33, 63 n. 59, 94–95 n. 88
Kennett, John, 75
Key West, Fla., 38, 140
Killborn, Curtis W., 156, 164
Kingsley, Rufus, 94
Knox, Henry, 102 n. 98

Lafourche region, La. 16, 17
Lafourche (steamboat), 126
Lake Pontchartrain, La., 9, 20, 22, 51, 167
Lane, James, 7, 8, 140 n. 64
Lane, W. P., 123 n. 32
Law, Richard A., 32, 50
Lawrence, Samuel, 13 n. 18
Lawrence, Kans., 140
Lewis (Louis), Joseph (Jules) P., 70
Lieber, G. N., 91, 94, 142, 145, 146
Lincoln, Abraham, 5, 7, 8, 11, 18, 21, 102, 119, 120, 146 n. 76, 165–66, 169, 172; mentioned, 43, 45, 94, 107, 109, 152, 157, 171
Lincoln, Mary Todd, 172
Louisiana Native Guards: enlistment, xvi, 11–13; black officers for, xvi–xvii, 13, 157–58; as Louisiana (Confederate) militia, 4, 5, 10–11, 11–12 n. 15, 13; color line and, 11–13; expectations of men, 12–13, 37; white officers for, 13; with white civilians, 15–16; pay issue, 42–43, 158 n. 1; as Corps d'Afrique, 110, 166; health of, 111; engineer regiment, 112, 113, 116–17; petition of, 159; as pioneers 157–58; as United States Colored Infantry (USCI), 166
—1st Regiment, xvi, 11, 13, 18, 19, 43, 45, 46, 61, 159; at Port Hudson, 112–13, 123 n. 33; mentioned, xvii, 42. *See also* Stafford, Spencer H.
—2nd Regiment: organized, 11, 14–15; black officers and, 14–15, 19, 32, 33–35, 37, 38, 114–16, 167–70; early duty and problems, 17, 19, 20; arrival at Ship Island and Fort Pike, 26; at Fort Pike, 26, 33–34, 44, 65, 115–16, 167; racial troubles involving, 28, 39–40, 42, 57–58, 92–93, 158–59; drills, dress parades, inspections, reviews of, 31, 51, 54, 57, 58, 63, 65, 75, 76, 78, 102; in building batteries, defenses, 35, 37, 48, 49, 51, 53, 54, 57, 95; in battle at Pascagoula, Miss., 40–42, 79–87, 88, 89, 91, 95; morale of, 42, 114, 125; importance of position at post, 62; as 2nd Regiment Corps d'Afrique, 110; health of, 117; as 74th USCI, 166, 167; records on, 167 n. 20. *See also* Daniels, Nathan W.; Hall, Alfred G.
—3rd Regiment, 11, 13, 19, 34, 45, 159–60; at Port Hudson, 112–13, 123 n. 33; mentioned, 42. *See also* Nelson, John
—4th Regiment, 45, 46, 61
Louisiana Regiments: Confederate, 5th Regiment Volunteers, 65; Union, 2nd Regiment Volunteers., 40 n. 40, 79
Lovell, Mansfield, 5

Madigan, John, 30, 38, 50
Major, J. P., 123 n. 32
12th Maine Volunteer Infantry, 138 n. 59
13th Maine Volunteer Infantry. *See* Rust, Henry; Daniels, Nathan W.
21st Maine Volunteer Infantry, 127 n. 42
Manton, Benjamin, 39, 42, 50, 54, 56, 73, 74, 80, 81, 83, 100, 122, 127, 130, 140–41
Martin, Theodore, 83
Massachusetts Volunteer Infantry regiments: 26th Mass., 129n; 30th Mass., 14; 31st Mass., 33, 95 n. 88; 41st Mass., 128 n. 44; 42nd Mass., 56 n. 46; Massachusetts 54th (black), xix–xx, 157
Merrimack (ship), 60
Mexico City, Mex., 74, 148 n. 79
Militia Act, 7

Index

Milliken's Bend, La., 157
Minnehaha (ship), 156
Mitchell, Joseph, 58 n. 48
Mobile, Ala.: Confederate activity at, 29–30, 40, 59–60, 116; defenses of, 48 n. 41, 65, 71–72, 103–104 n. 102; troops from, 81, 87, 89; suffering of population, 90–91; Daniels on delay in taking, 102; Mobile Point, 167
Monongahela (ship), 59
Monroe, Coleman, 91n, 100, 124
Moore, James, 84n
Moore, Thomas O., 4, 5
Morphy, Ernest, 33, 170; mentioned, 52 n. 42, 61 n. 56
Morris, Dr. [?], 99
Mumford, William, 6
Murillon, Monrose, 33, 34, 63 n. 59, 78, 94–95 n. 88

Nackir, Charles, 51
Nassau (ship), 47
National Anti-Slavery Standard, 174
Nelson, John A., 14, 34, 118–19, 127 n. 42, 152, 159, 160, 166–67. *See also* Louisiana Native Guards: 3rd Regiment
New Orleans, La.: assault on, 1–2, 9; defenders of, 2, 3, 4, 5; interracial/multicultural population of, 2–4; under Federal rule, 107, 134; epidemics in, 175–76
New Orleans *Delta*, 173
New Orleans *Era*, 84n, 88 n. 83
New Orleans *Picayune*, 55
New Orleans *Times*, 152, 173
New Orleans *Tribune*, 173, 174
New Orleans *Union (L'Union)*, 95, 169
New York *Tribune*, 51, 95, 173, 174
11th New York Volunteer Infantry, 13
176th New York Volunteer Infantry, 171
19th Corps, 21–22, 45
Northern Star (ship), 26
Noyes, James, 32–33, 62, 95, 146

Ohio, Army of the, 71
4th Ohio Cavalry, 75
Opelousas Railroad, 17, 27, 28 n. 6, 35, 47, 121, 158
Oregon (ship), 55
Oreto (Florida) (ship), 56
Owen, Robert Dale, 149, 171

Paine, Charles J., 40 n. 31
Palfrey, John C., 30, 31, 46, 95; charge against Daniels, 108, 118, 120, 122–23, 160–61, 170; on black troops, 161; later years of, 170; on black engineers, 170 n. 28
Parish Prison, 61
Pascagoula (East), Miss., battle at. *See* Louisiana Native Guards: 2nd Regiment
Pascagoula River, 55 n. 44
Pass Christian, La., 65 n. 62
Pass Manchac, La., 64
Patterson, Mr. [?]. *See* Ship Island, Miss.: Refugees
Peabody, William, 13 n. 18, 33n, 35n, 44, 115
Penfield, Joseph, 58 n. 48
Pensacola, Fla., 22, 64; mentioned, 38, 76, 148
Perkins, George H., 162–63; mentioned, 170
Peters, W. F., 94
Phelps, John W., 7, 8–9, 64
Phillips, Wendell, 68n, 169
Pickens, J. A., 19
Pierucci, Dr. Ceise, 83n, 136
Pinchback, P. B. S., 15, 33n, 35n, 44, 63 n. 59, 115, 168
Plaquemine, La., 123
Pointe Coupee Parish, La., 14, 58, 107, 127 n. 39
Pollard, Henry, 94
Ponchatoula River. *See* Pascagoula River
Porter, David D., 45, 59, 101 n. 97
Port Hudson, La.: assault on, xx, 42, 45, 53,

Index

112–14, 124. *See also* Louisiana Native Guards: 1st Regiment; Louisiana Native Guards: 3rd Regiment
Portland (Maine) *Argus*, 92
Prouty, Elijah K., 13 n. 18, 14, 32, 44, 91, 117–18, 125, 126, 140, 142, 143, 162–63, 170
Putnam, Israel, 102 n. 98
Putnam, O. H., 94

Quantrill, William, 140

Raceland, La., 19
Read, Mr. [?], 149, 150, 156
Refugees. *See* Ship Island, Miss.
Religio-Philosophical Journal, 174
Rey, Henry, 151
Rey, Octave, 33, 52 n. 42, 61 n. 56, 170
Reynolds, Frank, 122
Rhode Island Cavalry, 51
Richmond (ship), 59
Ringgold, Samuel, 62, 115, 169
Rochester *Express*, 174, 75
Rosa, Madam, 132, 138, 145
Rosecrans, William S., 152
Roudanez, Jean-Baptiste, 169
Rust, Henry, 26–27, 28, 29, 47, 48 n. 40, 159
Ruth (steamboat), 175

Sabine Pass, Tex., 56, 146 n. 77
St. Charles Hotel, 121, 132, 135, 163
St. Charles Parish, xxi, 143
St. James Hospital, 40 n. 31, 51
St. John, Vincent. *See* Ship Island, Miss.: Refugees
Salem Corner, N.Y., 101 n. 96
Sauvinet, Charles S., 38, 41, 68, 88, 95 n. 89, 156
Saxton, Rufus, 8, 11
Schaeffer, Bertine and Mary, 132, 134, 138, 146, 147, 156

Schara, Francis. *See* Ship Island, Miss.: Refugees
Sciota (ship), 162
Scott, Lucien, 33, 63 n. 59, 94–95 n. 88
Scott, Thomas, 84n
Scott, Winfield, 99
Selma (ship), 75
Shaw, Robert Gould, xix
Shepley, George, 143 n. 69
Sherman, Thomas W., 46, 52 n. 43, 53, 108, 112, 122, 160; mentioned, 62, 70, 83, 84, 95, 99, 104
Sherman, William T., mentioned, 59 n. 51
Sherman, William W., 43, 66, 70
Ship Island, Miss.: description of, 1, 25–26; Fort Massachusetts, 1, 26, 30, 160–61; lighthouse at, 1, 48, 51, 55, 56; importance of, 26, 38; prisoners at, 26, 38, 47–48, 59, 75, 82, 85, 98, 120; fear of attack on, 29, 30, 31, 116; defenses of, 29, 30–31, 48–49; contrabands at, 32, 62, 73; refugees at, 58, 65, 68, 69, 71–73, 75, 76–77, 91, 100; post school at, 95. *See also* Louisiana Native Guards: 2nd Regiment
Skinner, Dr. [?], 83n
Smith, Robert, 51
1st South Carolina Volunteers (black), xix, 7–8
Southern Pilot, 94
Stafford, Spencer H., 12 n. 15, 13, 15–16, 18, 20, 43, 46, 61 n. 57, 118, 127 n. 42, 151–52, 159–60, 166; mentioned, 61, 171. *See also* Louisiana Native Guards: 1st Regiment
Stanton, Edwin M., 8, 9–10, 45–46, 110, 148 n. 80, 149 n. 81
Stilwell, Captain [?], 56, 58, 61, 65, 66, 68
Stone, Charles P., 146 n. 75
Strausburg, William. *See* Ship Island, Miss.: Refugees
Strong, George, 131
Sumner, Charles, 99, 100

Index

Susquehanna (ship), 30
Swan, Robert, 84n
Switzerland (ship), 74n

Tappan, Samuel Forster, xxi
Taylor, Richard "Dick," 28–29 n. 6, 99, 111
Taylor, Van Meter, 51
Taylor, Zachary, 99
Thibles, Alec (and Mrs.), 124, 126, 131, 132, 135, 143, 144, 146, 153
Thibodaux, La., 17, 123 n. 32
Thomas, George H., 171
Thomas, Lorenzo, 36, 45, 103, 111 n. 9, 135, 139 n. 61, 146 n. 75
Todd, John Blair Smith, 172 n. 35
Tombigbee River, 56
Totten, Joseph G., 30
Touro Barracks, 15
Trask, Frank, 19
Tunbridge, John. *See* Ship Island, Miss.: Refugees
Turner, Joe, 84n, 91
Turner, Mrs. [?], 126, 132, 134, 135

Ullmann, Daniel, 45–46, 110, 115; mentioned, 127, 156, 157
L'Union (New Orleans), 95, 169
United States Colored Infantry (USCI), 111 n. 10; Corps d'Afrique as, 110–11; Louisiana Native Guards as, 166
United States Colored Troops (USCT), 111
Usher, R. G., 43n

Valmour, J. B., 153, 153–54 n. 91
Vance, Hamilton McNeil, xx, 145 n. 74, 171
Varney, Almon L., 138, 142

Vedder, Major [?], 142, 143
2nd Vermont Battery, 56 n. 46
8th Vermont Volunteer Infantry, 17, 19–20, 27, 31, 99 n. 94; as paroled prisoners, 28–29 n. 6, 47, 48; mentioned, 14, 118
Vicksburg campaign, 45, 59, 73, 98, 101, 103, 111–12, 113, 114; mentioned, 53, 69, 124, 136, 146
Victor, Francis, 63 n. 60, 75
Villeverd, Joseph, 19, 38, 66, 68, 79, 80, 83, 85, 143

Warmoth, Henry Clay, 168
Washington, Colman, 84n
Watson, George, 19
Wayne, Anthony, 102 n. 98
Weitzel, Godfrey, 17–18, 19, 20, 64–65, 120–21, 142, 146; mentioned, 45
Welch, James, 94
Wells, Dr. [?], 99, 122
Wibles, Alec (and Mrs.), 124, 126, 131, 132, 135, 143, 144, 146, 153
Wilberforce, William, 68n
Wilkinson, Samuel, 99 n. 95, 102 n. 100, 115
Williams, Mrs [?]. *See* Ship Island, Miss.: Refugees
Willis, Samuel, 32, 38, 66, 74, 83, 95, 104, 127 n. 41, 130; mentioned, 39
Wilson, Joseph T., 39, 40nn, 42n
Woods, John, 60 n. 54

Yazoo Pass, Miss., 59 n. 51

Zacharie, Isaac, 119